THE CLAY SANSKRIT LIBRARY

FOUNDED BY JOHN & JENNIFER CLAY

WWW.CLAYSANSKRITLIBRARY.COM

WWW.NYUPRESS.ORG

First Edition 2005

The Clay Sanskrit Library is co-published by
New York University Press
and the JJC Foundation.

Further information about this volume
and the rest of the Clay Sanskrit Library
is available on the following websites:
www.claysanskritlibrary.com
www.nyupress.org.

ISBN 0-8147-5706-5

Artwork by Robert Beer.
Typeset in Adobe Garamond at 10.25 : 12.3+pt.
Printed in Great Britain by St Edmundsbury Press Ltd,
Bury St Edmunds, Suffolk, on acid-free paper.
Bound by Hunter & Foulis, Edinburgh, Scotland.

MAHĀBHĀRATA
BOOK NINE

ŚALYA
VOLUME ONE

TRANSLATED BY
JUSTIN MEILAND

NEW YORK UNIVERSITY PRESS
JJC FOUNDATION
2005

Library of Congress Cataloging-in-Publication Data
Mahābhārata. Śalyaparvan. Adhyāya 1–29.
English & Sanskrit.
Mahabharata. Book 9, "Śalya." Vol. 1
edited and translated by Justin Meiland.
p. cm. – (The Clay Sanskrit library)
In English with Sanskrit parallel text;
includes translation from Sanskrit.
Includes bibliographical references and index.
ISBN 0-8147-5706-5 (cloth : alk. paper)
I. Meiland, J.,
II. Title. III. Series.

CONTENTS

CSL CONVENTIONS

SANSKRIT ALPHABETICAL ORDER

Vowels:	*a ā i ī u ū ṛ ṝ ḷ ḹ e ai o au ṃ ḥ*
Gutturals:	*k kh g gh ṅ*
Palatals:	*c ch j jh ñ*
Retroflex:	*ṭ ṭh ḍ ḍh ṇ*
Labials:	*p ph b bh m*
Semivowels:	*y r l v*
Spirants:	*ś ṣ s h*

GUIDE TO SANSKRIT PRONUNCIATION

a	b*u*t
ā, â	r*a*ther
i	s*i*t
ī, î	f*ee*
u	p*u*t
ū,û	b*oo*
ṛ	vocalic *r*, American p*ur*dy or English p*re*tty
ṝ	lengthened *ṛ*
ḷ	vocalic *l*, ab*le*
e, ê, ē	m*a*de, esp. in Welsh pronunciation
ai	b*i*te
o, ô, ō	r*o*pe, esp. Welsh pronunciation; Italian s*o*lo
au	s*ou*nd
ṃ	*anusvāra* nasalizes the preceding vowel
ḥ	*visarga*, a voiceless aspiration (resembling English *h*), or like Scottish lo*ch*, or an aspiration with a faint echoing of the preceding vowel so that *taiḥ* is pronounced *taih*^{i}
k	lu*ck*
kh	blo*ckh*ead
g	*g*o
gh	bi*gh*ead
ṅ	a*n*ger
c	*ch*ill
ch	mat*chh*ead
j	*j*og
jh	aspirated *j*, he*dgeh*og
ñ	ca*ny*on
ṭ	retroflex *t*, *t*ry (with the tip of tongue turned up to touch the hard palate)
ṭh	same as the preceding but aspirated
ḍ	retroflex *d* (with the tip of tongue turned up to touch the hard palate)
ḍh	same as the preceding but aspirated
ṇ	retroflex *n* (with the tip of tongue turned up to touch the hard palate)

t	French *t*out
th	ten*t h*ook
d	*d*inner
dh	guil*dh*all
n	*n*ow
p	*p*ill
ph	u*ph*eaval
b	*b*efore
bh	a*bh*orrent
m	*m*ind
y	*y*es
r	trilled, resembling the Italian pronunciation of *r*
l	*l*inger
v	*w*ord
ś	*sh*ore
ṣ	retroflex *sh* (with the tip of the tongue turned up to touch the hard palate)
s	hi*ss*
h	*h*ood

CSL PUNCTUATION OF ENGLISH

The acute accent on Sanskrit words when they occur outside of the Sanskrit text itself, marks stress, e.g. Ramáyana. It is not part of traditional Sanskrit orthography, transliteration or transcription, but we supply it here to guide readers in the pronunciation of these unfamiliar words. Since no Sanskrit word is accented on the last syllable it is not necessary to accent disyllables, e.g. Rama.

The second CSL innovation designed to assist the reader in the pronunciation of lengthy unfamiliar words is to insert an unobtrusive middle dot between semantic word breaks in compound names (provided the word break does not fall on a vowel resulting from the fusion of two vowels), e.g. Maha·bhárata, but Ramáyana (not Rama·áyana). Our dot echoes the punctuating middle dot (·) found in the oldest surviving forms of written Sanskrit, the Ashokan inscriptions of the third century BCE.

The deep layering of Sanskrit narrative has also dictated that we use quotation marks only to announce the beginning and end of every direct speech, and not at the beginning of every paragraph.

CSL PUNCTUATION OF SANSKRIT

The Sanskrit text is also punctuated, in accordance with the punctuation of the English translation. In mid-verse, the punctuation will not alter the *sandhi* or the scansion. Proper names are capitalized. Most

Sanskrit metres have four "feet" *(pāda):* where possible we print the common *śloka* metre on two lines. In the Sanskrit text, we use French *Guillemets* (e.g. *«kva saṃcicīrṣuḥ?»*) instead of English quotation marks (e.g. "Where are you off to?") to avoid confusion with the apostrophes used for vowel elision in *sandhi*.

Sanskrit presents the learner with a challenge: *sandhi* ("euphonic combination"). *Sandhi* means that when two words are joined in connected speech or writing (which in Sanskrit reflects speech), the last letter (or even letters) of the first word often changes; compare the way we pronounce "the" in "the beginning" and "the end."

In Sanskrit the first letter of the second word may also change; and if both the last letter of the first word and the first letter of the second are vowels, they may fuse. This has a parallel in English: a nasal consonant is inserted between two vowels that would otherwise coalesce: "a pear" and "an apple." Sanskrit vowel fusion may produce ambiguity. The chart at the back of each book gives the full *sandhi* system.

Fortunately it is not necessary to know these changes in order to start reading Sanskrit. For that, what is important is to know the form of the second word without *sandhi* (pre-*sandhi*), so that it can be recognized or looked up in a dictionary. Therefore we are printing Sanskrit with a system of punctuation that will indicate, unambiguously, the original form of the second word, i.e., the form without *sandhi*. Such *sandhi* mostly concerns the fusion of two vowels.

In Sanskrit, vowels may be short or long and are written differently accordingly. We follow the general convention that a vowel with no mark above it is short. Other books mark a long vowel either with a bar called a macron (*ā*) or with a circumflex (*â*). Our system uses the macron, except that for initial vowels in *sandhi* we use a circumflex to indicate that originally the vowel was short, or the shorter of two possibilities (*e* rather than *ai*, *o* rather than *au*).

When we print initial	before *sandhi* that vowel was
â,	*a*
î or *ê*,	*i*
û or *ô*,	*u*
âi,	*e*
âu,	*o*
ā,	*ā* (i.e., the same)

ī,	*ī* (i.e., the same)
ū,	*ū* (i.e., the same)
ē,	*ī*
ō,	*ū*
āi,	*ai*
āu,	*au*

', before *sandhi* there was a vowel *a*

FURTHER HELP WITH VOWEL SANDHI

When a final short vowel (*a*, *i* or *u*) has merged into a following vowel, we print ' at the end of the word, and when a final long vowel (*ā*, *ī* or *ū*) has merged into a following vowel we print " at the end of the word. The vast majority of these cases will concern a final *a* or *ā*.

Examples:

What before *sandhi* was *atra asti* is represented as *atr' âsti*

atra āste	*atr' āste*
kanyā asti	*kany" âsti*
kanyā āste	*kany" āste*
atra iti	*atr' êti*
kanyā iti	*kany" êti*
kanyā īpsitā	*kany" ēpsitā*

Finally, three other points concerning the initial letter of the second word:

(1) A word that before *sandhi* begins with *ṛ* (vowel), after *sandhi* begins with *r* followed by a consonant: *yatha" rtu* represents pre-*sandhi* *yathā ṛtu.*

(2) When before *sandhi* the previous word ends in *t* and the following word begins with *ś*, after *sandhi* the last letter of the previous word is *c* and the following word begins with *ch*: *syāc chāstravit* represents pre-*sandhi* *syāt śāstravit*.

(3) Where a word begins with *h* and the previous word ends with a double consonant, this is our simplified spelling to show the pre-*sandhi* form: *tad hasati* is commonly written as *tad dhasati*, but we write *tadd hasati* so that the original initial letter is obvious.

COMPOUNDS

We also punctuate the division of compounds (*samāsa*), simply by inserting a thin vertical line between words. There are words where the decision whether to regard them as compounds is arbitrary. Our principle has been to try to guide readers to the correct dictionary entries.

EXAMPLE

Where the Deva·nágari script reads:

कुम्भस्थली रक्षतु वो विकीर्णसिन्दूररेणुर्द्विरदाननस्य ।
प्रशान्तये विघ्नतमश्छटानां निष्ठ्यूतबालातपपल्लवेव ॥

Others would print:

kumbhasthalī rakṣatu vo vikīrṇasindūrareṇur dviradānanasya /
praśāntaye vighnatamaśchaṭānāṃ niṣṭhyūtabālātapapallaveva //

We print:

Kumbha|sthalī rakṣatu vo vikīrṇa|sindūra|reṇur dvirad'|ānanasya
praśāntaye vighna|tamaś|chaṭānāṃ niṣṭhyūta|bāl'|ātapa|pallav" êva.

And in English:

"May Ganésha's domed forehead protect you! Streaked with vermilion dust, it seems to be emitting the spreading rays of the rising sun to pacify the teeming darkness of obstructions."

"Nava·sáhasanka and the Serpent Princess" I.3 by Padma·gupta

INTRODUCTION

"The Book of Shalya" *(Śalya/parvan)* is the ninth book of the vast eighteen-book epic "The Maha·bhárata." Recounting the last day of the great battle between the Pándavas and the Káuravas, it describes the final destruction of the Káurava army and the Káurava king, Dur·yódhana. "Shalya" is divided into two clear halves, a division reflected by the two volumes of the Clay Sanskrit Library. Indeed, in some manuscript traditions the second half is considered to be a separate "book" (*parvan*) called "The Book of the Mace" *(Gadā/parvan)*.

The first half of the *Śalya/parvan* focuses on the slaughter of King Shalya and the final overthrow of the Káurava army, while the second half describes King Dur·yódhana's death at the hands of Bhima in a mace contest.

THE STORY SO FAR

In the briefest of outlines, the main story of the Maha·bhárata up to the point of "Shalya" is as follows. The narrative centers on a power struggle between two groups of cousins: the one hundred sons of King Dhrita·rashtra (the Káuravas), the eldest of whom is Dur·yódhana, and the five sons of Pandu (the Pándavas), the eldest of whom is Yudhi·shthira. In a game of dice devised by the adept gambler Shákuni (Dur·yódhana's uncle), Yudhi·shthira loses his kingdom to Dur·yódhana and is exiled along with his wife and brothers for thirteen years, the last year of which they have to spend incognito.

At the end of the prescribed period, the Pándavas are keen to claim back their kingdom, but prepare for war in case Dur·yódhana is intransigent. Envoys are sent to plead for the return of the kingdom by peaceful means, yet Dur·yódhana is obstinate. A war therefore takes place on the plains of Kuru·kshetra, which lasts for eighteen days. Bhishma is commander of the Káurava army for the first ten days but allows himself to be mortally wounded, whereupon Drona (the preceptor of both the Káuravas and the Pándavas) assumes command. After five days, Drona is killed by means of a trick. Karna, the devoted friend of Dur·yódhana and in fact the half brother of the Pándavas,[1] then becomes general of the army for two days before he is dishonorably killed by the Pándava Árjuna. Karna's death leaves the army in turmoil. It is at this juncture that the *Śalya/parvan* begins.

"SHALYA"

"Shalya" opens with the charioteer Sánjaya informing King Dhrita·rashtra that his son Dur·yódhana has been killed and his entire army destroyed. Despite his grief at hearing the news, Dhrita·rashtra asks Sánjaya to tell him every detail of how this disaster occurred. Sánjaya begins by describing the army's turmoil at the death of the great hero Karna. Although Dur·yódhana is urged to make peace after this setback, he insists that the war must continue and asks Ashva·tthaman to choose a new general for the depleted army. Ashva·tthaman chooses Shalya, who is duly consecrated. After much fighting, Shalya is killed by Yudhi·shthira, whereupon the Káurava army is left leaderless and practically vanquished.

The following chapters of this first half of the *Śalya/parvan* describe the final defeat of the Káurava army, including the death of Shákuni and Dur·yódhana's flight.

A sense of inevitability regarding the Káuravas' defeat pervades "Shalya". Previous to Shalya, there had been three generals: Bhishma, Drona and Karna, and the duration of their respective commands reveals a sure and steady decline from ten days, to five days, to two days. Predictably, Shalya's term is even shorter and lasts only half a day. That Shalya is destined to suffer the same fate as his predecessor is further suggested by the ways in which the *Śalya/parvan* echoes the previous book, the *Karṇa/parvan*. For example: in both books Sánjaya goes to tell Dhrita·rashtra of terrible calamities that have occurred, which Dhrita·rashtra asks to be told of in full; both describe scenes of grief over a recently deceased hero and the confusion of the Káurava army; both describe the election of a new general and constantly renewed hopes that the Pándavas will be destroyed, despite the frequent appearance of bad omens that spell doom for the Káuravas. This sense of repetition conveys the unavoidability of the Káuravas' defeat. Furthermore, as throughout the epic, "Shalya" is full of references to the role that fate or Time plays in determining the battle's outcome. Dhrita·rashtra, for example, laments at length over the power of fate (2.44):

> *My sons and grandsons are dead, mighty though they were, as are my friends and brothers—what else can this be but fate?*

In the light of this unstoppable process, the attempt that is made by the warrior Kripa (chapter 4) to persuade Dur·yódhana to sue for peace seems formulaic and futile: Dur·yódhana's willful rush toward death is simply inevitable.

The bewildering manner in which Dur·yódhana seems to be recklessly bent on destroying both himself and his own army is evoked by Árjuna, who expresses amazement at the irrationality of the Káuravas' continuous returns to battle (24.21ff.):

I do not know why the battle continued after Bhishma fell to the ground in that tumult. I believe that Dhrita·rashtra's followers must be utterly foolish and stupid to have returned to battle after Shántanu's son had fallen!

Afterward the carnage did not even cease when Drona was slaughtered—that best of Brahma-knowing men—nor when Radha's son or Vikárna was killed. Nor did the carnage even cease when the Káurava army had only a few survivors and Karna, that charioteer's son and tiger-like man, was killed together with his son.

Shalya's death is thus an inevitable aspect of this spiral toward the complete annihilation of the Káurava army.

SHALYA

The portrayal of Shalya is rather complex in the Maha·bhárata. As the king of the Madras (or Mádrakas), Shalya is depicted as a skillful and powerful fighter, a "great warrior" *(mahā/ratha)*,[2] who is to be feared in battle. Ashva·tthaman describes him as follows (6.18ff.):

Lineage, appearance, vigor, reputation, majesty—he possesses every virtue. [. . .] We will be able to achieve victory if we make this king our general, best of monarchs, just as the gods were victorious when they made Skanda their general!

The Káurava troops offer similar praise (7.10):

You have the power to conquer all the worlds in battle, along with their gods, demons and men; what then of the Srínjayas and Sómakas, who are mortal and belong to this world?

However, Shalya also displays less positive qualities. The reason he fights for the Káuravas is that he was lured into doing so by his weakness for luxury. Furthermore, his duplicity is revealed when, as the uncle of the Pándavas,[3] he agrees to Yudhi·shthira's request to lower Karna's energy when he is Karna's charioteer. This he does by repeatedly ridiculing Karna's claims that he will defeat the Pándavas and by praising Árjuna's power.[4] Yudhi·shthira himself describes his request as improper, "not to be done" *(a/kartavyam)*,[5] and Shalya's actions are presented as the opposite of how a charioteer should act. Indeed, as scholars have observed, the discordant relationship between Shalya and Karna acts as an effective foil to the exemplary friendship of charioteer and warrior that exists between Krishna and Árjuna (whose unity is highlighted by the phrase "the two Krishnas").[6] As Karna states, Shalya is acting as a foe (*a/mitra*) even while he pretends to be an ally.[7] Shalya thus plays the ambiguous role of being both a general of the Káurava army, who boasts that he will destroy the Pándavas, and a warrior who helps the Pándavas to defeat Karna, one of the Káuravas' greatest heroes. This irony is deepened by the fact that Yudhi·shthira, the very person who asked Shalya to aid the Pándavas in conquering Karna, is also the one who kills Shalya.[8]

Shalya's ambiguous portrayal is further extended by a long passage in the *Karṇa/parvan*, in which the Mádrakas are described as a people who practice a huge variety of sinful customs, for which the king is said to take on a sixth of the responsibility.[9] This passage, however, needs to be seen in context, since it is spoken by Karna, who is only too eager to criticize Shalya in retaliation for his charioteer's stinging words.

But despite problematic aspects of Shalya's character, it is noteworthy that Shalya's death is unique, in that he is the only one of the four generals—and indeed several other Káurava heroes, including Dur·yódhana—who is not killed by the Pándavas through questionable means.[10] On the contrary, he enjoys an honorable death worthy of a heroic warrior. The text thus firmly asserts that Shalya is killed in noble combat by a virtuous opponent (17.56):

> *Slain in honorable battle by the virtuous son of Righteousness, Shalya resembled a sacrificial fire that is extinguished after it has received proper oblations and offerings.*

The other generals, by contrast, are killed through actions that transgress the warrior code, the problematic nature of which the text is only too keen to explore. Bhishma is dishonorably killed when Árjuna uses Shikhándin as a shield, thereby taking advantage of Bhishma's vow not to fight against a woman, since Shikhándin had previously been a woman.[11] Drona is deceitfully killed by a trick when Yudhi·shthira tells him that Ashva·tthaman is dead—his statement is partly true because an elephant called Ashva·tthaman had been killed, but Drona believes that this refers to his son and therefore gives up his will to fight. In addition, Karna is killed in a morally questionable manner when he is unable to fight after his chariot becomes stuck in the ground.[12]

A major reason for Shalya's honorable death appears to be that it gives moral credibility to Yudhi·shthira, who is after all hailed as the King of Righteousness *(dharma/rājā)*. Although Yudhi·shthira had previously been instrumental in implementing many of the questionable tactics that led to the demise of the other generals, the text seems to feel the need to portray the king unproblematically when he is actually engaged in battle. This need for Yudhi·shthira to engage in "virtuous fighting" is all the more urgent given that he is generally not prominent in battle scenes. Indeed, the text itself expresses surprise at Yudhi·shthira's battle-fury (16.46):

> *It was a wonder to see Yudhi·shthira, the son of Kunti, become so brutal when previously he had been so mild and restrained.*

Although both Yudhi·shthira and Shalya are praised as powerful warriors, it is perhaps Yudhi·shthira's relative inexperience in fighting that makes Shalya a suitable opponent for the King, since it is stated elsewhere (by Krishna himself) that Shalya is less of an obstacle than previous generals (7.37):

> *Now that you have crossed the ocean of Drona and Bhishma and also the hell realm of Karna, do not drown in a cow's hoofprint when you confront Shalya with your troops!*

ALF HILTEBEITEL (1991:266ff.) has also pointed out other reasons why Shalya is an apposite opponent forYudhi·shthira, or—as the text states—Yudhi·shthira's "share" (*bhāga*). He argues that various passages in the Maha·bhárata closely identify Shalya with the earth, and that it is precisely the earth that Yudhi·shthira gains as his "share" when he destroys Shalya and thereby brings about the collapse of the Káurava army. This connection with the earth takes on a literal intimacy at Shalya's death (17.54ff.):

> *Drenched in blood and with every part of his body shattered, it was as if that bull among men had gone to greet the earth out of love, like a lover falling onto the breast of his dear beloved. The king seemed asleep, as if he were embracing the earth with all his limbs after he had enjoyed her like a dear beloved for a long period of time.*

Although there is perhaps a degree of dark humor in this image, it is also filled with poignancy, and the text's last description of Shalya leaves him glorified (17.57):

> *Even though he was lifeless—his heart pierced by the spear and his weapons and standard scattered—the king of the Madras did not lose any of his beauty.*

This connection between beauty and a warrior's death is, however, hardly unique to this passage but represents a continuation of a constant juxtaposition in the Maha·bhárata between images of violence and the horror of battle on the one hand and images of beauty and the magnificence of the warrior path on the other. "Shalya" thus describes lopped-off heads as looking like golden lotuses

(9.19), blood-drenched bodies as resembling red *kim·shuka* trees (9.24), and warriors with arrow-pierced foreheads as being like peaked mountains (10.15).

It is, however, not only Shalya's death that is portrayed in this first half of the *Śalya/parvan*; in fact, his slaughter occurs only halfway through the section. Numerous duels between warriors, containing quick-fire descriptions of attack and counterattack, are interspersed with more general accounts of the chaos of the battlefield, where headless torsos rise from the ground and rivers of blood flow teeming with the dead. Among the many heroes that are described, Shákuni—the very person who instigated the plan to seize the Pándavas' kingdom through a game of dice and who is described as "the root of the Kurus' evil" (28.60)—is killed by the Pándava Saha·deva. In addition, the narrator himself (Sánjaya) becomes embroiled in his own narrative by taking part in the battle for a while (25.47ff., 29.34ff.)—an apt situation, given that it is precisely Sánjaya's firsthand experience as a charioteer that gives him the authority to relate the events. Furthermore, the text also charts Dur·yódhana's gradual descent into humiliating defeat and, with it, the poignant evacuation of the Káurava camp. While Dur·yódhana continues to make speeches about the glory of dying in battle up until almost all the troops are killed, his decision to flee by disappearing into a lake is said to be made "out of fear" (29.23), and the previously great warrior becomes a wretched figure of humiliation and despair. With the Káurava army destroyed and their king disgraced, it is on this note of grief and tragedy that the first half of the book ends.

THE SANSKRIT TEXT

Finally, a few comments on the editions that have been used for this translation. The main text that has been employed is KINJAWADEKAR's edition of the "vulgate" established by Nila·kantha, a *Marāṭhī* brahmin living in the seventeenth century. I have also referred to variants found in two other editions of Nila·kantha's text, which were published in the nineteenth century in Bombay, and I have occasionally made use of the Critical Edition (where Nila·kantha variants are found in the critical apparatus under Dn). A full list of these variants and any emendations can be found on the CSL website.

NOTES

1 **Karna** is the first son of Kunti (the wife of Pandu), whom she conceives through the sun god Surya. To conceal her transgression, she abandons Karna at birth and he is raised by the charioteer Ádhiratha and his wife Radha.

2 The word ***mahā/ratha*** is used frequently in the Maha·bhárata as a general term for a skillful warrior. This is also how the word is glossed by the early commentary writer Vállabha·deva: "A *mahā/ratha* is a hero who has mastered all modes of fighting," (commenting on *Śiśupāla/vadha* 4.21: *sarvaṃ yuddha/vyavahāraṃ yo vetti sa śūro mahā/rathaḥ*). The expected interpretation of the word as a *bahu/vrīhi* compound, "he who has a great chariot," and hence "great charioteer" is rendered less likely (though occasionally it must be intended) by the evidence of Vedic texts (e.g. *Śata/patha/brāhmaṇa* 13.1.9) showing an accent on the second member of the compound, meaning it was originally intended to be a *karma/dhāraya* compound. MONIER-WILLIAMS (1899, s.v.) also notes that *ratha* by itself can mean "warrior" or "hero." I am indebted to Somadeva Vasudeva for this insight.

3 Shalya's sister is Madri, the mother of Nákula and Saha·deva.

4 See *Karṇa/parvan*, especially chapters 26 onward (Critical Edition). A further motive for Shalya's unseemly actions seems to be a sense of wounded pride—as a *kṣatriya*, Shalya should not be the chariot-driver of a mere *sūta* ("charioteer"); in fact, since Karna is himself the son of a *sūta*, it is he who should be Shalya's chariot-driver. See *Karṇa/parvan* 23.19ff (Critical Edition).

5 ***a/kartavyam***: *Udyoga/parvan* 8.27 (Critical Edition).

6 See HILTEBEITEL 1982:92ff. for this theme of friendship.

7 **Foe:** *Karṇa/parvan* 27.95 (Critical Edition).

8 This double-edged role as both warrior for the Káuravas and someone who acts on behalf of the Pándavas is echoed earlier in the epic in the figure of Bhishma, who is the general of the Káurava army but also tells the Pándavas how he can be destroyed.

9 See *Karṇa/parvan* 27.53ff. and 30.1ff. (Critical Edition); see also HILTEBEITEL 1990:272ff.

10 See HILTEBEITEL 1990:244ff. for the deaths of the four generals and especially 1990:266ff. for Shalya's death.

11 Importantly, however, Bhishma willingly tells the Pándavas how they can vanquish him. See *Bhīṣma/parvan* 112ff. (Critical Edition) for Bhishma's defeat.

12 For these passages, see *Droṇa/parvan* 164f. and *Karṇa/parvan* 66f. (Critical Edition).

BIBLIOGRAPHY – SANSKRIT TEXTS

The Mahābhāratam with the Bharata Bhawadeepa Commentary of Nīlakaṇṭha. Edited by RAMACHANDRASHASTRI KINJAWADEKAR. 1929–36. 7 vols. Poona: Chitrashala Press.

The Mahābhārata. [Critical Edition] Critically edited by V. K. SUKTHANKAR, S. K. BELVALKAR, P. L. VAIDYA, et al. 1933–66. 19 vols. Poona: Bhandarkar Oriental Research Institute.

The Mahābhārata with Nīlakaṇṭha's commentary. Edited by A. KHADILKAR. 1862–3. 8 vols. Bombay: Ganapati Krishnaji's Press.

Māghabhaṭṭa's Śiśupālavadha with the commentary Sandehaviṣauṣadhi of Vallabhadeva. Edited by RAM CHANDRA KAK and HARABHAṬṬA SHĀSTRĪ. 1935 (preface dated to 1941). Shrinagar: Kashmir Mercantile Press.

THE MAHA·BHÁRATA IN TRANSLATION

GANGULI, KISARI MOHAN (trans.) [early editions ascribed to the publisher, P. C. ROY]. 1884–99. *The Mahabharata of Krishna-Dwaipayana Vyasa*. 12 vols. Calcutta: Bharata Press.

VAN BUITENEN, J.A.B. (trans. and ed.). 1973–78. *The Mahābhārata* [Books 1–5]. 3 vols. Chicago: Chicago University Press.

SECONDARY SOURCES

BROCKINGTON, JOHN. 1998. *The Sanskrit Epics*. Leiden: Brill.

DONIGER, WENDY and SMITH, BRIAN K. (trans.). 1991. *The Laws of Manu*. New Delhi: Penguin Books India.

HILTEBEITEL, ALF. 1982. "Brothers, friends, and charioteers: Parallel episodes in the Irish and Indian epics." *Homage to Georges Dumézil*, ed. EDGAR C. POLOMÉ. *Journal of Indo-European Studies* Monographs 3. Washington: Insititute for the Study of Man. 85–111.

HILTEBEITEL, ALF. 1990. *The Ritual of Battle: Krishna in the Mahābhārata*. Albany: State University of New York Press.

M. MONIER-WILLIAMS. 1899. *A Sanskrit-English dictionary.* Oxford: Oxford University Press.

OBERLIES, THOMAS. 2003. *A grammar of epic Sanskrit*. Berlin: Walter de Gruyter.

SØRENSEN, SØREN. 1904–25. *An index to the names in the Mahābhārata*. London: Williams and Norgate.

1–2
DHRITA·RASHTRA GRIEVES

Nārāyaṇaṃ namas|kṛtya
　　Naraṃ c' âiva nar'|ôttamam
devīṃ Sarasvatīṃ c' âiva
　　tato *Jayam* udīrayet.

One should recite "The Victory"*
After one has honored Naráyana and Nara,
Who is supreme among men,
And the goddess Sarásvati.

JANAMEJAYA uvāca:

1.1 Evaṃ nipātite Karṇe samare Savyasācinā
alp'|âvaśiṣṭāḥ Kuravaḥ kim akurvata vai dvi|ja.
udīryamāṇaṃ ca balaṃ dṛṣṭvā rājā Suyodhanaḥ
Pāṇḍavaiḥ prāpta|kālaṃ ca kiṃ prāpadyata Kauravaḥ.
etad icchāmy ahaṃ śrotuṃ. tad ācakṣva dvi|j'|ôttama.
na hi tṛpyāmi pūrveṣāṃ śṛṇvānaś caritaṃ mahat.

VAIŚAMPĀYANA uvāca:

tataḥ Karṇe hate rājan Dhārtarāṣṭraḥ Suyodhanaḥ
bhṛśaṃ śok'|ârṇave magno nirāśaḥ sarvato 'bhavat.
1.5 «hā Karṇa hā Karṇa iti» śocamānaḥ punaḥ punaḥ
kṛcchrāt sva|śibiraṃ prāpto hata|śeṣair nṛ|paiḥ saha.
sa samāśvāsyamāno 'pi hetubhiḥ śāstra|niścitaiḥ
rājabhir n' âlabhac charma sūta|putra|vadhaṃ smaran.
sa daivaṃ balavan matvā bhavitavyaṃ ca pārthivaḥ
saṃgrāme niścayaṃ kṛtvā punar yuddhāya niryayau.
Śalyaṃ senā|patiṃ kṛtvā vidhivad rāja|puṅ|gavaḥ
raṇāya niryayau rājan hata|śeṣair nṛ|paiḥ saha.
tataḥ su|tumulaṃ yuddhaṃ Kuru|Pāṇḍava|senayoḥ
babhūva Bharata|śreṣṭha dev'|âsura|raṇ'|ôpamam.
1.10 tataḥ Śalyo mahā|rāja kṛtvā kadanam āhave
sa|sainyo 'tha sa madhy'|âhne dharma|rājena ghātitaḥ.

JANAM·ÉJAYA* said:

WHEN Savya·sachin, the left-handed Árjuna, had killed 1.1
Karna in battle in this way, what did the few remaining Kurus do, brahmin? When King Su·yódhana* saw that the Pándavas were agitating his army, how did the Káurava react when the time arrived? I yearn to hear this. Tell it to me, best of twice-born brahmins. I can never hear enough about the great deeds of my ancestors.

VAISHAM·PÁYANA said:

After Karna's death, Your Majesty, Su·yódhana, the son of
Dhrita·rashtra, sank deep into an ocean of grief and became
utterly despondent. Grieving again and again with cries of 1.5
"Oh! Karna! Oh! Karna!," he reached his camp strenuously,
accompanied by the surviving kings. Although the kings tried to console him with arguments based on scripture, he found no solace as he remembered the slaughter of the charioteer's son.*

Judging that it was fate and destiny that were powerful, King Dur·yódhana resolved to join battle and set out once again for war. After he had made Shalya general in the proper manner, that bull-like ruler departed for battle, Your Majesty, accompanied by the surviving kings. Then, best of Bharatas,* a tumultuous battle took place between the Kuru and Pándava armies; it was like a war between the gods and demons.

Although Shalya caused carnage in battle, he and his 1.10
soldiers were killed by the King of Righteousness* in the middle of the day, Your Majesty.

tato Duryodhano rājā hata|bandhū raṇ'|âjirāt
apasṛtya hradaṃ ghoraṃ viveśa ripu|jād bhayāt.
ath' âpar'|âhṇe tasy' âhnaḥ parivārya Suyodhanaḥ
hradād āhūya yuddhāya Bhīmasenena pātitaḥ.
tasmin hate mah"|êṣv|āse hata|śiṣṭās trayo rathāḥ
saṃrambhān niśi rāj'|êndra jaghnuḥ Pāñcāla|Somakān.

tataḥ pūrv'|âhṇa|samaye śibirād etya Sañjayaḥ
praviveśa purīṃ dīno duḥkha|śoka|samanvitaḥ.
1.15 sa praviśya purīṃ sūto bhujāv ucchritya duḥkhitaḥ
vepamānas tato rājñaḥ praviveśa niketanam,
ruroda ca nara|vyāghra «hā rājann iti» duḥkhitaḥ.

«aho bata vinaṣṭāḥ smo nidhanena mah"|ātmanaḥ!
vidhiś ca balavān atra pauruṣaṃ tu nirarthakam
Śakra|tulya|balāḥ sarve yath" âvadhyanta Pāṇḍavaiḥ.»

dṛṣṭv" âiva ca pure rājañ janaḥ sarvaḥ sa Sañjayam
kleśena mahatā yuktaṃ sarvato rāja|sattama
ruroda ca bhṛś'|ôdvigno «hā rājann iti» visvaram.
ā kumāraṃ nara|vyāghra tatra tatra samantataḥ
ārta|nādaṃ tataś cakre śrutvā vinihataṃ nṛ|pam.
1.20 dhāvataś c' âpy apaśyāmas tatra tān puruṣa'|rṣabhān
naṣṭa|cittān iv' ônmattān śokena bhṛśa|pīḍitān

tathā sa vihvalaḥ sūtaḥ praviśya nṛ|pati|kṣayam
dadarśa nṛ|pati|śreṣṭhaṃ prajñā|cakṣuṣam īśvaram
tathā c' āsīnam an|aghaṃ samantāt parivāritam
snuṣābhir Bharata|śreṣṭha Gāndhāryā Vidureṇa ca

At the death of his companions, King Dur·yódhana fled from the battlefield and entered a horrific lake out of fear of the enemy. Then, in the afternoon of that day, Su·yódhana was killed by Bhima·sena, who had surrounded him and summoned him out of the lake to fight. When that great archer was killed, O king of kings, the three surviving warriors slaughtered the Panchálas and Sómakas at night in a rage.

Sánjaya left the camp in the morning and arrived at the
city, distraught and filled with pain and grief. When he 1.15
entered the city, the charioteer raised his arms in anguish and entered King Dhrita·rashtra's palace, trembling. He wept, tiger among men, and exclaimed sorrowfully:

"Oh! My king! Alas! The death of this hero has destroyed us! If all these men, who rival Shakra* in strength, have been slaughtered by the Pándavas, then fate is powerful and human action has no purpose in this world."

As soon as the people in the city saw how Sánjaya was utterly affected by great sorrow, they all wept in deep distress, best of kings, screaming: "Oh! My king!" Here and there, they lamented on every side on hearing that the king had been struck down—including the very children, O tiger
among men. We even saw bull-like men running around 1.20
in the city and losing their minds like madmen under the heavy burden of their grief.

Full of anguish, the charioteer then entered the royal palace and saw his lord, that best of kings, who has wisdom for his eyes. The virtuous king was sat down, O best of Bharatas, surrounded on all sides by his daughters-in-law, as well as by Gandhári and Vídura and his other friends and

tath" ânyaiś ca su|hṛdbhiś ca jñātibhiś ca hit'|âiṣibhiḥ
tam eva c' ârthaṃ dhyāyantaṃ Karṇasya nidhanaṃ prati.

rudann ev' âbravīd vākyaṃ rājānaṃ Janamejaya
n' âtihṛṣṭa|manāḥ sūto bāṣpa|saṃdigdhayā girā:

1.25 «Sañjayo 'haṃ nara|vyāghra. namas te Bharata'|rṣabha.
Madr'|âdhipo hataḥ Śalyaḥ Śakuniḥ Saubalas tathā
Ulūkaḥ puruṣa|vyāghra Kaitavyo dṛḍha|vikramaḥ.
Saṃśaptakā hatāḥ sarve Kāmbojāś ca Śakaiḥ saha
mlecchāś ca pārvatīyāś ca Yavanāś ca nipātitāḥ.

prācyā hatā mahā|rāja dākṣiṇātyāś ca sarvaśaḥ.
udīcyāś ca hatāḥ sarve pratīcyāś ca nar'|ôttamāḥ.
rājāno rāja|putrāś ca sarve te nihatā nṛ|pa.

Duryodhano hato rājā yath"|ôktaṃ Pāṇḍavena ha.
bhagna|saktho mahā|rāja śete pāṃsuṣu rūṣitaḥ.
Dhṛṣṭadyumno hato rājan Śikhaṇḍī cāpa|rājitaḥ
Uttamaujā Yudhāmanyus tathā rājan Prabhadrakāḥ.

1.30 Pañcālāś ca nara|vyāghra Cedayaś ca niṣūditāḥ.
tava putrā hatāḥ sarve Draupadeyāś ca Bhārata.
Karṇa|putro hataḥ śūro Vṛṣasenaḥ pratāpavān.
narā vinihatāḥ sarve gajāś ca vinipātitāḥ.
rathinaś ca nara|vyāghra hayāś ca nihatā yudhi.
kiṃcic|cheṣaṃ ca śibiraṃ tāvakānāṃ kṛtaṃ prabho.

relatives who wished him well. He was brooding over the very matter of Karna's death.

As he wept sorrowfully, O Janam·éjaya, the charioteer addressed the king with a voice choked with tears:

"Tiger among men, I am Sánjaya. I bow before you, bull 1.25
of the Bharatas. Shalya, the king of the Madras, is dead. So, too, is Shákuni, the son of Súbala, and also, tiger among men, courageous Ulúka, the son of the gambler Shákuni. The Samshháptakas are all dead, as are the Kambójas and Shakas. The foreigners, mountain people, and Yávanas have been slaughtered.

The Easterners and all those from the South have died, Your Majesty. The Northerners have also all been killed, as have the Westerners, those best of men. All the kings and princes have been slain, O king.

As he predicted, the Pándava Bhima·sena has killed King Dur·yódhana.* His thighs smashed, Dur·yódhana lies in the dust, smeared with blood, great king. Dhrishta·dyumna is dead, Your Majesty, as is Shikhándin, splendid with his bow. Uttamáujas, Yudha·manyu, and the Prabhádrakas have also been killed, O king.

The Panchálas and the Chedis have been slain, tiger 1.30
among men. All your sons have died, descendant of Bharata, as have Dráupadi's sons. Karna's son, that mighty hero Vrisha·sena, is dead. All the men have been struck down and the elephants have been killed. The charioteers and the horses have been slaughtered in battle, tiger among men. Only a small part of your troops' camp remains, my lord.

Pāṇḍavānāṃ Kurūṇāṃ ca samāsādya paras|param
prāyaḥ strī|śeṣaṃ abhavaj jagat kālena mohitam.
sapta Pāṇḍavataḥ śeṣā Dhārtarāṣṭrās trayo rathāḥ:
te c' âiva bhrātaraḥ pañca Vāsudevo 'tha Sātyakiḥ,
Kṛpaś ca Kṛtavarmā ca Drauniś ca jayatāṃ varaḥ.
tath" âpy ete mahā|rāja rathino nṛ|pa|sattama
akṣauhiṇīnāṃ sarvāsāṃ sametānāṃ jan'|ēśvara.
1.35 ete śeṣā mahā|rāja sarve 'nye nidhanaṃ gatāḥ.
kālena nihataṃ sarvaṃ jagad vai Bharata'|rṣabha
Duryodhanaṃ vai purataḥ kṛtvā vairaṃ ca Bhārata.»

VAIŚAMPĀYANA uvāca:

etac chrutvā vacaḥ krūraṃ Dhṛtarāṣṭro jan'|ēśvaraḥ
nipapāta sa rāj'|êndro gata|sattvo mahī|tale.
tasmin nipatite bhūmau Viduro 'pi mahā|yaśāḥ
nipapāta mahā|rāja śoka|vyasana|karṣitaḥ.
Gāndhārī ca nṛ|pa|śreṣtha sarvāś ca Kuru|yoṣitaḥ
patitāḥ sahasā bhūmau śrutvā krūraṃ vacas tadā.
niḥsaṃjñaṃ patitaṃ bhūmau tad" āsīd rāja|maṇḍalam
pralāpa|yuktaṃ mahati citraṃ nyastaṃ paṭe yathā.
1.40 kṛcchreṇa tu tato rājā Dhṛtarāṣṭro mahī|patiḥ
śanair alabhata prāṇān putra|vyasana|karṣitaḥ.
labdhvā tu sa nṛ|paḥ saṃjñāṃ vepamānaḥ su|duḥkhitaḥ
udīkṣya ca diśaḥ sarvāḥ kṣattāraṃ vākyaṃ abravīt:
«vidvan Kṣattar mahā|prājña tvaṃ gatir Bharata'|rṣabha
mam' â|nāthasya su|bhṛśaṃ putrair hīnasya sarvaśaḥ.»

As a result of this conflict between the Pándavas and the Kurus, the world—bewildered by Time—mostly consists of the women that have been left behind. On the Pándavas' side seven heroes remain: the five brothers, Vásu·deva* and Sátyaki. And there are three warriors on Dhrita·rashtra's side: Kripa, Krita·varman and Ashva·tthaman, the son of Drona, that best of conquerors. These charioteers are what remain of all the armies that were mustered, lord of the
people. All the others, great king, have been slaughtered. 1.35
By championing Dur·yódhana and his enmity, the entire world has been destroyed by Time, bull of the Bharatas."

VAISHAM·PÁYANA said:

On hearing these terrible words, Dhrita·rashtra, the lord of the people and king of kings, fell to the ground unconscious. When he fell, glorious Vídura also collapsed, Your Majesty, pained by grief and suffering. Gandhári and all the Kuru women, O best of kings, suddenly fell to the ground, too, when they heard this terrible news. Whereupon the lamenting royal court also collapsed on the floor unconscious, like a picture stretched out on a large canvas.

Pained by his son's misfortune, king Dhrita·rashtra, the 1.40
lord of the earth, slowly and strenuously regained his life-breath. When he had regained consciousness, the king stared in every direction, trembling in great anguish, and addressed Vídura the Kshattri:*

"Wise and learned Kshattri, bull of the Bharatas, you are my refuge—I am utterly helpless and have lost all my sons."

evam uktvā tato bhūyo visaṃjño nipapāta ha.
taṃ tathā patitaṃ dṛṣṭvā bāndhavā ye 'sya ke cana
śītais te siṣicus toyair vivyajur vyajanair api.
sa tu dīrgheṇa kālena pratyāśvasto nar'|âdhipaḥ.
tūṣṇīṃ dadhyau mahī|pālaḥ putra|vyasana|karśitaḥ
niḥśvasañ jihma|ga iva kuṃbha|kṣipto viśāṃ pate.
1.45 Sañjayo 'py arudat tatra dṛṣṭvā rājānam āturam
tathā sarvāḥ striyaś c' âiva Gāndhārī ca yaśasvinī.
tato dīrgheṇa kālena Viduraṃ vākyam abravīt
Dhṛtarāṣṭro nara|śreṣtha muhyamāno muhur muhuḥ:
«gacchantu yoṣitaḥ sarvā Gāndhārī ca yaśasvinī
tath" ême su|hṛdaḥ sarve. bhrāmyate me mano bhṛśam.»
evam uktas tataḥ Kṣattā tāḥ striyo Bharata'|rṣabha
visarjayām āsa śanair vepamānāḥ punaḥ punaḥ
niścakramus tataḥ sarvāḥ striyo Bharata|sattama
su|hṛdaś ca tathā sarve dṛṣṭvā rājānam āturam.
1.50 tato nara|patiṃ tūrṇaṃ labdha|saṃjñaṃ paran|tapa
avaikṣat Sañjayo dīnaṃ rodamānaṃ bhṛś'|āturam.
prāñjalir niḥśvasantaṃ ca taṃ nar'|êndraṃ muhur muhuḥ
samāśvāsayata Kṣattā vacasā madhureṇa ha.

VAIŚAMPĀYANA UVĀCA:

2.1 VISṚṢṬĀSV ATHA nārīṣu Dhṛtarāṣṭro 'mbikā|sutaḥ
vilalāpa mahā|rāja duḥkhād duḥkhataraṃ gataḥ.
sa|dhūmam iva niḥśvasya karau dhunvan punaḥ punaḥ
vicintya ca mahā|rāja vacanaṃ c' êdam abravīt.

Saying this, he again fell unconscious. When they saw him thus fall, all his relatives sprinkled him with cool water and fanned him. After a long period, the king was revived. Pained by his son's disaster, the protector of the earth stayed silent and sighed deeply like a snake caught in a pot, Your Majesty.

Sánjaya wept on seeing his king so sick, as did glorious 1.45
Gandhári and all the women. Fainting again and again, O best of men, Dhrita·rashtra spoke to Vídura after a long time:

"Let all the women leave, including glorious Gandhári. And let all my friends leave, too. My mind is reeling violently."

Addressed in this way, the Kshattri gently ushered out the women, who were trembling constantly, bull of the Bharatas. Seeing that their king was sick, all the women left, as did all the friends present, best of Bharatas.

Sánjaya stared at the distraught king, who had quickly re- 1.50
gained consciousness but who still wept and suffered greatly, O destroyer of enemies. With his hands folded in respect, the Kshattri used soothing words to console that lord of men as he sighed repeatedly.

VAISHAM·PÁYANA said:

YOUR MAJESTY, when all the women had been sent away, 2.1
Dhrita·rashtra, the son of Ámbika, lamented and felt even greater pain than before. Breathing out sighs that seemed to contain smoke and waving his arms repeatedly, he brooded and then spoke these words, great king.

DHṚTARĀṢṬRA uvāca:

aho bata mahad duḥkhaṃ yad ahaṃ Pāṇḍavān raṇe
kṣemiṇaś c' â|vyayāṃś c' âiva tvattaḥ sūta śṛṇomi vai.
vajra|sāram ayaṃ nūnaṃ hṛdayaṃ su|dṛḍhaṃ mama
yac chrutvā nihatān putrān dīryate na sahasradhā.
2.5 cintayitvā vayas teṣām bāla|krīḍāṃ ca Sañjaya
hatān putrān a|śeṣeṇa dīryate me bhṛśaṃ manaḥ.

a|netratvād yad eteṣāṃ na me rūpa|nidarśanam
putra|sneha|kṛtā prītir nityam eteṣu dhāritā.
bāla|bhāvam atikrāntān yauvana|sthāṃś ca tān aham
madhya|prāptāṃs tathā śrutvā hṛṣṭa āsaṃ tad" ân|agha.
tān adya nihatāñ śrutvā hat'|aiśvaryān hat'|âujasaḥ
na labheyaṃ kva cic chāntiṃ putr'|ādhibhir abhiplutaḥ.

ehy ehi putra rāj'|êndra mam' â|nāthasya sāṃpratam!
tvayā hīno mahā|bāho kāṃ nu yāsyāmy ahaṃ gatiṃ?
2.10 kathaṃ tvaṃ pṛthivī|pālāṃs tyaktvā tāta samāgatān
śeṣe vinihato bhūmau prākṛtaḥ ku|nṛ|po yathā?
gatir bhūtvā mahā|rāja jñātīnāṃ su|hṛdāṃ tathā
andhaṃ vṛddhaṃ ca māṃ vīra vihāya kva nu yāsyasi?

sā kṛpā sā ca te prītiḥ sā ca rājan su|mānitā!
kathaṃ vinihataḥ Pārthaiḥ saṃyugeṣv a|parājitaḥ?
ko nu mām utthitaṃ vīra «tāta tāt' êti» vakṣyati
«mahā|rāj' êti» «satataṃ loka|nāth' êti» c' â|sakṛt?

DHRITA·RASHTRA said:

Alas! It causes me great suffering, charioteer, to hear you say that the Pándavas are not only safe but also unharmed in battle. This hard heart of mine must be made of diamond that it does not shatter into a thousand pieces when I hear
that my sons are dead. When I think of their age, Sánjaya, 2.5
and the games they used to play as children, and when I consider that every one of my sons has been killed, my mind falls apart terribly.

Although I have never seen what my sons look like, because of my blindness, I have always loved them with a father's affection. When I heard that they had passed beyond childhood and become youths and then adults, I was joyful, virtuous Sánjaya. Today, I have learned that they are dead, their strength and vigor destroyed, and I cannot find peace anywhere, overwhelmed as I am by distress for my sons.

Come back, come back to me, my son, my king of kings, helpless as I am! What course can I take now that I have
lost you, mighty-armed son? Why, my boy, did you leave 2.10
the assembled rulers of the earth and do you now lie struck down on the ground like an ordinary, insignificant king? Where are you going, my great king and hero, abandoning me in my blindness and old age, when you are the refuge of your relatives and friends?

You had such compassion, love and pride, O king! How were you killed by the sons of Pritha if you were invincible in battle? Who will speak to me when I wake up, O hero, repeatedly saying, "Father, father! Great king! Lord of the world forever!"? Embracing me around my neck, your eyes

parişvajya ca māṃ kaṇṭhe snehena klinna|locanaḥ
«anuśādh' îti» Kauravya tat sādhu vada me vacaḥ.
2.15 nanu nām' âham aśrauṣaṃ vacanaṃ tava putraka:
«bhūyasī mama pṛthv" îyaṃ yathā Pārthasya no tathā.
Bhagadattaḥ Kṛpaḥ Śalya Āvantyo 'tha Jayadrathaḥ,
Bhūriśravāḥ Somadatto mahā|rājaś ca Bāhlikaḥ,
Aśvatthāmā ca Bhojaś ca Māgadhaś ca mahā|balaḥ,
Bṛhadbalaś ca Kāś"|īśaḥ Śakuniś c' âpi Saubalaḥ,
mlecchāś ca śata|sāhasrāḥ Śakāś ca Yavanaiḥ saha,
Sudakṣiṇaś ca Kāmbojas Trigart'|âdhipatis tathā,
Bhīṣmaḥ pitā|mahaś c' âiva Bhāradvājo 'tha Gautamaḥ,
Śrutāyuś c' Âyutāyuś ca Śatāyuś c' âpi vīryavān,
2.20 Jalasandho 'th' Ārṣyaśṛṅgī rākṣasas c' âpy Alāyudhaḥ,
Alambuṣo mahā|bāhuḥ Subāhuś ca mahā|rathaḥ,
ete c' ânye ca bahavo rājāno rāja|sattama
mad|artham udyatāḥ sarve prāṇāṃs tyaktvā dhanāni ca.
　tesāṃ madhye sthito yuddhe bhrātṛbhiḥ parivāritaḥ
yodhayiṣyāmy ahaṃ Pārthān Pañcālāṃś c' âiva sarvaśaḥ
Cedīṃś ca nṛ|pa|śārdūla Draupadeyāṃś ca saṃyuge
Sātyakiṃ Kuntibhojaṃ ca rākṣasaṃ ca Ghaṭotkacam.
eko 'py eṣāṃ mahā|rāja samarthaḥ sannivāraṇe
samare Pāṇḍaveyānāṃ saṃkruddho hy abhidhāvatām.
2.25 kiṃ punaḥ sahitā vīrāḥ kṛta|vairāś ca Pāṇḍavaiḥ
atha vā sarva ev' âite Pāṇḍavasy' ânuyāyibhiḥ
yotsyante saha rāj'|êndra haniṣyanti ca tān mṛdhe.
Karṇas tv' eko mayā s'|ârdhaṃ nihaniṣyati Pāṇḍavān.
tato nṛ|patayo vīrāḥ sthāsyanti mama śāsane.

wet with affection, say these fine words to me again, Káurava: "Instruct me!"

My dear son, did I not hear you say the following words? 2.15
You said: "This great earth is as much ours as it is the son of Pritha's. All the following kings—and many others—have given up their lives and wealth and rallied to my cause, O best of monarchs: Bhaga·datta, Kripa and Shalya; the king of Avánti and Jayad·ratha; Bhuri·shravas, Soma·datta and the great king Báhlika; Ashva·tthaman, the Bhojan Krita·varman and the mighty king of Mágadha; Brihad·bala, and the king of Kashi, and Shákuni, the son of Súbala; a hundred thousand foreigners, as well as the Shakas and Yávanas; the Kambója king Sudákshina and the king of Tri·garta; my grandfather Bhishma, the son of Bharad·vaja,* too, and the grandson of Gótama;* Shrutáyush, Ayutáyush and mighty
Shatáyush; Jala·sandha, and the son of Rishya·shringa, and 2.20
the demon Aláyudha; mighty-armed Alámbusha and the great warrior Subáhu.

Standing in their midst and surrounded by my brothers in war, I will fight all the Parthas* and Panchálas in battle, as well as the Chedis, the sons of Dráupadi, Sátyaki, Kunti·bhoja and the demon Ghatótkacha, tiger-like king. When filled with rage, even one of these allies is capable of resisting
the Pándavas as they charge forward in battle. What then if 2.25
these heroes are united in their feuds against the Pándavas? Every one of these kings will fight against the Pándava's followers and kill them in battle, king of kings. However, only Karna and I will kill the Pándavas themselves. After that, these heroic kings will live under my rule.

yaś ca teṣāṃ praṇetā vai Vāsudevo mahā|balaḥ
na sa saṃnahyate rājann iti» mām abravīd vacaḥ.

tasy' âtha vadataḥ sūta bahuśo mama sannidhau
śaktito hy anupaśyāmi nihatān Pāṇḍavān raṇe.

teṣāṃ madhye sthitā yatra hanyante mama putrakāḥ
vyāyacchamānāḥ samare kim anyad bhāga|dheyataḥ?

2.30 Bhīṣmaś ca nihato yatra loka|nāthaḥ pratāpavān
Śikhaṇḍinaṃ samāsādya mṛg'|êndra iva jambukam,
Droṇaś ca brāhmaṇo yatra sarva|śastr'|âstra|pāra|gaḥ
nihataḥ Pāṇḍavaiḥ saṃkhye kim anyad bhāga|dheyataḥ?

Karṇaś ca nihataḥ saṃkhye divy'|âstra|jño mahā|balaḥ
Bhūriśravā hato yatra Somadattaś ca saṃyuge
Bāhlikaś ca mahā|rājaḥ kim anyad bhāga|dheyataḥ?

Bhagadatto hato yatra gaja|yuddha|viśāradaḥ
Jayadrathaś ca nihataḥ kim anyad bhāga|dheyataḥ?

Sudakṣiṇo hato yatra Jalasandhaś ca Pauravaḥ
Śrutāyuś c' Âyutāyuś ca kim anyad bhāga|dheyataḥ?

2.35 mahā|balas tathā Pāṇḍyaḥ sarva|śastra|bhṛtāṃ varaḥ
nihataḥ Pāṇḍavaiḥ saṃkhye kim anyad bhāga|dheyataḥ?

As for the leader of the Pándavas—the mighty Vásu·deva—he will not put on armor, Your Majesty."

This is what he told me several times, O charioteer, and I imagined as best I could that the Pándavas would die in battle.

But when my dear sons are dead, even though they were in such company and fought hard in battle, what else can this be but fate?

When Bhishma, the mighty lord of the world, has been 2.30
struck down after he clashed against Shikhándin like a lion against a jackal; and when the brahmin Drona, skilled in every form of weaponry, has been killed in battle by the Pándavas, what else can this be but fate?

When mighty Karna has been struck down in battle, even though he was expert in divine weaponry; and when Bhuri·shravas, Soma·datta and the great king Báhlika have been killed in war, what else can this be but fate?

When Bhaga·datta is dead, even though he was skilled in elephant warfare, and when Jayad·ratha has been slain, what else can this be but fate?

When Sudákshina and the Páurava Jala·sandha have been killed, as well as Shrutáyush and Ayutáyush, what else can this be but fate?

When the mighty Pandya, the best of all those who wield 2.35
weapons, has also been killed by the Pándavas in battle, what else can this be but fate?

Bṛhadbalo hato yatra Māgadhaś ca mahā|balaḥ
Ugrāyudhaś ca vikrāntaḥ pratimānaṃ dhanuṣmatām
Āvantyo nihato yatra Traigartaś ca jan'|âdhipaḥ
Saṃśaptakāś ca nihatāḥ kim anyad bhāga|dheyataḥ?

Alambuṣas tathā rājan rākṣasaś c' âpy Alāyudhaḥ
Āăyaśṛṅgiś ca nihataḥ kim anyad bhāga|dheyataḥ?

Nārāyaṇā hatā yatra gopālā yuddha|dur|madāḥ
mlecchāś ca bahu|sāhasrāḥ kim anyad bhāga|dheyataḥ?

2.40 Śakuniḥ Saubalo yatra Kaitavyaś ca mahā|balaḥ
nihataḥ sa|balo vīraḥ kim anyad bhāga|dheyataḥ?

ete c' ânye ca bahavaḥ kṛt'|âstrā yuddha|dur|madāḥ
rājāno rāja|putrāś ca śūrāḥ parigha|bāhavaḥ
nihatā bahavo yatra kim anyad bhāga|dheyataḥ?

yatra śūrā mah"|êṣv|āsāḥ kṛt'|âstrā yuddha|dur|madā
bahavo nihatā sūta Mah"|êndra|sama|vikramāḥ
nānā|deśa|samāvṛttāḥ kṣatriyā yatra Sañjaya
nihatāḥ samare sarve kim anyad bhāga|dheyataḥ?

putrāś ca me vinihatāḥ pautrāś c' âiva mahā|balāḥ
vayasyā bhrātaraś c' âiva kim anyad bhāga|dheyataḥ?

When Brihad·bala and the mighty king of Mágadha are dead, as well as bold Ugráyudha, that paradigm of archers; and when the king of Avánti has been struck down as well as the king of Tri·garta, that lord of people; and when the Samshháptakas have been slaughtered, what else can this be but fate?

Alámbusha, the demon Aláyudha and the son of Rishya·shringa have likewise been slain, Your Majesty—what else can this be but fate?

When the Naráyana cowherds are dead—so difficult to defeat in battle—along with many thousands of foreigners, what else can this be but fate?

When Shákuni, the heroic son of Súbala, has been slain 2.40
together with his army, as well as Ulúka, the mighty son of the gambler,* what else can this be but fate?

When these and many others have been killed—kings and princes with arms like iron bars, and heroes skilled in weaponry and difficult to conquer in battle—what else can this be but fate?

When many heroic and great archers have been slain, O charioteer, even though they were skilled in weaponry, difficult to conquer in battle, and equal to great Indra in strength; when all these warriors from different countries have been killed in battle, Sánjaya, what else can this be but fate?

My sons and grandsons are dead, mighty though they were, as are my friends and brothers—what else can this be but fate?

2.45 bhāga|dheya|samāyukto dhruvam utpadyate naraḥ.
yas tu bhāgya|samāyuktaḥ sa śubhaṃ prāpnuyān naraḥ.
ahaṃ viyuktas tair bhāgyaiḥ putraiś c' âiv' êha Sañjaya.
katham adya bhaviṣyāmi vṛddhaḥ śatru|vaśaṃ gataḥ?
n' ânyad atra paraṃ manye vana|vāsād ṛte prabho.
so 'haṃ vanaṃ gamiṣyāmi nirbandhur jñāti|saṃkṣaye.
na hi me 'nyad bhavec chreyo van'|âbhyupagamād ṛte
imām avasthāṃ prāptasya lūna|pakṣasya Sañjaya.

Duryodhano hato yatra Śalyaś ca nihato yudhi
Duḥśāsano Viviṃśaś ca Vikarṇaś ca mahā|balaḥ,
2.50 kathaṃ hi Bhīmasenasya śroṣye 'haṃ śabdam uttamam
ekena samare yena hataṃ putra|śataṃ mama?
a|sakṛd vadatas tasya Duryodhana|vadhena ca
duḥkha|śok'|âbhisaṃtapto na śroṣye paruṣā giraḥ.

VAIŚAMPĀYANA uvāca:

evaṃ vṛddhaś ca saṃtaptaḥ pārthivo hata|bāndhavaḥ
muhur muhur muhyamānaḥ putr'|ādhibhir abhiplutaḥ.
vilapya su|ciraṃ kālaṃ Dhṛtarāṣṭro 'mbikā|sutaḥ
dīrgham uṣṇaṃ sa niḥśvasya cintayitvā parābhavam,
duḥkhena mahatā rājan saṃtapto Bharata'|rṣabhaḥ
punar Gāvalgaṇiṃ sūtaṃ paryapṛcchad yathā|tatham.

DHṚTARĀṢṬRA uvāca:

2.55 Bhīṣma|Droṇau hatau śrutvā sūta|putraṃ ca ghātitam
senā|patiṃ praṇetāraṃ kam akurvata māmakāḥ?
yaṃ yaṃ senā|praṇetāraṃ yudhi kurvanti māmakāḥ

From birth, mankind is surely directed by fate. When 2.45
a man prospers, it is because of his fortune. I have been deprived of such fortune in this world, Sánjaya, as well as of my sons. How can I, an old man, surrender to my enemies today? There is, I believe, nothing left for me in this world than to live in the forest, my lord. Since I have no relatives and my kinsmen have perished, I will enter the forest. For when my wings are cut off and I am in this state, there is nothing better for me than to enter the forest, Sánjaya.

Now that Dur·yódhana is dead and Shalya slain in battle,
as are Duhshásana, Vivímsha and mighty Vikárna, how can 2.50
I listen to the great voice of Bhima·sena, who alone killed my one hundred sons in battle? Tormented by suffering and grief, I cannot bear to hear his cruel words as he repeatedly speaks about the slaughter of Dur·yódhana.

VAISHAM·PÁYANA continued:

In this way, as he fainted again and again, the old king felt anguish at losing his relatives and became overwhelmed by distress for his sons. After lamenting a long time, Dhrita·rashtra, the son of Ámbika, breathed deep and hot sighs as he pondered his defeat. But although tormented by great suffering, the bull of the Bharatas once again asked that charioteer, the son of Gaválgana, to describe what had happened, Your Majesty.

DHRITA·RASHTRA said:

When my troops learned that Bhishma and Drona were 2.55
dead and that the charioteer's son had been killed, whom did they make their general and leader? Whoever is made general by my troops is very quickly killed by the Pánda-

a|ciren' âiva kālena taṃ taṃ nighnanti Pāṇḍavāḥ.
raṇa|mūrdhni hato Bhīṣmaḥ paśyatāṃ vaḥ Kirīṭinā.
evam eva hato Droṇaḥ sarveṣām eva paśyatām.
evam eva hataḥ Karṇaḥ sūta|putraḥ pratāpavān
sa rājakānāṃ sarveṣāṃ paśyatāṃ vaḥ Kirīṭinā.

pūrvam ev' âham ukto vai Vidureṇa mah"|ātmanā
Duryodhan'|âparādhena praj" êyaṃ vinaśiṣyati.
2.60 ke cin na samyak paśyanti mūḍhāḥ samyag avekṣya ca.
tad idaṃ mama mūḍhasya tathā|bhūtaṃ vacaḥ sma tat
yad abravīt sa dharm'|ātmā Viduro dīrgha|darśivān.
tat tathā samanuprāptaṃ vacanaṃ satya|vādinaḥ
daiv'|ôpahata|cittena yan mayā na kṛtaṃ purā
a|nayasya phalaṃ tasya brūhi Gāvalgaṇe punaḥ.

ko vā mukham anīkānāṃ āsīt Karṇe nipātite?
Arjunaṃ Vāsudevaṃ ca ko vā pratyudyayau rathī?
ke 'rakṣan dakṣiṇaṃ cakraṃ Madra|rājasya saṃyuge
vāmaṃ ca yoddhu|kāmasya; ke vā vīrasya pṛṣṭhataḥ?
kathaṃ ca vaḥ sametānāṃ Madra|rājo mahā|rathaḥ
nihataḥ Pāṇḍavaiḥ saṃkhye putro vā mama Sañjaya?
2.65 brūhi sarvaṃ yathā|tattvaṃ Bharatānāṃ mahā|kṣayam
yathā ca nihataḥ saṃkhye putro Duryodhano mama,
Pañcālāś ca yathā sarve
nihatāḥ sa|pad'|ânugāḥ
Dhṛṣṭadyumnaḥ Śikhaṇḍī ca
Draupadyāḥ pañca c' ātma|jāḥ,
Pāṇḍavāś ca yathā muktās tath" ôbhau Mādhavau yudhi
Kṛpaś ca Kṛtavarmā ca Bhāradvājasya c' ātma|jaḥ.
yad yathā yādṛśaṃ c' âiva yuddhaṃ vṛttaṃ ca sāmpratam
akhilaṃ śrotum icchāmi. kuśalo hy asi Sañjaya.

vas. Diadem-adorned Árjuna killed Bhishma at the front of the battle under all your eyes. Drona was killed in the very same way while everyone was looking on. Karna, the mighty charioteer's son, was also killed in exactly this way by diadem-adorned Árjuna under the eyes of all you kings.

Great-spirited Vídura once told me that Dur·yódhana's
wrongdoing would destroy our race. There are fools who 2.60
do not see things properly, even when they are looking straight at them. I was that kind of fool when righteous and farsighted Vídura told me the truth. Son of Gaválgana, tell me once again the fruit of the fault I committed in the past when I did not follow the words of this truth-speaker, my mind destroyed by fate.

Who became head of the armies when Karna died? Which charioteer rose up against Árjuna and Vásu·deva? Who protected the right and left wheels of the king of the Madras* in battle when he was eager for war? And who protected that hero's rear? How did the Pándavas kill that mighty warrior, the king of the Madras, on the battlefield if you were all gathered together? How was my son killed, Sánjaya?

Tell me everything truthfully about the great destruction 2.65
of the Bharatas—how my son Dur·yódhana died in battle, and how all the Panchálas and their followers were killed, as well as Dhrishta·dyumna, Shikhándin and the five sons of Dráupadi. Tell me, too, how the Pándavas and the two Mádhavas* escaped death in battle, and also how Kripa, Krita·varman and the grandson of Bharad·vaja* survived. I want to know everything fully—how the battle happened and the type of battle it was. For you are skilled in speaking, Sánjaya.

3–5
SURRENDER REJECTED

SAÑJAYA uvāca:

3.1 ŚṚṆU RĀJANN avahito yathā vṛtto mahān kṣayaḥ
Kurūṇāṃ Pāṇḍavānāṃ ca samāsādya paras|param.
nihate sūta|putre tu Pāṇḍavena mah"|ātmanā,
vidruteṣu ca sainyeṣu samānīteṣu c' â|sakṛt,
ghore manuṣya|dehānām ājau nara|vara|kṣaye.
yat tat Karṇe hate Pārthaḥ siṃha|nādam ath' âkarot
tadā tava sutān rājan prāviśat su|mahad bhayam.
na sandhātum anīkāni na c' âiv' âtha parākrame
āsīd buddhir hate Karṇe tava yodhasya kasya cit.
3.5 vaṇijo nāvi bhinnāyām a|gādhe viplavā iva
a|pāre pāram icchanto hate dvīpe Kirīṭinā.
sūta|putre hate rājan vitrastāḥ śara|vikṣatāḥ
a|nāthā nātham icchanto mṛgāḥ siṃh'|ârditā iva.
bhagna|śṛṅgā iva vṛṣāḥ śīrṇa|daṃṣṭrā iv' ôragāḥ
pratyupāyāma* sāy'|âhne nirjitāḥ Savyasācinā.
hata|pravīrā vidhvastā nikṛttā niśitaiḥ śaraiḥ
sūta|putre hate rājan putrās te prādravaṃs tataḥ.
vidhvasta|kavacāḥ sarve kāndiśīkā vicetasaḥ
anyonyam abhinighnanto vīkṣamāṇā bhayād diśaḥ.
3.10 «mām eva nūnaṃ Bībhatsur mām eva ca Vṛkodaraḥ
abhiyāt' îti» manvānāḥ petur mamluś ca Bhārata.

SÁNJAYA said:

LISTEN CAREFULLY, Your Majesty, to how a great slaughter took place between the Kurus and the Pándavas after they clashed together. 3.1

When the heroic Pándava had killed the charioteer's son, and the troops were repeatedly fleeing and rallying, there was a terrible carnage of human bodies in battle and the destruction of excellent men.* When the son of Pritha shouted a lion-roar at Karna's slaughter, a huge fear overtook your sons, Your Majesty. Indeed, after Karna died, not one of your warriors had the resolve to control their regiments, let alone show courage in battle.

They were like merchants who were without rafts after 3.5
being shipwrecked in the ocean, and who sought the shore in the boundless sea after their island had been destroyed by diadem-adorned Árjuna. Wounded by arrows and terrified after the death of the charioteer's son, they yearned for a leader—leaderless as they were—and were like deer hounded by a lion, Your Majesty. Like bulls with broken horns or snakes that had had their fangs removed, we returned in the evening, defeated by Savya·sachin.

When their hero was slaughtered, your sons fled at the death of the charioteer's son, crushed and lacerated by sharp arrows, O king. Fearfully looking in every direction, they even began to kill each other as they all ran away madly,
their armor destroyed. Thinking, "It is I whom Bibhátsu* 3.10
is chasing! It is I whom Vrikódara* is chasing!," they fell and languished, descendant of Bharata.

aśvān anye gajān anye rathān anye mahā|rathāḥ
āruhya java|sampannāḥ pādātān prajahur bhayāt.
kuñjaraiḥ syandanā bhagnāḥ sādinaś ca mahā|rathaiḥ.
padāti|saṅghāś c' âśv'|âughaiḥ palāyadbhir bhṛśaṃ hatāḥ.

vyāla|taskara|saṃkīrṇe s'|ârtha|hīnā yathā vane
tathā tvadīyā nihate sūta|putre tad" âbhavan.
hat'|ārohās tathā nāgāś chinna|hastās tath" âpare
sarvaṃ Pārtha|mayaṃ lokam apaśyan vai bhay'|ârditāḥ.
3.15 tān prekṣya dravataḥ sarvān Bhīmasena|bhay'|ârditān
Duryodhano 'tha svaṃ sūtaṃ hā|hā|kṛtv" âivam abravīt:

«n' âtikramiṣyate Pārtho dhanuṣ|pāṇim avasthitam
jaghane yuddhyamānaṃ māṃ. tūrṇam aśvān pracodaya!
samare yudhyamānaṃ hi Kaunteyo māṃ Dhanañjayaḥ
n' ôtsahet' âpy atikrāntuṃ velām iva mah"|ârṇavaḥ.
ady' Ârjunaṃ sa|Govindaṃ māninaṃ ca Vṛkodaram
nihatya śiṣṭāñ śatrūṃs ca Karṇasy' ân|ṛṇyam āpnuyām.»

tac chrutvā Kuru|rājasya śūr'|ārya|sadṛśaṃ vacaḥ
sūto hema|paricchannāñ śanair aśvān acodayat.
3.20 gaj'|âśva|ratha|hīnās tu pādātāś c' âiva māriṣa
pañca|viṃśati|sāhasrāḥ prādravañ śanakair iva.
tān Bhīmasenaḥ saṃkruddho Dhṛṣṭadyumnaś ca Pārṣataḥ
balena catur|aṅgeṇa parikṣipy' âhanac charaiḥ.
pratyayudhyaṃs tu te sarve Bhīmasenaṃ sa|Pārṣatam
Pārtha|Pārṣatayoś c' ânye jagṛhus tatra nāmanī.

Abandoning the foot soldiers in their fear, some mighty warriors climbed swiftly onto horses, others onto elephants, and others onto chariots. Chariots were crushed by elephants, and horsemen by huge chariots. Hordes of infantrymen were brutally killed by packs of fleeing horses.

When the charioteer's son died, your soldiers resembled people that had lost their caravan in a forest full of animals and thieves. Elephants that had lost their riders, or that had had their trunks lopped off, viewed the entire world as being permeated by the son of Pritha, so stricken were they with
fear. When he saw that his men were all fleeing and stricken 3.15
with fear of Bhima·sena, Dur·yódhana shouted loudly and said this to his charioteer:

"The son of Pritha will not overcome me if I stand in the rear and fight, bow in hand. Drive on the horses quickly! Dhanan·jaya,* the son of Kunti, will not be able to conquer me when I fight in battle, just as the great ocean cannot surpass the shore. Today I will remove my debt to Karna by killing Árjuna and Go·vinda,* as well as proud Vrikódara and my other enemies, too."

Hearing the king of the Kurus say these words—so suitable to a heroic noble—the charioteer gently urged on his gold-decked horses.

Then, my lord, twenty-five thousand foot soldiers slowly 3.20
advanced forward, men who had lost their elephants, horses and chariots. Angry Bhima·sena and Dhrishta·dyumna, the grandson of Príshata, surrounded these troops with their fourfold army and began to slaughter them with their arrows. The foot soldiers, however, all fought back against

akrudhyata raṇe Bhīmas tair mṛdhe pratyavasthitaiḥ.
so 'vatīrya rathāt tūrṇaṃ gadā|pāṇir ayudhyata.
na tān ratha|stho bhūmi|ṣṭhān dharm'|āpekṣī Vṛkodaraḥ
yodhayām āsa Kaunteyo bhuja|vīryam upāśritaḥ.
3.25 jāta|rūpa|paricchannāṃ pragṛhya mahatīṃ gadām
nyavadhīt tāvakān sarvān daṇḍa|pāṇir iv' Ântakaḥ.

pādātayo hi saṃrabdhās tyakta|jīvita|bāndhavāḥ
Bhīmam abhyadravan saṃkhye pataṅgā iva pāvakam.
āsādya Bhīmasenaṃ te saṃrabdhā yuddha|dur|madāḥ
vineśuḥ sahasā dṛṣṭvā bhūta|grāmā iv' Ântakam.
śyenavad vyacarad Bhīmaḥ khaḍgena gadayā tathā
pañca|viṃśati|sāhasrāṃs tāvakānām vyapothayat.
hatvā tat puruṣ'|ânīkaṃ Bhīmaḥ satya|parākramaḥ
Dhṛṣṭadyumnaṃ puraskṛtya punas tasthau mahā|balaḥ.

3.30 Dhanañjayo rath'|ânīkam anvapadyata vīryavān
Mādrī|putrau ca Śakuniṃ Sātyakiś ca mahā|balaḥ
javen' âbhyapatan hṛṣṭā ghnanto Dauryodhanaṃ balaṃ.
tasy' âśva|vāhān su|bahūṃs te nihatya śitaiḥ śaraiḥ
tam anvadhāvaṃs tvaritās; tatra yuddham avartata.

Bhima·sena and the grandson of Príshata; some even challenged them by calling out their names.

Bhima became filled with battle-fury against these men who confronted him in war. Descending quickly from his chariot, he fought them, mace in hand. Relying on the strength of his arms, Vrikódara, the son of Kunti, fought according to the rules of warfare by not standing on his
chariot against men that stood on the ground. Taking his 3.25
enormous gold-covered mace, he slew all your soldiers as if he were Death wielding his staff.

At their kinsmen's loss of life, the enraged foot soldiers charged against Bhima in battle, like moths flying into a flame. When they attacked Bhima·sena in their rage, the troops—although difficult to conquer in battle—perished as soon as they saw him, like creatures who look upon Death. Bhima swooped like a hawk with his sword and mace, and crushed those twenty-five thousand of your troops. After destroying that division of men, mighty Bhima—who has truth as his strength—once again took up position behind Dhrishta·dyumna.

Powerful Dhanan·jaya, meanwhile, moved against the 3.30
chariot division, while mighty Sátyaki and the sons of Madri* swiftly rushed with joy against Shákuni, slaughtering Dur·yódhana's army as they did so. After slaying multitudes of Shákuni's horsemen with their sharp arrows, they quickly charged against Shákuni himself. A battle then ensued in that area.

tato Dhanañjayo rājan rath'|ânīkam agāhata
viśrutaṃ triṣu lokeṣu Gāṇḍīvaṃ vyākṣipan dhanuḥ.
Kṛṣṇa|sārathim āyāntaṃ dṛṣṭvā śveta|hayaṃ ratham
Arjunaṃ c' âpi yoddhāraṃ tvadīyāḥ paryavārayan.
viprahīna|rath'|âśvāś ca śaraiś ca parivāritāḥ
pañca|viṃśati|sāhasrāḥ Pārtham ārchan padātayaḥ.
3.35 hatvā tat puruṣ'|ânīkaṃ Pañcālānāṃ mahā|rathaḥ
Bhīmasenaṃ puras|kṛtya na cirāt pratyadṛśyata,
mahā|dhanur|dharaḥ śrīmān a|mitra|gaṇa|mardanaḥ
putraḥ Pañcāla|rājasya Dhṛṣṭadyumno mahā|yaśāḥ.
pārāvata|sa|varṇ'|âśvaṃ kovidāra|vara|dhvajam
Dhṛṣṭadyumnaṃ raṇe dṛṣṭvā tvadīyāḥ prādravan bhayāt.

Gāndhāra|rājaṃ śīghr'|âstram anusṛtya yaśasvinau
a|cirāt pratyadṛśyetāṃ Mādrī|putrau sa|Sātyakau.
Cekitānaḥ Śikhaṇḍī ca Draupadeyāś ca māriṣa
hatvā tvadīyaṃ su|mahat sainyaṃ śaṅkhān ath' âdhaman.
3.40 te sarve tāvakān prekṣya dravato vai parāñ|mukhān
abhyadhāvanta nighnanto vṛṣāñ jitvā vṛṣā iva.

sen"|âvaśeṣaṃ taṃ dṛṣṭvā tava putrasya Pāṇḍavaḥ
avasthitaṃ Savyasācī cukrodha balavan nṛ|pa.
tata enaṃ śarai rājan sahasā samavākirat
rajasā c' ôdgaten' âtha na sma kiñ cana dṛśyate.
andhakārīkṛte loke śarībhūte mahī|tale
diśaḥ sarvā mahā|rāja tāvakāḥ prādravan bhayāt.

Dhanan·jaya penetrated the chariot division, Your Majesty, firing his Gandíva bow, which is renowned throughout the three worlds. Seeing the white-horsed chariot approaching, with Krishna as its driver and Árjuna as its warrior, your soldiers surrounded it. Twenty-five thousand infantrymen confronted the son of Pritha, even though they were deprived of their horses and chariots and enveloped by arrows. But Dhrishta·dyumna—that famous prince of Pan- 3.35
chála who wields a mighty bow, that glorious destroyer of enemy hordes and great warrior of the Panchálas—was soon seen slaughtering that division of troops with Bhima·sena in front of him. Your troops fled in fear when they saw Dhrishta·dyumna in battle, his horses the color of pigeons and his standard made of fine *kovidára* material.

Sátyaki and the glorious sons of Madri were soon seen attacking the king of Gandhára, whose weapons are swift. Chekitána, Shikhándin and the sons of Dráupadi destroyed your great army, my lord, and then blew their conches.
On seeing that all your men were fleeing with their backs 3.40
turned, they chased after them, killing them like bulls conquering bulls.

The Pándava Savya·sachin then grew angry when he saw the remainder of your son's army still standing firm, mighty king. He violently covered them with arrows, Your Majesty, and nothing was visible from the dust that arose. The world became dark and the earth turned into arrows. And your men fearfully fled in every direction, great king.

bhajyamāneṣu sarveṣu Kuru|rājo viśāṃ pate
pareṣām ātmanaś c' âiva sainye te samupādravat.
3.45 tato Duryodhanaḥ sarvān ājuhāv' âtha Pāṇḍavān
yuddhāya Bharata|śreṣṭha devān iva purā Baliḥ.
ta enam abhigarjantaṃ sahitāḥ samupādravan
nānā|śastra|sṛjaḥ kruddhā bhartsayanto muhur muhuḥ.
Duryodhano 'py a|saṃbhṛāntas tān arīn vyadhamac charaiḥ.
tatr' âdbhutam apaśyāma tava putrasya pauruṣam
yad enaṃ Pāṇḍavāḥ sarve na śekur ativartitum.
n' âtidūr'|âpayātaṃ ca kṛta|buddhiṃ palāyane
Duryodhanaḥ svakaṃ sainyam apaśyad bhṛśa|vikṣatam.
tato 'vasthāpya rāj'|êndra kṛta|buddhis tav' ātma|jaḥ
harṣayann iva tān yodhāṃs tato vacanam abravīt:
3.50 «na taṃ deśaṃ prapaśyāmi pṛthivyām parvateṣu ca
yatra yā tān na vo hanyuḥ Pāṇḍavāḥ; kiṃ sṛtena vaḥ?
sv|alpaṃ c' âiva balaṃ teṣāṃ Kṛṣṇau ca bhṛśa|vikṣatau.
yadi sarve 'tra tiṣṭhāmo dhruvaṃ no vijayo bhavet.
viprayātāṃs tu vo bhinnān Pāṇḍavāḥ kṛta|kilbiṣān
anusṛtya haniṣyanti. śreyo naḥ samare vadhaḥ.
sukhaḥ sāṃgrāmiko mṛtyuḥ
kṣatra|dharmeṇa yudhyatām.
mṛto duḥkhaṃ na jānīte.
pretya c' ân|antyam aśnute.
śṛṇvantu kṣatriyāḥ sarve yāvanto 'tra samāgatāḥ:
dviṣato Bhīmasenasya vaśam eṣyatha vidrutāḥ;

When all his soldiers were scattered in this way, the king of the Kurus began to attack both the enemy's troops and his own, O lord of the people.

Dur·yódhana then challenged all the Pándavas to fight, 3.45
best of Bharatas, just as Bali* challenged the gods in the past. Enraged, the Pándavas grouped together and attacked Dur·yódhana as he roared, deriding him repeatedly and hurling various weapons at him. Dur·yódhana, however, did not waver but dispersed the enemies with his arrows. We then witnessed your son's remarkable courage in that battle, as all the Pándavas failed to overpower him.

On seeing that his troops were heavily wounded and intent on flight—although not yet very far away—Dur·yódhana restrained them, king of kings. With a resolute mind, your son then made a speech to his soldiers, as if gladdening them:

"I do not see any place on the earth or in the mountains 3.50
where the Pándavas have not killed you. What then is the use of your fleeing? Their army is only very small and the two Krishnas are heavily wounded. If we all stand firm here, our victory should be certain. The Pándavas will pursue and kill you, if you commit the sin of fleeing and breaking up. It is better for us to die in battle.

Happiness comes from death in battle for those who fight according to the warrior code. A dead man knows no suffering. After he dies, he attains eternity. Let all the warriors gathered here listen: if you flee, you will fall under the control of the enemy Bhima·sena. You must not abandon the practices of your ancestors! There is no worse action for a
warrior than flight. For there is no better path to heaven, 3.55

pitā|mahair ācaritaṃ na dharmaṃ hātum arhatha.
3.55 n' ânyat karm' âsti pāpīyāḥ kṣatriyasya palāyanāt.
na yuddha|dharmāc chreyān hi
panthāḥ svargasya Kauravāḥ.
su|cireṇ' ârjitāl lokān
sadyo yuddhāt samaśnute.»

tasya tad vacanaṃ rājñaḥ pūjayitvā mahā|rathāḥ punar ev' âbhyavartanta kṣatriyāḥ Pāṇḍavān prati parājayam a|mṛṣyantaḥ kṛta|cittāś ca vikrame. tataḥ pravavṛte yuddhaṃ punar eva su|dāruṇam tāvakānāṃ pareṣāṃ ca dev'|âsura|raṇ'|ôpamam.

Yudhiṣṭhira|purogāṃś ca sarva|sainyena Pāṇḍavān anvadhāvan mahā|rāja putro Duryodhanas tava.

SAÑJAYA uvāca:

4.1 PATITĀN RATHA|nīḍāṃś ca rathāṃs c' âpi mah"|ātmanām
raṇe ca nihatān nāgān dṛṣṭvā pattīṃś ca māriṣa,
āyodhanaṃ c' âtighoraṃ Rudrasy' ākrīḍa|saṃnibham
a|prakhyātiṃ gatānāṃ tu rājñāṃ śata|sahasraśaḥ,
vimukhe tava putre tu śok'|ôpahata|cetasi
bhṛś'|ôdvigneṣu sainyeṣu dṛṣṭvā Pārthasya vikramam
dhyāyamāneṣu sainyeṣu duḥkhaṃ prāpteṣu Bhārata,
balānāṃ mathyamānānāṃ śrutvā ninadam uttamam
abhijñānaṃ nar'|êndrāṇāṃ vikṣataṃ prekṣya saṃyuge,
4.5 kṛp"|āviṣṭaḥ Kṛpo rājan vayaḥ|śīla|samanvitaḥ
abravīt tatra tejasvī so 'bhisṛtya jan'|âdhipam
Duryodhanaṃ manyu|vaśād vākyaṃ vākya|viśāradaḥ:

«Duryodhana nibodh' êdaṃ yat tvāṃ vakṣyāmi Kaurava. śrutvā kuru mahā|rāja yadi te rocate 'n|agha.

Káuravas, than the code of war. Through battle, one instantly attains worlds that others obtain after a long time."

Applauding the king's words, those great, martial charioteers once again advanced against the Pándavas, unable to endure defeat and their hearts set on valor. Once again a gruesome battle took place between your troops and the enemy, like a battle between the gods and demons.

Your son Dur·yódhana and all his soldiers then attacked the Pándavas, who were led by Yudhi·shthira, Your Majesty.

SÁNJAYA said:

MY LORD, WHEN Kripa saw the fallen chariots and char- 4.1
iot platforms of the heroes, as well as the elephants and infantrymen that had been slaughtered in battle. And when he saw the horrific battlefield, which resembled Rudra's playground, and the ignominious end of hundreds and thousands of kings. And when, descendant of Bharata, Kripa saw the valor of the Partha, while your son on the other hand fled—his mind destroyed by grief—and your troops brooded in anguish and utter despair. And when he heard crushed soldiers screaming loudly and saw the shattered
mementos of kings in battle. Then, Your Majesty, splen- 4.5
did Kripa—who is compassionate, mature and virtuous—approached King Dur·yódhana and angrily addressed him with these words, skilled as he was in speech:

"Dur·yódhana, descendant of Kuru, listen to what I have to say! And after you have listened, act—if it so pleases you, O faultless, great king.

na yuddha|dharmāc chreyān vai panthā rāj'|êndra vidyate
yaṃ samāśritya yudhyante kṣatriyāḥ kṣatriya'|rṣabha.
putro bhrātā pitā c' âiva svasrīyo mātulas tathā
saṃbandhi|bāndhavāś c' âiva yodhyā vai kṣatra|jīvinā.
vadhe c' âiva paro dharmas tath" â|dharmaḥ palāyane.
te sma ghorāṃ samāpannā jīvikāṃ jīvit'|ârthinaḥ.
tad atra prativakṣyāmi kiñ cid eva hitaṃ vacaḥ:
4.10 hate Bhīṣme ca Droṇe ca Karṇe c' âiva mahā|rathe,
Jayadrathe ca nihate tava bhrātṛṣu c' ân|agha
Lakṣmaṇe tava putre ca kiṃ śeṣaṃ paryupāsmahe?
yeṣu bhāraṃ samāsādya rājye matim akurmahi.
te saṃtyajya tanūr yātāḥ śūrā Brahma|vidāṃ gatim.
vayaṃ tv iha vinā|bhūtā guṇavadbhir mahā|rathaiḥ
kṛpaṇaṃ vartayiṣyāma* pātayitvā nṛ|pān bahūn.
sarvair api ca jīvadbhir Bībhatsur a|parājitaḥ.
Kṛṣṇa|netro mahā|bāhur devair api dur|āsadaḥ.
Indra|kārmuka|tuly'|ābham Indra|ketum iv' ôcchritam
vānaraṃ ketum āsādya saṃcacāla mahā|camūḥ.
4.15 siṃha|nādāc ca Bhīmasya Pāñcajanya|svanena ca
Gāṇḍīvasya ca nirghoṣāt saṃhṛṣyanti manāṃsi naḥ.
carant" îva mahā|vidyun muṣṇantī nayana|prabhām
alātam iva c' āviddhaṃ Gāṇḍīvaṃ samadṛśyata.
jāmbūnada|vicitraṃ ca dhūyamānaṃ mahad dhanuḥ
dṛśyate dikṣu sarvāsu vidyud abhra|ghaneṣv iva.
śvetāś ca vega|saṃpannāḥ śaśi|kāśa|sama|prabhāḥ

King of kings, there is no better path to heaven than the code of war. It is this that warriors follow when they wage battle, bull-like kshatriya. A warrior can fight against his son, brother, father, nephew, uncle, kinsmen or relatives. It is right to be intent on slaughter and wrong to be concerned with fleeing. Warriors practice a terrifying way of life if they want to survive.

Let me give you some useful advice on this matter.

If Bhishma, Drona and the great warrior Karna are dead, 4.10
and if Jayad·ratha, your brothers and your son Lákshmana have been killed, what is there left for us to do, faultless king? It was on these heroes that we placed the burden when we set our hearts on kingship. They have left their bodies and reached the realm of the Brahma-knowers. We, on the other hand, will slaughter many kings and then lead a miserable existence in this world, separated from these virtuous warriors.

Even while all these men were alive, Bibhátsu was unconquered. Even the gods would find it difficult to attack mighty-armed Árjuna, who has Krishna for his eyes. Our huge army trembled when it approached Árjuna's monkey-banner, which was raised like the banner of Indra and shone
like Indra's bow.* Our senses were robbed by Bhima's lion- 4.15
roar, by the blare of the Pancha·janya conch,* and by the noise of the Gandíva* bow. Quivering like lightning and blinding our eyes,* the Gandíva seemed to be wielded* like a firebrand. When that great bow shakes, glittering with gold, it can be seen in every direction, like lightning in rain clouds. Speedy white horses are yoked to Árjuna's chariot; splendid as the moon or *kasha* grass, they seem to devour

pibanta iva c' ākāśaṃ rathe yuktās tu vājinaḥ.
uhyamānāś ca Kṛṣṇena vāyun" êva balāhakāḥ
jāmbūnada|vicitr'|âṅgā vahante c' Ârjunaṃ raṇe.
4.20 tāvakaṃ tad balaṃ rājann Arjuno 'stra|viśāradaḥ
gahanaṃ śiśire kakṣaṃ dadāh' âgnir iv' ôlbaṇaḥ.
gāhamānam anīkāni Mah"|êndra|sadṛśa|prabham
Dhanañjayam apaśyāma catur|daṃṣṭram iva dvi|pam.
vikṣobhayantaṃ senāṃ te trāsayantaṃ ca pārthivān
Dhanañjayam apaśyāma nalinīm iva kuñjaram.
trāsayantaṃ tathā yodhān dhanur ghoṣena Pāṇḍavam
bhūya enam apaśyāma siṃhaṃ mṛga|gaṇān iva.
sarva|loka|mah"|êṣv|āsau vṛṣabhau sarva|dhanvināṃ
āmukta|kavacau Kṛṣṇau loka|madhye viceratuḥ.
4.25 adya sapta|daś'|âhāni vartamānasya Bhārata
saṃgrāmasy' âti|ghorasya vadhyatāṃ c' âbhito yudhi.
vāyun" êva vidhūtāni tava sainyāni sarvataḥ
śarad|ambho|da|jālāni vyaśiryanta samantataḥ
tām nāvam iva paryastāṃ vāta|dhūtāṃ mah"|ârṇave
tava senāṃ mahā|rāja Savyasācī vyakampayat.
kva nu te sūta|putro 'bhūt? kva nu Droṇaḥ sah'|ânugaḥ?
ahaṃ kva ca kva c' ātmā te Hārdikyaś ca tathā kva nu?
Duḥśāsanaś ca te bhrātā bhrātṛbhiḥ sahitaḥ kva nu
bāṇa|gocara|saṃprāptaṃ prekṣya c' âiva Jayadratham
4.30 sambandhinas te bhrātṝṃś ca sahāyān mātulāṃs tathā
sarvān vikramya miṣato lokam ākramya mūrdhani?

the sky. Driven by Krishna, as clouds are by the wind, their legs glittering with gold, the horses carry Árjuna on the battlefield.

Árjuna—skilled in archery—scorched that army of yours, 4.20
Your Majesty, like a violent fire incinerates a thick and dry forest in the winter. We saw Dhanan·jaya penetrating your regiments like a four-tusked elephant, splendid as great Indra. We saw Dhanan·jaya throwing your army into confusion and terrifying the kings, like an elephant disturbs a lotus pond. We saw the Pándava once again terrifying the warriors with the sound of his bow, like a lion terrifies herds of deer. The two Krishnas—the greatest archers in the entire world and bulls of all bowmen—rampaged in everyone's midst, clad in armor.

Today, descendant of Bharata, is the seventeenth day of 4.25
this terrible, ongoing war and of men being slaughtered everywhere in battle. Your troops have been scattered on all sides, like clusters of autumn clouds dispersed in every direction by the wind. Your army has been shaken by Savya·sachin, great king, like a boat tossed about by the wind and reeling on the vast ocean.

Where was that charioteer's son of yours? Where was Drona and his followers? Where was I? Where were you? Where was Krita·varman, the son of Hrídika? And where was your brother Duhshásana and his brothers, when Árjuna saw
that Jayad·ratha was within range of his arrows and—under 4.30
their very eyes—attacked all your relatives, brothers, allies and uncles, and strode across everyone's head?

Jayadratho hato rājan kiṃ nu śeṣam upāsmahe?
ko h' îha sa pumān asti yo vijeṣyati Pāṇḍavam?
tasya c' âstrāṇi divyāni vividhāni mah"|ātmanaḥ.
Gāṇḍīvasya ca nirghoṣo dhairyāṇi harate hi naḥ.
naṣṭa|candrā yathā rātriḥ sen" êyaṃ hata|nāyakā
nāga|bhagna|drumā śuṣkā nad" îv' ākulatāṃ gatā.
dhvajinyāṃ hata|netrāyāṃ yath"|êṣṭaṃ śveta|vāhanaḥ
cariṣyati mahā|bāhuḥ kakṣeṣv agnir iva jvalan.
4.35 Sātyakeś c' âiva yo vego Bhīmasenasya c' ôbhayoḥ
dārayec ca girīn sarvān śoṣayec c' âiva sāgarān.
uvāca vākyaṃ yad Bhīmaḥ sabhā|madhye viśāṃ pate
kṛtaṃ tat sa|phalaṃ tena, bhūyaś c' âiva kariṣyati.
pramukha|sthe tadā Karṇe balaṃ Pāṇḍava|rakṣitaṃ
dur|āsadaṃ tadā guptaṃ vyūḍhaṃ Gāṇḍīva|dhanvanā.
yuṣmābhis tāni cīrṇāni yāny a|sādhūni sādhuṣu
a|kāraṇa|kṛtāny eva. teṣāṃ vaḥ phalam āgatam.
ātmano 'rthe tvayā loko yatnataḥ sarva āhṛtaḥ.
sa te saṃśayitas tāta ātmā ca Bharata'|rṣabha.
4.40 rakṣa Duryodhan' ātmānaṃ. ātmā sarvasya bhājanam.
bhinne hi bhājane tāta diśo gacchati tad|gatam.
hīyamānena vai sandhiḥ paryeṣṭavyaḥ samena ca
vigraho vardhamānena. matir eṣā Bṛhaspateḥ.

If Jayad·ratha has been killed, Your Majesty, what is there left for us to do? What man in this world can conquer the Pándava? The weapons of that hero are divine and diverse. The noise of his Gandíva bow robs us of our courage. Your army is like a moonless night, now that its leader is dead. It is in disarray, like a dried-up river in which the trees have been broken by elephants.

Like a fire burning in dry forests, mighty-armed Árjuna will roam as he likes with his white horses through your
leaderless army. The power of both Sátyaki and Bhima 4.35
could burst through every mountain and dry up the oceans. The words that Bhima said in the assembly hall have been fulfilled, lord of the people, and he will fulfill them still further.* Even when Karna stood at our head, their arrayed army was still difficult to defeat, guarded as it was by the Gandíva bow and protected by the Pándavas.

You have committed deeds that are wicked for good people to do and that were performed without reason. The fruit of these actions of yours has now arrived. You zealously rallied together the entire world for your own cause. Now it and yourself, my child, are in danger, bull of the Bharatas.
Protect yourself, Dur·yódhana; for you are the vessel of ev- 4.40
erything. When a vessel is broken, my boy, all that is in it disperses everywhere. A balanced man should seek peace when he is weak and conflict when he is strong; this is the creed of Brihas·pati.

te vayaṃ Pāṇḍu|putrebhyo
hīnāḥ sva|bala|śaktitaḥ.
tad atra Pāṇḍavaiḥ sārdhaṃ
sandhiṃ manye kṣamaṃ prabho.
na jānīte hi yaḥ śreyaḥ śreyasaś c' âvamanyate
sa kṣipraṃ bhraśyate rājyān na ca śreyo 'nuvindati.
praṇipatya hi rājānaṃ rājyaṃ yadi labhema hi
śreyaḥ syān, na tu mauḍhyena rājan gantuṃ parābhavam.

4.45 Vaicitravīrya|vacanāt kṛpā|śīlo Yudhiṣṭhiraḥ
viniyuñjīta rājye tvāṃ Govinda|vacanena ca.
yad brūyādd hi Hṛṣīkeśo rājānam a|parājitam
Arjunaṃ Bhīmasenaṃ ca sarve kuryur a|saṃśayam.
n' âtikramiṣyate Kṛṣṇo vacanaṃ Kauravasya tu
Dhṛtarāṣṭrasya manye 'haṃ n' âpi Kṛṣṇasya Pāṇḍavaḥ.
etat kṣemam ahaṃ manye tava Pārthair na vigraham.
na tvāṃ bravīmi kārpaṇyān na prāṇa|parirakṣaṇāt.
pathyaṃ rājan bravīmi tvāṃ. tat parāsuḥ smariṣyasi.»
iti vṛddho vilapy' âitat Kṛpaḥ Śāradvato vacaḥ
dīrgham uṣṇaṃ ca niḥśvasya śuśoca ca mumoha ca.

SAÑJAYA uvāca:

5.1 EVAM UKTAS tato rājā Gautamena tapasvinā
niḥśvasya dīrgham uṣṇaṃ ca tūṣṇīm āsīd viśāṃ pate.
tato muhūrtaṃ sa dhyātvā Dhārtarāṣṭro mahā|manāḥ
Kṛpaṃ Śāradvataṃ vākyam ity uvāca paran|tapaḥ:

As for the strength of our army, we have been weakened by the sons of Pandu. Given our situation, I think that peace with the Pándavas is appropriate, my lord. Those who do not know what is good and who disregard what is good quickly lose their kingship and do not acquire the good. If by bowing to King Yudhi·shthira we keep our kingship, that would be good. It would not be good to be defeated out of foolishness, Your Majesty.

Yudhi·shthira is compassionate and would entrust you 4.45
with kingship if Vichítra·virya's son* and Go·vinda request it. Whatever Hrishi·kesha* says to the undefeated king, or to Árjuna and Bhima·sena, will certainly be followed by everyone. Krishna will not go against the words of the Káurava Dhrita·rashtra; nor do I think that the Pándava will disobey Krishna. The safe thing, I believe, is for you not to fight against the sons of Pritha. I tell you this not out of weakness nor in order to save my life. I am telling you what is appropriate, Your Majesty; you will remember this when you are about to die."

Lamenting in this way and breathing out long and hot sighs, old Kripa, the son of Sharádvat, grieved and then fainted.

SÁNJAYA said:

WHEN THE ASCETIC grandson of Gótama addressed him 5.1
in this way, the king stayed silent, lord of the people, breathing out long and hot sighs. Then, after pondering awhile, the proud son of Dhrita·rashtra, that destroyer of enemies, said this to Kripa, the son of Sharádvat:

«yat kiñ cit su|hṛdā vācyaṃ tat sarvaṃ śrāvito hy aham.
kṛtaṃ ca bhavatā sarvaṃ prāṇān saṃtyajya yudhyatā.
gāhamānam anīkāni yudhyamānaṃ mahā|rathaiḥ
Pāṇḍavair atitejobhir lokas tvām anudṛṣṭavān.
5.5 su|hṛdā yad idaṃ vākyaṃ bhavatā śrāvito hy aham.
na māṃ prīṇāti tat sarvaṃ mumūrṣor iva bheṣajam.
hetu|kāraṇa|saṃyuktaṃ hitaṃ vacanam uttamam
ucyamānaṃ mahā|bāho na me vipr'|âgrya rocate.
rājyād vinirhṛto 'smābhiḥ kathaṃ so 'smāsu viśvaset?
akṣa|dyūte ca nṛ|patir jito 'smābhir mahā|dhanaḥ
sa kathaṃ mama vākyāni śraddaddhyād bhūya eva tu?
tathā dautyena saṃprāptaḥ Kṛṣṇaḥ Pārtha|hite rataḥ
pralabdhaś ca Hṛṣīkeśas tac ca karm' â|vicāritam
sa ca me vacanaṃ brahman katham ev' âbhimanyate?
vilalāpa ca yat Kṛṣṇā sabhā|madhye sameyuṣī
na tan marṣayate Kṛṣṇo na rājya|haraṇaṃ tathā.
5.10 eka|prāṇāv ubhau Kṛṣṇāv anyonyam abhisaṃśritau
purā yac chrutam ev' āsīd adya paśyāmi tat prabho.
svasrīyaṃ nihataṃ śrutvā duḥkhaṃ svapiti Keśavaḥ.
kṛt'|āgaso vayaṃ tasya. sa mad|arthaṃ kathaṃ kṣamet?
Abhimanyor vināśena na śarma labhate 'rjunaḥ.
sa kathaṃ madd|hite yatnaṃ prakariṣyati yācitaḥ?
madhyamaḥ Pāṇḍavas tīkṣṇo Bhīmaseno mahā|balaḥ
pratijñātaṃ ca ten' ôgraṃ. bhajyet' âpi na saṃnamet.
ubhau tau baddha|nistriṃśāv ubhau c' ābaddha|kaṅkaṭau
kṛta|vairāv ubhau vīrau yamāv api Yam'|ôpamau.

"Everything that you have told me is what should be
said by a friend. Offering up your life, you have also done
everything in battle. The world has watched you plunging
into armies and fighting against the Pándavas, fierce and
mighty warriors though they are. You have told me what a 5.5
friend should say. None of it, however, gratifies me, just as
medicine cannot gratify a man who is about to die. Although
your words are reasoned, beneficial and excellent, they do
not please me, mighty-armed champion of the brahmins.

Why would Yudhi·shthira trust us after we have deprived
him of his kingdom? Why would he believe my words again
after we beat him in dice—and he with so much wealth?*
Likewise, brahmin, why would Krishna Hrishi·kesha have
any regard for my words after we acted wrongly and de-
ceived him when he came to us as a messenger, delighting
in helping the Parthas?* Krishna cannot forgive the fact that
dark Dráupadi lamented when she came into the middle of
the assembly hall, nor that we usurped the kingdom.*

I had previously only heard that the two Krishnas* have 5.10
one life-breath and depend on each other; today I see that it
is true, my lord. Késhava's sleep was full of sorrow after he
learned that his nephew had been killed. We have wronged
him. Why would he pardon that for my sake?

Árjuna can find no solace after Abhimányu's death.* Why would he make the effort to help me if he was asked? Bhima·sena, the second son of Pandu, is fierce and powerful and has made a formidable vow. He may break but he will not bend. Swearing hostility, the heroic twins, who resemble Yama,* have both strapped on their armor and taken up their swords.

5.15 Dhṛṣṭadyumnaḥ Śikhaṇḍī ca kṛta|vairau mayā saha.
tau kathaṃ madd|hite yatnaṃ kuryātāṃ dvi|ja|sattama?
Duḥśāsanena yat Kṛṣṇā eka|vastrā rajas|valā
parikliṣṭā sabhā|madhye sarva|lokasya paśyataḥ.
tathā vivasanāṃ dīnāṃ smaranty ady' âpi Pāṇḍavāḥ
na nivārayituṃ śakyāḥ saṃgrāmāt te paran|tapāḥ.
yadā ca Draupadī kliṣṭā mad|vināśāya duḥkhitā
ugraṃ tepe tapaḥ Kṛṣṇā bhartṝṇām artha|siddhaye.
sthaṇḍile nityadā śete yāvad vairasya yātanam
nikṣipya mānaṃ darpaṃ ca Vāsudeva|sahodarā
Kṛṣṇāyāḥ preṣyavad bhūtvā śuśrūṣāṃ kurute sadā.
5.20 iti sarvaṃ samunnaddham, na niryāti kathañ cana.
Abhimanyor vināśena sa sandheyaḥ kathaṃ mayā?
kathaṃ ca rājā bhuktv" êmāṃ pṛthivīṃ sāgar'|âmbarām
Pāṇḍavānāṃ prasādena bhokṣye rājyam ahaṃ katham?
upary upari rājñāṃ vai jvalitvā bhās|karo yathā
Yudhiṣṭhiraṃ kathaṃ paścād anuyāsyāmi dāsavat?
kathaṃ bhuktvā svayaṃ bhogān dattvā dāyāṃś ca puṣkalān
kṛpaṇaṃ vartayiṣyāmi kṛpaṇaiḥ saha jīvikām?
n' âbhyasūyāmi te vākyam uktaṃ snigdhaṃ hitaṃ tvayā.
na tu sandhim ahaṃ manye prāpta|kālaṃ kathañ cana.
5.25 su|nītam anupaśyāmi su|yuddhena paran|tapa.
n' âyaṃ klībayituṃ kālaḥ. saṃyoddhuṃ kāla eva naḥ.

Dhrishtha·dyumna and Shikhándin have formed feuds 5.15
against me; why would they make the effort to help me, best of brahmins? Wearing a single cloth and covered in dust, dark Dráupadi was wronged by Duhshásana in the middle of the assembly hall under the eyes of the entire world. Even today the Pándavas still remember how she was naked and wretched; those enemy-destroyers cannot be turned from war. When dark Dráupadi was wronged, she suffered pain and underwent severe austerities in order to destroy me and fulfill her brothers' goals. She constantly lies on the bare ground out of vengeance, and Vásu·deva's sister continuously attends to dark Dráupadi like a servant, discarding her honor and pride.

Everything has thus swollen up, and there is no way that 5.20
it will dissipate. How can peace be made with me after Abhimányu's death? How can I take pleasure in a kingdom through the grace of the Pándavas when I have already enjoyed this sea-clad earth as a king? How can I trail behind Yudhi·shthira like a slave when I have blazed like the sun over and above monarchs? How can I live a wretched life alongside wretched people when I have independently enjoyed wealth and given abundant gifts?

I am not angry at your kind and beneficial words. But I
do not at all think that the time has come for peace. The 5.25
correct conduct, in my view, is to fight well, destroyer of enemies. This is not the time to act like a eunuch. It is time for us to make war.

iṣṭaṃ me bahubhir yajñair. dattā vipreṣu dakṣiṇāḥ.
prāptāḥ kāmāḥ śrutā vedāḥ. śatrūṇāṃ mūrdhni ca sthitam.
bhṛtyā me su|bhṛtās tāta, dīnaś c' âbhyuddhṛto janaḥ.
n' ôtsahe 'dya dvi|ja|śreṣṭha Pāṇḍavān vaktum īdṛśam.
jitāni para|rāṣṭrāṇi sva|rāṣṭram anupālitam.
bhuktāś ca vividhā bhogās. tri|vargaḥ sevito mayā.
pitṝṇāṃ gatam ān|ṛṇyaṃ kṣatra|dharmasya c' ôbhayoḥ.

na sukhaṃ dhruvam ast' îha. kuto rāṣṭraṃ? kuto yaśaḥ?
iha kīrtir vidhātavyā sā ca yuddhena n' ânyathā.
5.30 gṛhe yat kṣatriyasy' âpi nidhanaṃ tad vigarhitam.
a|dharmaḥ su|mahān eṣa yac chayyā|maraṇaṃ gṛhe.
araṇye yo vimuñceta saṃgrāme vā tanuṃ naraḥ
kratūn āhṛtya mahato mahimānaṃ sa gacchati.
kṛpaṇaṃ vilapann ārto jaray" âbhipariplutaḥ
mriyate rudatāṃ madhye jñātīnāṃ na sa pūruṣaḥ.

tyaktvā tu vividhān bhogān prāptānāṃ paramāṃ gatim
ap' îdānīṃ su|yuddhena gaccheyaṃ yat sa|lokatām.
śūrāṇāṃ ārya|vṛttānāṃ saṃgrāmeṣv a|nivartinām
dhīmatāṃ satya|sandhānāṃ sarveṣāṃ kratu|yājinām,
5.35 śastr'|âvabhṛtha|pūtānāṃ dhruvaṃ vāsas tri|viṣṭape
mudā nūnaṃ prapaśyanti yuddhe hy apsarasāṃ gaṇāḥ.
paśyanti nūnaṃ pitaraḥ pūjitān sura|saṃsadi
apsarobhiḥ parivṛtān modamānāṃs tri|viṣṭape.
panthānam a|marair yātaṃ śūraiś c' âiv' â|nivartibhiḥ

I have made many sacrifices, and I have given gifts to brahmins. I have attained my desires, listened to the Vedas, and stood on the heads of my enemies. I have supported my dependents well, my friend, and I have raised the people out of distress. I could not bear to say such words to the Pándavas today, best of brahmins. I have conquered the kingdoms of others and protected my own kingdom. I have enjoyed pleasures of various kinds and followed the three-fold path.* I have paid my debt to my ancestors and also to the warrior code.

There is no stable happiness in this world. What is the point of a kingdom and what of prestige? It is glory that one should strive for in this world, and that can be achieved only through battle. It is reprehensible for a warrior to die at 5.30
home. To die in bed in one's house is a very great wrong. A man attains greatness by giving up his body in the forest or in battle, after he has performed many sacrifices. Whoever dies in the middle of his weeping relatives, overcome by old age and lamenting miserably in distress, is not a man.

Giving up diverse possessions, I will now join, through virtuous battle, those who have reached the highest state. Heroes who behave nobly, who do not flee in battle, who are wise and true to their vows, who perform sacrifices and who 5.35
are cleansed by the purification of weapons—all these men certainly dwell in heaven. Bands of nymphs surely watch them with joy as they fight in battle. Their ancestors surely look upon them as they are honored in the abode of the gods, joyfully surrounded by nymphs in heaven. We will ascend the path that unites us with these men and that has been traveled by the gods and by heroes who have not fled,

api taiḥ saṃgataṃ mārgaṃ vayam adhyāruhemahi,
pitā|mahena vṛddhena tath" ācāryeṇa dhīmatā
Jayadrathena Karṇena tathā Duḥśāsanena ca.
ghaṭamānā mad|arthe 'smin hatāḥ śūrā jan'|âdhipāḥ
śerate lohit'|âkt'|âṅgāḥ saṃgrāme śara|vikṣatāḥ
5.40 uttam'|âstra|vidaḥ śūrā yath"|ôkta|kratu|yājinaḥ
tyaktvā prāṇān yathā|nyāyam Indra|sadmasu dhiṣṭhitāḥ.*
taiḥ svayaṃ racito mārgo dur|gamo hi punar bhavet
saṃpatadbhir mahā|vegair yāsyadbhir iha sad|gatim.
ye mad|arthe hatāḥ śūrās teṣāṃ kṛtam anusmaran
ṛṇaṃ tat pratiyuñjāno na rājye mana ādadhe.
ghātayitvā vayasyāṃś ca bhrātṝn atha pitā|mahān
jīvitaṃ yadi rakṣeyaṃ loko māṃ garhayed dhruvam.
kīdṛśaṃ ca bhaved rājyaṃ mama hīnasya bandhubhiḥ
sakhibhiś ca viśeṣeṇa praṇipatya ca Pāṇḍavam?
5.45 so 'ham etādṛśaṃ kṛtvā jagato 'sya parābhavam
su|yuddhena tataḥ svargaṃ prāpsyāmi na tad anyathā.»
evaṃ Duryodhanen' ôktaṃ sarve saṃpūjya tad vacaḥ
«sādhu sādhv iti» rājānaṃ kṣatriyāḥ saṃbabhāṣire.
parājayam a|śocantaḥ kṛta|cittāś ca vikrame
sarve su|niścitā yoddhum udagra|manaso 'bhavan.
tato vāhān samāśvāsya sarve yuddh'|âbhinandinaḥ
ūne dvi|yojane gatvā pratyatiṣṭhanta Kauravāḥ.
ākāśe vidrume puṇye prasthe Himavataḥ śubhe
aruṇāṃ Sarasvatīṃ prāpya papuḥ sasnuś ca te jalam.

as well as by my venerable grandfather* and by my wise teacher,* and by Jayad·ratha, Karna and Duhshásana.

Heroic kings who strove for my cause have been killed and lie on the battlefield, pierced by arrows and their limbs smeared with blood. Heroes who were expert in the highest 5.40
weaponry and who performed the prescribed sacrifices, have duly given up their lives and taken their places in Indra's abode. They paved this path by themselves. But it has once again become difficult to tread for those who are still in this world and who are about to enter that good state, rushing there with great speed.

Remembering the deeds of these heroes who died for my sake, I will pay back that debt and I will not lend a thought to kingship. The world would certainly criticize me if I were to protect my own life after I have caused the deaths of my friends, brothers and grandfathers. What kind of kingship would I have if I were deprived of my relatives and friends, and especially if I bowed before the Pándava?
After I have thus destroyed this world, I will reach heaven 5.45
through virtuous battle. It cannot be otherwise."

All the warriors applauded Dur·yódhana's words and agreed with the king, saying, "Excellent! Excellent!" No longer grieving over their defeat, they set their hearts on valor and all became fiercely determined to fight. Delighted at the prospect of battle, the Káuravas all roused their animals and, after going a little less than two leagues, set up camp. When they reached the red Sarásvati River on the open, treeless plateau of the Hímavat mountains, which was sacred and auspicious, they drank and bathed in its waters.

5.50 tava putra|kṛt'|ôtsāhāḥ paryavartanta te tataḥ.
paryavasthāpya c' ātmānam anyonyena punas tadā
sarve rājan nyavartanta kṣatriyāḥ kāla|coditāḥ.

The warriors stayed there, enthused by your son, and af- 5.50
ter repeatedly encouraging themselves as well as each other,
they all took their rest, Your Majesty, driven on by Time.

6–7
THE NEW GENERAL

SAÑJAYA UVĀCA:

6.1 ATHA HAIMAVATE prasthe sthitvā yuddh'|âbhinandinaḥ
sarva eva mahā|yodhās tatra tatra samāgatāḥ.
Śalyaś ca Citrasenaś ca Śakuniś ca mahā|rathaḥ
Aśvatthāmā Kṛpaś c' âiva Kṛtavarmā ca Sātvataḥ,
Suṣeṇo 'riṣṭasenaś ca Dhṛtasenaś ca vīryavān
Jayatsenaś ca rājānas te rātrim uṣitās tataḥ.
raṇe Karṇe hate vīre trāsitā jita|kāśibhiḥ
n' âlabhan śarma te putrā Himavantam ṛte girim.
6.5 te 'bruvan sahitās tatra rājānaṃ Śalya|sannidhau
kṛta|yatnā raṇe rājan saṃpūjya vidhivat tadā:
«kṛtvā senā|praṇetāraṃ parāṃs tvaṃ yoddhum arhasi
yen' âbhiguptāḥ saṃgrāme jayem' â|su|hṛdo vayam.»
tato Duryodhanaḥ sthitvā rathe ratha|var'|ôttamam
sarva|yuddha|vibhāga|jñaṃ antaka|pratimaṃ yudhi,
sv|aṅgaṃ pracchanna|śirasaṃ kambu|grīvaṃ priyaṃ|vadam,
vyākośa|padma|patr'|âkṣaṃ vyāghr'|āsyaṃ Meru|gauravam
Sthāṇor vṛṣasya sadṛśaṃ skandha|netra|gati|svaraiḥ
puṣṭa|śliṣṭ'|āyata|bhujaṃ su|vistīrṇa|var'|ôrasam,
6.10 bale jave ca sadṛśaṃ Aruṇ'|ânuja|vātayoḥ
ādityasy' ârciṣā tulyaṃ buddhyā c' Ôśanasā samam,
kānti|rūpa|mukh'|âiśvaryais tribhiś candramasā samam
kāñcan'|ôtpala|saṃghātaiḥ sadṛśaṃ śliṣṭa|sandhikam,
su|vṛtt'|ôru|kaṭī|jaṃghaṃ su|pādaṃ sv|aṅgulī|nakham
smṛtvā smṛtv" âiva tu guṇān Dhātrā yatnād vinirmitam,

SÁNJAYA said:

ALL THE GREAT warriors then gathered here and there 6.1
on the Hímavat plateau, delighted at the prospect of battle. Shalya, Chitra·sena and the mighty warrior Shákuni; Ashva·tthaman, Kripa and Krita·varman, the Sátvata; Sushéna, Árishta·sena, mighty Dhrita·sena and Jayat·sena—all these kings spent the night there.

When heroic Karna died in battle, your sons were terrified by the conquering Pándavas and could find shelter only
in the Hímavat mountains. Assembled in that place, they 6.5
honored King Dur·yódhana in the proper fashion and, in the presence of Shalya, addressed him with the following words, intent as they were upon war:

"You should fight the enemy after you have elected an army leader. Protected by him in battle, we will conquer our foes."

Standing on his chariot, your son Dur·yódhana then went up to Ashva·tthaman, that champion of excellent warriors. Ashva·tthaman: who knows every type of weapon and who is like Death in battle; who has handsome limbs, a covered head, a neck with three lines like a conch, and fine speech; whose eyes are like the petals of an open lotus, whose face is like that of a tiger, and who has the dignity of Meru; who resembles the bull of Sthanu* in his shoulders, eyes, gait and voice; whose arms are strong, well formed and
long, and whose chest is extremely broad and fine; whose 6.10
strength and speed is like that of Áruna's brother* or the wind, and who resembles a ray of the sun; who equals Úshanas in intellect and rivals the moon in the three excellent qualities of splendor, beauty and countenance; who looks

sarva|lakṣaṇa|saṃpannaṃ nipuṇaṃ śruti|sāgaram
jetāraṃ taras" âriṇāṃ a|jeyam aribhir balāt,
daś'|âṅgaṃ yaś catuṣ|pādam iṣv|astraṃ veda tattvataḥ
s'|âṅgāṃś ca caturo vedān samyag ākhyāna|pañcamān,
6.15 ārādhya try|ambakaṃ yatnād vratair ugrair mahā|tapāḥ
a|yoni|jāyām utpanno Droṇen' â|yoni|jena yaḥ,
tam a|pratima|karmāṇaṃ rūpeṇ' â|pratimaṃ bhuvi
pāra|gaṃ sarva|vidyānāṃ guṇ'|ârṇavam a|ninditam,
tam abhety' ātma|jas tubhyam Aśvatthāmānam abravīt:
«yaṃ puraskṛtya sahitā yudhi jeṣyāma Pāṇḍavān
guru|putro 'dya sarveṣām asmākaṃ paramā gatiḥ
bhavāṃs tasmān niyogāt te ko 'stu senā|patir mama?»

DRAUNIR uvāca:

«ayaṃ kulena rūpeṇa tejasā yaśasā śriyā
sarvair guṇaiḥ samuditaḥ Śalyo no 'stu camū|patiḥ.
bhāgineyān nijāṃs tyaktvā kṛta|jño 'smān upāgataḥ.
mahā|seno mahā|bāhur mahā|sena iv' âparaḥ.
6.20 enaṃ senā|patiṃ kṛtvā nṛ|patiṃ nṛ|pa|sattama

like clusters of golden lotuses and who has a body with well-connected joints; who has well-rounded thighs, buttocks and legs, as well as handsome feet, fingers and nails; who bears all the auspicious marks and who was created with care by the Arranger, after He constantly brought to mind various virtues; who is clever and an ocean of learning; who conquers his enemies vigorously but cannot be forcefully conquered by his foes; who has complete knowledge of archery in its ten branches and four sections, and who knows the four Vedas and their branches perfectly, as well as the Ak-
hyánas as a fifth; who was born from a mother not born in a 6.15
womb and was conceived by Drona—himself not born in a womb—after that great ascetic had strenuously worshipped three-eyed Shiva with fierce vows.

Approaching that blameless ocean of virtues, who is unrivaled in his actions, unparalleled on earth in his beauty, and a master of all forms of knowledge, your son said these words to Ashva·tthaman:

"As the teacher's son, you are today the highest refuge of us all. Tell us therefore who should be the general of my army and who can lead us in unity to defeat the Pándavas in battle."

The SON OF DRONA replied:

"Let Shalya be the leader of our army. Lineage, appearance, vigor, reputation, majesty—he possesses every virtue. Abandoning his own nephews, he has remembered his debts and come over to our side. With his great army and mighty
arms, he is like a second Skanda!* We will be able to achieve 6.20
victory if we make this king our general, best of monarchs,

śakyaḥ prāptuṃ jayo 'smābhir devaiḥ Skandam iv' ājitam.»

tath"|ôkte Droṇa|putreṇa sarva eva nar'|âdhipāḥ
parivārya sthitāḥ Śalyaṃ jaya|śabdāṃś ca cakrire.
yuddhāya ca matiṃ cakrur āveśaṃ ca paraṃ yayuḥ.
tato Duryodhano bhūmau sthitvā ratha|vare sthitaṃ
uvāca prāñjalir bhūtvā Droṇa|Bhīṣma|samaṃ raṇe:

«ayaṃ sa kālaḥ samprāpto mitrāṇāṃ mitra|vatsala
yatra mitram a|mitraṃ vā parīkṣante budhā janāḥ.
sa bhavān astu naḥ śūraḥ praṇetā vāhanī|mukhe!
raṇaṃ yāte ca bhavati Pāṇḍavā manda|cetasaḥ
bhaviṣyanti sah'|âmātyāḥ Pañcālāś ca nirudyamāḥ.»

6.25 Duryodhana|vacaḥ śrutvā Śalyo Madr'|âdhipas tadā
uvāca vākyaṃ vākya|jño rājānaṃ rāja|sannidhau.

ŚALYA uvāca:

yat tu māṃ manyase rājan Kuru|rāja karomi tat
tvat|priy'|ârthaṃ hi me sarvaṃ prāṇā rājyaṃ dhanāni ca.

DURYODHANA uvāca:

saināpatyena varaye tvām ahaṃ mātul' â|tulam.
so 'smān pāhi yudhāṃ śreṣṭha Skando devān iv' āhave!
abhiṣicyasva rāj'|êndra devānām iva Pāvakiḥ!
jahi śatrūn raṇe vīra mah"|êndro dānavān iva!

just as the gods were victorious when they made Skanda their general."*

When the son of Drona said these words, all the kings stood around Shalya and cried out shouts of victory. Setting their hearts on battle, they became filled with immense frenzy. Dur·yódhana then stepped onto the ground and, with his hands folded in respect, said these words to Shalya, who stood on a fine chariot, a rival to Drona and Bhishma in battle:

"The time has now come, loyal friend, for the wise to distinguish between friends and enemies. May you be our hero and leader at the head of our army! The Pándavas will become weak-willed when you enter into battle, and the Panchálas and their companions will lose their passion."

Hearing Dur·yódhana's speech and skilled as he was in 6.25
speaking, Shalya, the king of the Madras, said these words before that king of kings.

SHALYA said:

Your Majesty, king of the Kurus, I will do whatever you think right. Everything I have I give as a favor to you, whether my life, my kingdom or my wealth.

DUR·YÓDHANA replied:

My uncle, I choose you as general, for you are without rival. Protect us, best of warriors, just as Skanda protected the gods in battle! Be consecrated, king of kings, just as Skanda, the son of Fire,* was consecrated as leader of the gods! Kill our enemies in battle, O hero, just as great Indra killed the demons!

SAÑJAYA uvāca:

7.1 ETAC CHRUTVĀ vaco rājño Madra|rājaḥ pratāpavān
Duryodhanaṃ tadā rājan vākyam etad uvāca ha:
«Duryodhana mahā|bāho śṛṇu vākya|vidāṃ vara.
yāv etau manyase Kṛṣṇau ratha|sthau rathināṃ varau
na me tulyāv ubhāv etau bāhu|vīrye kathañ cana.
udyatāṃ pṛthivīṃ sarvāṃ sa|sur'|âsura|mānavām
yodhayeyaṃ raṇa|mukhe saṃkruddhaḥ, kim u Pāṇḍavān?
vijeṣyāmi raṇe Pārthān Somakāṃś ca samāgatān
ahaṃ senā|praṇetā te bhaviṣyāmi; na saṃśayaḥ.
7.5 taṃ ca vyūhaṃ vidhāsyāmi na tariṣyanti yaṃ pare
iti satyaṃ bravīmy eṣa Duryodhana; na saṃśayaḥ.»
evam uktas tato rājā Madr'|âdhipatim añjasā
abhyaṣiñcata senāyāṃ madhye Bharata|sattama
vidhinā śāstra|dṛṣṭena hṛṣṭa|rūpo viśāṃ pate.
abhiṣikte tatas tasmin siṃha|nādo mahān abhūt
tava sainye 'bhyavādyanta vāditrāṇi ca Bhārata.
hṛṣṭāś c' āsaṃs tathā yodhā Madrakāś ca mahā|rathāḥ
tuṣṭuvuś c' âiva rājānaṃ Śalyam āhava|śobhinam:
«jaya rājaṃś! ciraṃ jīva! jahi śatrūn samāgatān!
tava bāhu|balaṃ prāpya Dhārtarāṣṭrā mahā|balāḥ
nikhilāḥ pṛthivīṃ sarvāṃ praśāsantu hata|dviṣaḥ!
7.10 tvaṃ hi śakto raṇe jetuṃ sa|sur'|âsura|mānavān;
martya|dharmāṇa iha tu kim u Sṛñjaya|Somakān?»

SÁNJAYA said:

YOUR MAJESTY, on hearing the words of the king, the glorious ruler of the Madras said this to Dur·yódhana: 7.1

"Mighty-armed Dur·yódhana, best of those skilled in speech, listen to my words. You have judged the two chariot-riding Krishnas to be the best of charioteers. But neither of them can in any way rival me in the strength of my arms. In my rage, I could fight at the forefront of the battle against the entire earth if it rose up against me, along with its gods, demons and men. What then of the Pándavas? I will conquer the sons of Pritha in battle, as well as the assembled
Sómakas. I will be your general; have no doubt. And I will 7.5
arrange the army so that it cannot be overcome by our enemies. What I say is true, Dur·yódhana; have no doubt."

Immediately after this speech, best of Bharatas, the king joyfully consecrated the ruler of the Madras in the middle of the army in the manner prescribed by scripture. After Shalya's consecration, there was a loud lion-roar and music was played among your troops, descendant of Bharata. The soldiers were delighted, as were the Mádrakas, those great warriors. Praising King Shalya, who is radiant in battle, they said:

"Victory to you, Your Majesty! May you live long! And may you destroy the assembled enemies! Through the power of your arms, may all the powerful sons of Dhrita·rashtra slaughter their enemies and wield command over the entire
earth! For you have the power to conquer all the worlds in 7.10
battle, along with their gods, demons and men;* what then of the Srínjayas and Sómakas, who are mortal and belong to this world?"

evaṃ saṃpūjyamānas tu Madrāṇām adhipo balī
harṣaṃ prāpa tadā vīro dur|āpam a|kṛt'|ātmabhiḥ.

ŚALYA uvāca:

adya c' âhaṃ raṇe sarvān Pañcālān saha Pāṇḍavaiḥ
nihaniṣyāmi vā rājan svargaṃ yāsyāmi vā hataḥ.
adya paśyantu māṃ lokā vicarantam a|bhītavat
adya Pāṇḍu|sutāḥ sarve Vāsudevaḥ sa|Sātyakiḥ,
Pañcālāś Cedayaś c' âiva Draupedayāś ca sarvaśaḥ
Dhṛṣṭadyumnaḥ Śikhaṇḍī ca sarve c' âpi Prabhadrakāḥ
7.15 vikramaṃ mama paśyantu dhanuṣaś ca mahad balam
lāghavaṃ c' âstra|vīryaṃ ca bhujayoś ca balaṃ yudhi!
adya paśyantu me Pārthāḥ siddhāś ca saha cāraṇaiḥ
yādṛśaṃ me balaṃ bāhvoḥ sampad astreṣu yā ca me!
adya me vikramaṃ dṛṣṭvā Pāṇḍavānāṃ mahā|rathāḥ
pratīkāra|parā bhūtvā ceṣṭantāṃ vividhāḥ kriyāḥ!
adya sainyāni Pāṇḍūnāṃ drāvayiṣye samantataḥ.
Droṇa|Bhīṣmāv ati vibho sūta|putraṃ ca saṃyuge
vicariṣye raṇe yudhyan priy'|ârthaṃ tava Kaurava.

SAÑJAYA uvāca:

abhiṣikte tathā Śalye tava sainyeṣu māna|da
na Karṇa|vyasanaṃ ke cin menire tatra Bhārata.
7.20 hṛṣṭāḥ su|manasaś c' âiva babhūvus tatra sainikāḥ
menire nihatān Pārthān Madra|rāja|vaśaṃ gatān.
praharṣaṃ prāpya senā tu tāvakī Bharata'|rṣabha
tāṃ rātriṃ sukhinī suptā harṣa|cittā ca s" âbhavat.

Praised in this way, the heroic and mighty king of the Madras felt a joy that is difficult for those with imperfect souls to attain.

SHALYA said:

On this day, Your Majesty, I will either kill all the Panchálas and the Pándavas in battle or I will die and reach heaven. On this day let the world see me rampaging fearlessly. On this day let all the sons of Pandu, as well as Vásu·deva, Sátyaki, the Panchálas, Chedis, all the sons of Dráupadi, Dhrishta·dyumna, Shikhándin and all the Prabhádrakas see my 7.15
valor, the huge strength of my bow, my speed, the power of my weapons and the might of my arms in battle! On this day let the Parthas, *siddha*s and *chárana*s observe the kind of strength I have in my arms and my accomplishment in weaponry!* Let the mighty warriors of the Pándavas adopt various strategies to counteract my actions when they see my prowess today! On this day I will rout the troops of the Pandus on every side. Excelling Drona, Bhishma and the charioteer's son in battle, I will rampage on the battlefield, fighting as a favor to you, Káurava.

SÁNJAYA said:

After Shalya had been consecrated in this way, none of your troops there thought about Karna's disaster, honor-giving descendant of Bharata. Joyful and in good spirits, 7.20
the soldiers now thought about the death of the Parthas and their surrender to the king of the Madras. Feeling such joy, your army slept happily during the night and their minds were elated, bull of the Bharatas.

sainyasya tava taṃ śabdaṃ śrutvā rājā Yudhiṣṭhiraḥ
Vārṣṇeyam abravīd vākyaṃ sarva|kṣatrasya paśyataḥ:
«Madra|rājaḥ kṛtaḥ Śalyo Dhārtarāṣṭreṇa Mādhava
senā|patir mah"|êṣv|āsaḥ sarva|sainyeṣu pūjitaḥ.
etaj jñātvā yathā|bhūtaṃ kuru Mādhava yat kṣamam.
bhavān netā ca goptā ca. vidhatsva yad an|antaram.»
7.25 tam abravīn mahā|rāja Vāsudevo jan'|âdhipam:
«Ārtāyanim ahaṃ jāne yathā|tattvena Bhārata.
vīryavāṃś ca mahā|tejā mah"|ātmā ca viśeṣataḥ.
kṛtī ca citra|yodhī ca saṃyukto lāghavena ca.
yādṛg Bhīṣmo yathā Droṇo yādṛk Karṇaś ca saṃyuge
tādṛśas tad|viśiṣṭo vā Madra|rājo mato mama.
yudhyamānasya tasy' âhaṃ cintayānaś ca Bhārata
yoddhāraṃ n' âdhigacchāmi tulya|rūpaṃ jan'|âdhipa.
Śikhaṇḍy|Arjuna|Bhīmānāṃ Sātvatasya ca Bhārata
Dhṛṣṭadyumnasya ca tathā balen' âbhyadhiko raṇe
7.30 Madra|rājo mahā|rāja siṃha|dvi|rada|vikramaḥ
vicariṣyaty abhīḥ kāle kālaḥ kruddhaḥ prajāsv iva.
tasy' âdya na prapaśyāmi pratiyoddhāram āhave
tvām ṛte puruṣa|vyāghra śārdūla|sama|vikramam.
sa|deva|loke kṛtsne 'smin n' ânyas tvattaḥ pumān bhavet
Madra|rājaṃ raṇe kruddhaṃ yo hanyāt Kuru|nandana.
ahany ahani yudhyantaṃ kṣobhayantaṃ balaṃ tava
tasmāj jahi raṇe Śalyaṃ Maghavān iva Śambaram!

On hearing this noise coming from your army, King Yu-dhi·shthira spoke to Krishna of the Vrishni clan, while all the warriors looked on:

"O Mádhava, Shalya—that king of the Madras and great archer who is honored among all troops—has been made general by the son of Dhrita·rashtra. Seeing this to be true, do what is appropriate, Mádhava. You are our leader and protector. Arrange what has to be done next."

Vásu·deva then said this to the ruler of the people, great 7.25
king:

"I know Artáyani* thoroughly, descendant of Bharata. He has vigor, immense power and an exceptionally great spirit. He is accomplished, skilled in various forms of battle, and agile. I consider the king of the Madras to be like Bhishma, Drona or Karna in battle, or perhaps even better. When I think of him fighting, lord of the people, I can see no warrior that is equal to him. In his strength, he surpasses Shikhándin, Árjuna, Bhima, Sátyaki the Sátvata and Dhri-
shta·dyumna in battle, descendant of Bharata. With the 7.30
bravery of a lion or elephant, the ruler of the Madras will rampage everywhere when the moment arrives, great king, like Time itself when it is angry with creatures.

I can see no one today who could oppose him in battle, except for you, tiger-like man—you who have the strength of a tiger. In this entire world with all its gods, there is truly no man other than you, delight of the Kurus, who could kill the king of the Madras when he is enraged in battle. Day after day, he agitates and fights your troops. Therefore kill Shalya in battle, like Mághavat killed Shámbara!* This invincible hero is honored by the son of Dhrita·rashtra;

a|jeyaś c' âpy asau vīro Dhārtarāṣṭreṇa sat|kṛtaḥ;
tav' âiva hi jayo nūnaṃ hate Madr'|ēśvare yudhi.
tasmin hate hataṃ sarvaṃ Dhārtarāṣṭra|balaṃ mahat.
7.35 etac chrutvā mahā|rāja vacanaṃ mama sāmpratam
pratyudyāhi raṇe Pārtha Madra|rājaṃ mahā|ratham!
jahi c' âinaṃ mahā|bāho Vāsavo Namuciṃ yathā!
na c' âiv' âtra dayā kāryā mātulo 'yaṃ mam' êti vai.
kṣatra|dharmaṃ puraskṛtya jahi Madra|jan'|ēśvaram!
Droṇa|Bhīṣm'|ârṇavaṃ tīrtvā Karṇa|pātāla|saṃbhavam
mā nimajjasva sa|gaṇaḥ Śalyam āsādya goṣ|padam!
yac ca te tapaso vīryaṃ yac ca kṣātraṃ balaṃ tava
tad darśaya raṇe sarvaṃ jahi c' âinaṃ mahā|ratham!»

etāvad uktvā vacanaṃ Keśavaḥ para|vīra|hā
jagāma śibiraṃ sāyaṃ pūjyamāno 'tha Pāṇḍavaiḥ.
7.40 Keśave tu tadā yāte Dharma|putro Yudhiṣṭhiraḥ
visṛjya sarvān bhārtṛṃś ca Pañcālān atha Somakān
suṣvāpa rajanīṃ tāṃ tu viśalya iva kuñjaraḥ.

te ca sarve mah"|êṣv|āsāḥ Pañcālāḥ Pāṇḍavās tathā
Karṇasya nidhane hṛṣṭāḥ suṣupus tāṃ niśāṃ tadā.
gata|jvaraṃ mah"|êṣv|āsaṃ tīrṇa|pāraṃ mahā|ratham
babhūva Pāṇḍaveyānāṃ sainyaṃ ca muditaṃ nṛ|pa
sūta|putrasya nidhane jayaṃ labdhvā ca māriṣa.

victory would therefore surely be yours if you killed the lord of the Madras in battle. If Shalya was killed, all of Dhrita·rashtra's great army would be destroyed.

Listen to these words of mine, great king and son of 7.35
Pritha, and rise up in battle against that mighty warrior the king of the Madras! Kill him, mighty-armed Yudhi·sh-thira, just as Vásava killed Námuchi!* You should not feel compassion because he is your uncle. Make the warrior code your priority and kill the lord of the Madras! Now that you have crossed the ocean of Drona and Bhishma and also the hell realm of Karna, do not drown in a cow's hoofprint when you confront Shalya with your troops! Reveal on the battlefield all the force of your ascetic power and all your martial strength. Slaughter this mighty warrior!"

Saying these words, Késhava, that destroyer of enemy heroes, retired to his tent in the evening, honored by the
Pándavas. After Késhava's departure, Yudhi·shthira, the son 7.40
of Righteousness, dismissed all his brothers, as well as the Panchálas and the Sómakas, and slept during the night like an elephant that has had thorns removed from its body.*

Those great archers, the Panchálas and Pándavas, also all went to sleep for the night, joyful at Karna's death. Its anxieties dispelled, the army of the Pándavas—with its great archers and mighty warriors—seemed to have reached the further shore, Your Majesty, and felt joy at its victory in destroying the charioteer's son, my lord.

8–10
THE BATTLE RESUMES

SAÑJAYA uvāca:

8.1 VYATĪTĀYĀṂ rajanyāṃ tu rājā Duryodhanas tadā
abravīt tāvakān sarvān «saṃnahyantāṃ mahā|rathāḥ.»
rājñaś ca matam ājñāya samanahyata sā camūḥ.
ayojayan rathāṃs tūrṇaṃ paryadhāvaṃs tath" âpare.
akalpyanta ca mātaṅgāḥ, samanahyanta pattayaḥ,
rathān āstaraṇ'|ôpetāṃś cakrur anye sahasraśaḥ.
vāditrāṇāṃ ca ninadaḥ prādur āsīd viśāṃ pate
āyodhan'|ârthaṃ yodhānāṃ balānāṃ c' âpy udīryatām.
8.5 tato balāni sarvāṇi senā|śiṣṭāni Bhārata
prasthitāni vyadṛśyanta mṛtyuṃ kṛtvā nivartanam
Śalyaṃ senā|patiṃ kṛtvā Madra|rājaṃ mahā|rathāḥ
pravibhajya balaṃ sarvam anīkeṣu vyavasthitāḥ.
tataḥ sarve samāgamya putreṇa tava sainikāḥ
Kṛpaś ca Kṛtavarmā ca Drauniḥ Śalyo 'tha Saubalaḥ
anye ca pārthivāḥ śeṣāḥ samayaṃ cakrur ādṛtāḥ:
«na na ekena yoddhavyaṃ kathañ cid api Pāṇḍavaiḥ.
yo hy ekaḥ Pāṇḍavair yudhyed yo vā yudhyantaṃ utsṛjet,
sa pañcabhir bhaved yuktaḥ pātakaiś c' ôpapātakaiḥ.
anyonyaṃ parirakṣadbhir yoddhavyaṃ sahitaiś ca naḥ.»
8.10 evaṃ te samayaṃ kṛtvā sarve tatra mahā|rathāḥ
Madra|rājaṃ puraskṛtya tūrṇam abhyadravan parān.
tath" âiva Pāṇḍavāḥ sarve vyūhya sainyaṃ mahā|raṇe
abhyayuḥ Kauravān rājan yotsyamānāḥ samantataḥ.
tad balaṃ Bharata|śreṣṭha kṣubdh'|ârṇava|sama|svanam
samuddhūt'|ârṇav'|ākāram uddhūta|ratha|kuñjaram.

SÁNJAYA said:

AFTER THE NIGHT had passed, King Dur·yódhana addressed all your troops, saying, "Arm yourselves, great warriors!" Hearing the king's command, the army began to make preparations. Some swiftly yoked their chariots, while others hurried about. Elephants were equipped, and foot soldiers put on their armor. Thousands of others furnished chariots with covers. There was the noise of musical instruments and of troops and warriors who were roused for battle, lord of the people. 8.1

All the army's remaining soldiers were then seen to be 8.5
prepared, descendant of Bharata, determined to die before fleeing. Having made Shalya, the king of the Madras, their general, the great warriors sectioned out the entire army and took up position in their divisions. All the troops then gathered together with your son, including Kripa, Krita·varman, the son of Drona, Shalya, the son of Súbala, and the other remaining kings, and solemnly made this pact:

"No one under any circumstance must fight the Pándavas alone. Whoever does fight the Pándavas alone, or abandons a fellow warrior, will incur the five major sins and the minor sins.* We must fight together, protecting one another."

After making this pact, all the great warriors on the bat- 8.10
tlefield swiftly charged against the enemy, led by the king of the Madras.

In the same way, Your Majesty, all the Pándavas drew up their army on the great battlefield and advanced against the Káuravas, ready to fight on all sides. Their force roared like a stormy ocean, and with its heaving chariots and elephants, it looked like a billowing sea, best of Bharatas.

DHṚTARĀṢṬRA uvāca:

Droṇasya c' âiva Bhīṣmasya Rādheyasya ca me śrutam
pātanaṃ śaṃsa me bhūyaḥ Śalyasy' âtha sutasya me.
kathaṃ raṇe hataḥ Śalyo dharma|rājena Sañjaya
Bhīmena ca mahā|bāhuḥ putro Duryodhano mama?

SAÑJAYA uvāca:

8.15 kṣayaṃ manuṣya|dehānāṃ tathā nāg'|âśva|saṃkṣayam
śṛṇu rājan sthiro bhūtvā saṃgrāmaṃ śaṃsato mama.
āśā balavatī rājan putrāṇāṃ te 'bhavat tadā
hate Droṇe ca Bhīsme ca sūta|putre ca pātite
Śalyaḥ Pārthān raṇe sarvān nihaniṣyati māriṣa.
tām āśāṃ hṛdaye kṛtvā samāśvāsya ca Bhārata
Madra|rājaṃ ca samare samāśritya mahā|ratham
nāthavantaṃ tad" ātmānam amanyanta sutās tava.
yadā Karṇe hate Pārthāḥ siṃha|nādaṃ pracakrire
tadā tu tāvakān rājann āviveśa mahad bhayam.
8.20 tān samāśvāsya yodhāṃs tu Madra|rājaḥ pratāpavān
vyūhya vyūhaṃ mahā|rāja sarvato|bhadram ṛddhimat.
pratyudyayau raṇe Pārthān Madra|rājaḥ pratāpavān
vidhunvan kārmukaṃ citraṃ bhāra|ghnaṃ vegavattaram.
ratha|pravaram āsthāya saindhav'|âśvaṃ mahā|rathaḥ
tasya sūto mahā|rāja ratha|stho 'śobhayad ratham.
sa tena saṃvṛto vīro rathen' â|mitra|karṣaṇaḥ
tasthau śūro mahā|rāja putrāṇāṃ te bhaya|praṇut.

DHRITA·RASHTRA said:

I have already heard about the fall of Drona, Bhishma and the son of Radha. Tell me further about the fall of Shalya and my son. How was Shalya killed in battle by the King of Righteousness, O Sánjaya? And how was my mighty-armed son Dur·yódhana killed by Bhima?

SÁNJAYA said:

Be strong, Your Majesty, and listen to the slaughter of 8.15
human bodies and the destruction of elephants and horses, as I tell you of the battle.

After Drona, Bhishma and the charioteer's son had been killed, Your Majesty, your sons had high hopes that Shalya would kill all the sons of Pritha in battle. Encouraged and keeping this hope in their hearts, your sons depended on that great warrior, the king of the Madras, in battle and considered themselves to have a protector, descendant of Bharata.

When the sons of Pritha made a lion-roar at the death
of Karna, a great fear overtook your troops, Your Majesty. 8.20
Encouraging these soldiers, the glorious king of the Madras drew up the army into the effective *sárvato·bhadra* formation.* The mighty king of the Madras then advanced against the sons of Pritha in battle, wielding his glistening bow, which was strong and extremely swift. That mighty warrior climbed onto an excellent chariot that was driven by Sindhu horses, and his driver made the chariot look glorious as he stood on the vehicle, great king. Guarded by this chariot, that manly hero stood there, vexing his enemies and dispelling your sons' fears, mighty king.

prayāṇe Madra|rājo 'bhūn mukhaṃ vyūhasya daṃśitaḥ
Madrakaiḥ sahito vīraiḥ Karṇa|putraiś ca dur|jayaiḥ.
8.25 Duryodhano 'bhavan madhye rakṣitaḥ Kuru|puṅ|gavaiḥ
savye 'bhūt Kṛtavarmā ca Trigartaiḥ parivāritaḥ.
Gautamo dakṣiṇe pārśve Śakaiṣ ca Yavanaiḥ saha
Aśvatthāmā pṛṣṭhato 'bhūt Kāmbojaiḥ parivāritaḥ.
hay'|ânīkena mahatā Saubalaś c' âpi saṃvṛtaḥ
prayayau sarva|sainyena Kaitavyaś ca mahā|rathaḥ.

Pāṇḍavāś ca mah"|êṣv|āsā vyūhya sainyam arin|damāḥ
tridhā bhūtā mahā|rāja tava sainyam upādravan.
Dhṛṣṭadyumnaḥ Śikhaṇḍī ca Sātyakiś ca mahā|rathaḥ
Śalyasya vāhinīṃ hantum abhidudruvur āhave.
8.30 tato Yudhiṣṭhiro rājā sven' ânīkena saṃvṛtaḥ
Śalyam ev' âbhidudrāva jighāṃsur Bharata'|rṣabha.
Hārdikyaṃ ca mah"|êṣv|āsaṃ Arjunaḥ śatru|sainya|hā
Saṃśaptaka|gaṇāṃś c' âiva vegito 'bhividudruve.
Gautamaṃ Bhīmaseno vai Somakāś ca mahā|rathāḥ
abhyadravanta rāj'|êndra jighāṃsantaḥ parān yudhi.
Mādrī|putrau tu Śakunim Ulūkaṃ ca mahā|ratham
sa|sainyau saha|senau tāv upatasthatur āhave.

tath" âiv' âyutaśo yodhās tāvakāḥ Pāṇḍavān raṇe
abhyavartanta saṃkruddhā vividh'|āyudha|pāṇayaḥ.

During that advance, the king of the Madras stood at the head of the army, clad in armor. He was accompanied by the Madra heroes and by the sons of Karna, who are difficult to conquer. Dur·yódhana stood in the center, protected by 8.25
the bull-like Kurus, while Krita·varman stood on the left, surrounded by the Tri·gartas. The grandson of Gótama* was on the right flank, together with the Shakas and Yávanas, while Ashva·tthaman stood in the rear, surrounded by the Kambójas. Accompanied by a large cavalry, Shákuni, the son of Súbala, advanced forward with all his troops; with him was Ulúka, that great warrior and gambler's son.

The Pándavas—those great archers and enemy-tamers—drew up their army and attacked your soldiers in three groups, great king. Dhrishta·dyumna, Shikhándin and the mighty warrior Sátyaki charged against Shalya's army on the battlefield in order to destroy it.

Surrounded by his own regiment, King Yudhi·shthira 8.30
then charged against Shalya himself, eager to kill him, bull of the Bharatas. Árjuna, that destroyer of enemy armies, swiftly attacked the great archer Krita·varman, that son of Hrídika, and the Samsháptaka troops. Eager to kill their enemies in battle, Bhima·sena and those great warriors, the Sómakas, charged against the grandson of Gótama, king of kings. Meanwhile, the two sons of Madri confronted Shákuni and the great warrior Ulúka with their soldiers and armies in battle.

In the same manner, myriads of your troops furiously attacked the Pándavas on the battlefield, wielding various weapons.

DHṚTARĀṢṬRA uvāca:

8.35 hate Bhīṣme mah"|êṣv|āse Droṇe Karṇe mahā|rathe
Kuruṣv alp'|âvaśiṣṭeṣu Pāṇḍaveṣu ca saṃyuge,
su|saṃrabdheṣu Pārtheṣu parākrānteṣu Sañjaya
māmakānāṃ pareṣāṃ ca kiṃ śiṣṭam abhavad balam?

SAÑJAYA uvāca:

yathā vayaṃ pare rājan yuddhāya samupasthitāḥ
yāvac c' āsīd balaṃ śiṣṭaṃ saṃgrāme tan nibodha me.
ekādaśa sahasrāṇi rathānāṃ Bharata'|rṣabha
daśa danti|sahasrāṇi sapta c' âiva śatāni ca,
pūrṇe śata|sahasre dve hayānāṃ tatra Bhārata
patti|koṭyas tathā tisro, balam etat tav' âbhavat.
8.40 rathānāṃ ṣaṭ|sahasrāṇi ṣaṭ|sahasrāś ca kuñjarāḥ
daśa c' âśva|sahasrāṇi patti|koṭī ca Bhārata,
etad balaṃ Pāṇḍavānām abhavac cheṣam āhave.

eta eva samājagmur yuddhāya Bharata'|rṣabha.
evaṃ vibhajya rāj'|êndra Madra|rāja|vaśe sthitāḥ
Pāṇḍavān pratyudīyāma jaya|gṛddhāḥ pramanyavaḥ
tath" âiva Pāṇḍavāḥ śūrāḥ samare jita|kāśinaḥ
upayātā nara|vyāghrāḥ Pañcālāś ca yaśasvinaḥ.

ime te ca bal'|âughena paras|para|vadh'|âiṣiṇaḥ
upayātā nara|vyāghrāḥ pūrvāṃ sandhyāṃ prati prabho.
8.45 tataḥ pravavṛte yuddhaṃ ghora|rūpaṃ bhayānakam
tāvakānāṃ pareṣāṃ ca nighnatām itar'|êtaram.

DHRITA·RASHTRA said:

After that great archer Bhishma had been killed, along 8.35
with Drona and the mighty warrior Karna, and when there were only a few Kurus and Pándavas left in the battle, what was the remaining strength of both my troops and the enemy when the sons of Pritha advanced in a rage, Sánjaya?

SÁNJAYA said:

Listen, Your Majesty, to how both we and the enemy were drawn up for war, and the size of the forces that remained in the battle. Eleven thousand chariots, ten thousand seven hundred elephants, a total of two hundred thousand horses on the battlefield, and thirty million infantry—this was
the size of your army, descendant of Bharata. Six thousand 8.40
chariots, six thousand elephants, ten thousand horses, and ten million infantry—this was the size of the Pándavas' remaining army in battle, descendant of Bharata.

Such were the forces that confronted each other to wage war, bull of the Bharatas. Organized in this way, we took up position under the command of the king of the Madras and furiously advanced against the Pándavas, greedy for victory, king of kings. In the same way, the heroic Pándavas—those conquerors in battle and tigers among men—advanced together with the glorious Panchálas.

Desiring to kill each other, these tiger-like men advanced
at dawn with a sea of troops, my lord. There was then a 8.45
hideous and terrifying battle between your troops and the enemy, as both sides slaughtered one another.

SAÑJAYA UVĀCA:

9.1 TATAḤ PRAVAVṚTE yuddhaṃ Kurūṇāṃ bhaya|vardhanam
Sṛñjayaiḥ saha rāj'|êndra ghoraṃ dev'|âsur'|ôpamam.
narā rathā gaj'|âughāś ca sādinaś ca sahasraśaḥ
vājinaś ca parākrāntāḥ samājagmuḥ paras|param.
gajānāṃ bhīma|rūpāṇāṃ dravatāṃ niḥsvano mahān
aśrūyata yathā kāle jala|dānāṃ nabhas|tale.
nāgair abhyāhatāḥ ke cit sa|rathā rathino 'patan.
vyadravanta raṇe vīrā drāvyamāṇā mad'|ôtkaṭaiḥ.
9.5 hay'|âughān pāda|rakṣāṃś ca rathinas tatra śikṣitāḥ
śaraiḥ saṃpreṣayām āsuḥ para|lokāya Bhārata.
sādinaḥ śikṣitā rājan parivārya mahā|rathān
vicaranto raṇe 'bhyaghnan prāsa|śakty|ṛṣṭibhis tathā.
dhanvinaḥ puruṣāḥ ke cit parivārya mahā|rathān
ekaṃ bahava āsādya preṣayeyur Yama|kṣayam.
nāgān ratha|varāṃś c' ânye parivārya mahā|rathāḥ
s'|ântar'|āyodhinaṃ jaghnur dravamāṇaṃ mahā|ratham.
tathā ca rathinaṃ kruddhaṃ vikirantaṃ śarān bahūn
nāgā jaghnur mahā|rāja parivārya samantataḥ.
9.10 nāgo nāgam abhidrutya rathī ca rathinaṃ raṇe
śakti|tomara|nārācair nijaghne tatra Bhārata.
pādātān avamṛdnanto ratha|vāraṇa|vājinaḥ
raṇa|madhye vyadṛśyanta kurvanto mahad ākulam.
hayāś ca paryadhāvanta cāmarair upaśobhitāḥ
haṃsā Himavataḥ prasthe pibanta iva medinīm.

SÁNJAYA said:

A TERRIFYING and horrific battle then ensued between the Kurus and the Sríñjayas, king of kings; it was like a battle between the gods and demons. Men, chariots, hordes of elephants, thousands of cavalrymen and brave horses all clashed together. A vast noise was heard of elephants charging forward with terrifying appearances, just like the sound of thunderclouds in the sky during the rainy season. Some charioteers were hit by elephants and fell down along with their chariots. Heroes fled across the battlefield, routed by the crazed animals. 9.1

Skilled charioteers sent streams of horses to the other world with their arrows, along with men who guarded elephant legs, descendant of Bharata. Rampaging across the battlefield, trained horsemen surrounded great warriors, Your Majesty, and killed them with javelins, lances and spears. Some archers surrounded great warriors and sent them to Yama's abode, attacking them, many against one. Other great warriors encircled elephants and fine chariots and killed mighty warriors as they charged and fought in duels.* Elephants likewise surrounded single charioteers on every side, great king, and killed them as they furiously sprayed out volleys of arrows. 9.5

Elephants attacked elephants in the battle, and charioteers attacked charioteers; they then killed each other on the battlefield with lances, spears and arrows, descendant of Bharata. Chariots, elephants and horses were seen crushing foot soldiers in the middle of the battlefield and creating immense chaos. Horses galloped around, adorned wih yak tails, and resembled swans that devour the ground on the 9.10

teṣāṃ tu vājināṃ bhūmiḥ khuraiś chinnā viśāṃ pate
aśobhata yathā nārī kara|jaiḥ kṣata|vikṣatā.

vājināṃ khura|śabdena ratha|nemi|svanena ca
pattīnāṃ c' âpi śabdena nāgānāṃ bṛṃhitena ca,
9.15 vāditrāṇāṃ ca ghoṣeṇa śaṅkhānāṃ ninadena ca
abhavan nāditā bhūmir nirghātair iva Bhārata.
dhanuṣāṃ kūjamānānāṃ śastr'|âughānāṃ ca dīpyatām
kavacānāṃ prabhābhiś ca na prājñāyata kiñ cana.

bahavo bāhavaś chinnā nāga|rāja|kar'|ôpamāḥ
udveṣṭanto viceṣṭanto vegaṃ kurvanti dāruṇam.
śirasāṃ ca mahā|rāja patatāṃ dharaṇī|tale
cyutānām iva tālebhyas tālānām śrūyate svanaḥ.
śirobhiḥ patitair bhāti rudhir'|ârdrair vasun|dharā
tapanīya|nibhaiḥ kāle nalinair iva Bhārata.
9.20 udvṛtta|nayanais tais tu gata|sattvaiḥ su|vikṣataiḥ
vyabhrājata mahī rājan puṇḍarīkair iv' āvṛtā.
bāhubhiś candan'|ādigdhaiḥ sa|keyūrair mahā|dhanaiḥ
patitair bhāti rāj'|êndra mahā|Śakra|dhvajair iva.
ūrubhiś ca nar'|êndrāṇāṃ vinikṛttair mah"|āhave
hasti|hast'|ôpamair anyaiḥ saṃvṛtaṃ tad raṇ'|âṅganam.
kabandha|śata|saṃkīrṇaṃ chattra|cāmara|saṃkulam
senā|vanaṃ tac chuśubhe vanaṃ puṣp'|ācitaṃ yathā.

Hímavat plateau. Carved up by the hooves of these horses, the earth looked beautiful, lord of the people, just like a woman who has been scratched by her lover's nails.

The earth resounded with the rumbling of horse hooves, the clamor of chariot wheels, the shouts of foot soldiers, the trumpeting of elephants, the peal of instruments and 9.15
the blare of conches; it was as if it echoed with thunder storms, descendant of Bharata. The gleam of armor, and the glistening of twanging bows and multitudes of weapons, meant that nothing could be perceived clearly.

Numerous arms quivered and writhed with violent jerks, chopped off like the trunks of royal elephants. One could hear the thud of heads falling to the ground, just like that of coconuts falling from palm trees, great king. The earth glistened with blood-soaked fallen heads that looked like golden lotuses in season, descendant of Bharata. As if cov- 9.20
ered with lotuses, Your Majesty, the earth shone with these lifeless, mutilated heads, their eyes wide open. Fallen arms, which were smeared with sandalwood and bore expensive bracelets, made the earth gleam as if they were Shakra's lofty banners, king of kings. The battlefield was covered with the thighs of kings that had been torn off in the great battle and that looked like elephant trunks. Strewn with hundreds of torsos and covered with parasols and yak tails, that forest of an army looked radiant, just like a wood carpeted with flowers.

tatra yodhā mahā|rāja vicaranto hy a|bhītavat
dṛśyante rudhir'|âkt'|âṅgāḥ puṣpitā iva kiṃśukāḥ.
9.25 mātaṅgāś c' âpy adṛśyanta śara|tomara|pīḍitāḥ
patantas tatra tatr' âiva chinn'|âbhra|sadṛśā raṇe.
gaj'|ânīkaṃ mahā|rāja vadhyamānaṃ mah"|ātmabhiḥ
vyadīryata diśaḥ sarvā vāta|nunnā ghanā iva.
te gajā ghana|saṃkāśāḥ petur urvyāṃ samantataḥ
vajra|nunnā iva babhuḥ parvatā yuga|saṃkṣaye.
hayānāṃ sādibhiḥ sārdhaṃ patitānāṃ mahī|tale
rāśayaḥ sma pradṛśyante giri|mātrās tatas tataḥ.

saṃjajñe raṇa|bhūmau tu para|loka|vahā nadī
śoṇit'|ôdā rath'|āvartā dhvaja|vṛkṣ" âsthi|śarkarā
9.30 bhuja|nakrā dhanuḥ|srotā hasti|śailā hay'|ôpalā
medo|majjā|kardaminī chattra|haṃsā gad"|ôḍu|pā,
kavac'|ôṣṇīṣa|saṃchannā patākā|rucira|drumā
cakra|cakr'|âvalī|juṣṭā tri|veṇu|daṇḍak'|āvṛtā,
śūrāṇāṃ harṣa|jananī bhīrūṇāṃ bhaya|vardhinī
prāvartata nadī raudrā Kuru|Sṛñjaya|saṃkulā.
tāṃ nadīṃ para|lokāya vahantīm atibhairavām
terur vāhana|naubhis te śūrāḥ parigha|bāhavaḥ.

vartamāne tathā yuddhe nirmaryāde viśāṃ pate
catur|aṅga|kṣaye ghore pūrva|dev'|âsur'|ôpame
9.35 vyākrośan bāndhavān anye tatra tatra paran|tapa
krośadbhir dayitair anye bhay'|ārtā na nivartire.

Warriors were seen rampaging fearlessly on the battlefield, their limbs smeared with blood and resembling flowering *kim·shuka** trees, great king. Elephants were seen falling 9.25
here and there in the battle like broken clouds, overwhelmed by arrows and spears. Slaughtered by great-spirited warriors, a division of elephants was torn apart in every direction, like clouds dispelled by the wind. On every side, cloud-like elephants fell to the ground; they looked like mountains that had been toppled by thunderbolts at the dissolution of an eon. Here and there one could see mountain-size piles of horses that had fallen to the ground along with their horsemen.

A river arose on the battlefield that flowed to the other world. Its waters were blood, its eddies were chariots, its trees were banners and its pebbles were bones. Its crocodiles were 9.30
arms, its streams were bows, its rocks were elephants and its stones were horses. Its marshes were fat and marrow, its swans were parasols, and its rafts were maces. Littered with armor and turbans, its beautiful trees were flags. Abounding in wheels and teeming with three-bannered chariots and poles, this horrifying river flowed full of Kurus and Srínjayas, inspiring delight in heroes and filling the timid with dread. Using their animals as boats, the heroes—with arms like iron bars—crossed that terrifying river that flowed to the other world.

During this horrific, unbounded battle, lord of the people, in which fourfold armies* were destroyed and which resembled a battle in the past between the gods and demons, troops screamed everywhere for their relatives, while others, 9.35

nirmaryāde tathā yuddhe vartamāne bhayānake
Arjuno Bhīmasenaś ca mohayāṃ cakratuḥ parān.
sā vadhyamānā mahatī senā tava nar'|âdhipa
amuhyat tatra tatr' âiva yoṣin mada|vaśād iva.

mohayitvā ca tāṃ senāṃ Bhīmasena|Dhanañjayau
dadhmatur vāri|jau tatra siṃha|nādāṃś ca cakratuḥ.
śrutv" âiva tu mahā|śabdaṃ Dhṛṣṭadyumna|Śikhaṇḍinau
dharma|rājaṃ puraskṛtya Madra|rājam abhidrutau.
9.40 tatr' āścaryam apaśyāma ghora|rūpaṃ viśāṃ pate
Śalyena saṃgatāḥ śūrā yad ayudhyanta bhāgaśaḥ.

Mādrī|putrau tu rabhasau kṛt'|âstrau yuddha|dur|madau
abhyayātāṃ tvar'|āyuktau jigīṣantau paran|tapa.
tato nyavartata balaṃ tāvakaṃ Bharata'|rṣabha
śaraiḥ praṇunnaṃ bahudhā Pāṇḍavair jita|kāśibhiḥ.
vadhyamānā camūḥ sā tu putrāṇāṃ prekṣatāṃ tava
bheje diśo mahā|rāja praṇunnā śara|vṛṣṭibhiḥ.

hā|hā|kāro mahāñ jajñe yodhānāṃ tava Bhārata
«tiṣṭha tiṣṭh' êti» c' âpy āsīd drāvitānāṃ mah"|ātmanām
9.45 kṣatriyāṇāṃ tad" ânyonyaṃ saṃyuge jayam icchatām.

prādravann eva saṃbhagnāḥ Pāṇḍavais tava sainikāḥ.
tyaktvā yuddhe priyān putrān bhrātṝn atha pitā|mahān
mātulān bhāgineyāṃś ca vayasyān api Bhārata,
hayān dvi|pāṃs tvarayanto yodhā jagmuḥ samantataḥ
ātma|trāṇa|kṛt'|ôtsāhās tāvakā Bharata'|rṣabha.

who were stricken with fear, were unable to flee because of their screaming loved ones, O scorcher of enemies.

During this terrifying, unbounded battle, Árjuna and Bhima·sena bewildered their enemies. Like an intoxicated woman, that great army of yours became confused in every direction as it was massacred, lord of men.

After they had bewildered your army, Bhima·sena and Dhanan·jaya sounded their conches on the battlefield and shouted out lion-roars. Hearing that great noise and headed by the King of Righteousness, Dhrishta·dyumna and Shikhándin attacked the ruler of the Madras. We then saw a 9.40
terrible wonder on that battlefield, lord of the people, as those heroes confronted Shalya and fought him in turn.

The two violent sons of Madri, who were skilled in archery and difficult to subdue in battle, swiftly charged forward in their eagerness to attack, O enemy-scorcher. Your troops then retreated, bull of the Bharatas, repelled by swarms of arrows that were fired by the conquering Pándavas. Slaughtered under your sons' very eyes, the army fled in every direction, driven away by showers of arrows, great king.

Your troops screamed out loud cries, descendant of Bharata, while heroic warriors, who had been routed but still de- 9.45
sired victory in battle, shouted to each other: "Stop! Stop!"

Your soldiers fled, crushed by the Pándavas. Abandoning their dear sons, brothers, grandfathers, uncles, nephews and friends in the battle, your troops sped on their horses and elephants and fled on all sides, determined to save themselves, bull of the Bharatas.

SAÑJAYA uvāca:

10.1 TAT PRABHAGNAṂ balaṃ dṛṣṭvā Madra|rājaḥ pratāpavān
uvāca sārathiṃ: «tūrṇaṃ coday' âśvān mahā|javān!
eṣa tiṣṭhati vai rājā Pāṇḍu|putro Yudhiṣṭhiraḥ
chattreṇa dhriyamāṇena pāṇḍureṇa virājatā.
atra māṃ prāpaya kṣipraṃ paśya me sārathe balam.
na samartho hi me Pārthaḥ sthātum adya puro yudhi.»
evam uktas tataḥ prāyān Madra|rājasya sārathiḥ
yatra rājā satya|sandho Dharma|putro Yudhiṣṭhiraḥ.
10.5 prāpatat tac ca sahasā Pāṇḍavānāṃ mahad balam
dadhār' âiko raṇe Śalyo vel" ôdvṛttam iv' ârṇavam.
Pāṇḍavānāṃ bal'|âughas tu Śalyam āsādya māriṣa
vyatiṣṭhata tadā yuddhe sindhor vega iv' â|calam.
Madra|rājaṃ tu samare dṛṣṭvā yuddhāya dhiṣṭhitam*
Kuravaḥ sannyavartanta mṛtyuṃ kṛtvā nivartanam.
teṣu rājan nivṛtteṣu vyūḍh'|ânīkeṣu bhāgaśaḥ
prāvartata mahā|raudraḥ saṃgrāmaḥ śoṇit'|ôdakaḥ.
samārchac Citrasenaṃ tu Nakulo yuddha|dur|madaḥ.
tau paras|param āsādya citra|kārmuka|dhāriṇau
10.10 meghāv iva yath"|ôdvṛttau dakṣiṇ'|ôttara|varṣiṇau
śara|toyaiḥ siṣicatus tau paras|param āhave.
n' ântaraṃ tatra paśyāmi Pāṇḍavasy' êtarasya ca:
ubhau kṛt'|âstrau balinau ratha|caryā|viśāradau
paras|para|vadhe yattau chidr'|ânveṣaṇa|tat|parau.

SÁNJAYA said:

WHEN THE GLORIOUS king of the Madras saw that his army had been crushed, he said this to his charioteer: "Drive on my swift horses quickly! King Yudhi·shthira, the son of Pandu, is standing over there under a white, gleaming umbrella. Take me there quickly, charioteer, and observe my strength! For today the son of Pritha will be unable to stand before me in battle!" 10.1

Addressed in this way, the charioteer of the ruler of the Madras advanced toward King Yudhi·shthira, that son of Righteousness, who is true to his word.

Shalya then violently attacked the great army of the Pán- 10.5
davas and restrained it on his own in battle, just as the shore contains the surging sea. Indeed, the mass of the Pándava army came to a standstill when it encountered Shalya in battle, just as when the force of a river comes up against a mountain. Although they had resolved to die rather than flee, the Kurus withdrew when they saw the king of the Madras intent on war in that battle. After they had retreated and drawn up their ranks into various divisions, a terrible battle ensued, Your Majesty, in which blood flowed like water.

Nákula, who is difficult to defeat in battle, then clashed against Chitra·sena. Confronting each other with glistening bows, they showered one another with torrents of arrows
on the battlefield, just as swollen clouds pour rain in the 10.10
north or south. I could see no difference between the Pándava and his opponent: both were accomplished archers and both were powerful and skilled in charioteering; both

Citrasenas tu bhallena pītena niśitena ca
Nakulasya mahā|rāja muṣṭi|deśe 'cchinad dhanuḥ.
ath' âinaṃ chinna|dhanvānaṃ rukma|puṅkhaiḥ śilā|śitaiḥ
tribhiḥ śarair a|saṃbhrānto lalāṭe vai samārpayat.
hayāṃś c' âsya śarais tīkṣṇaiḥ preṣayām āsa mṛtyave
tathā dhvajaṃ sārathiṃ ca tribhis tribhir apātayat.
10.15 sa śatru|bhuja|nirmuktair lalāṭa|sthais tribhiḥ śaraiḥ
Nakulaḥ śuśubhe rājaṃs tri|śṛṅga iva parvataḥ.
sa chinna|dhanvā virathaḥ khaḍgam ādāya carma ca
rathād avātarad vīraḥ śail'|âgrād iva kesarī.
padbhyām āpatatas tasya śara|vṛṣṭiṃ samāsṛjat.
Nakulo 'py agrasat tāṃ vai carmaṇā laghu|vikramaḥ.
citrasena|rathaṃ prāpya citra|yodhī jita|śramaḥ
āruroha mahā|bāhuḥ sarva|sainyasya paśyataḥ.
sa|kuṇḍalaṃ sa|mukuṭaṃ su|nasaṃ sv|āyat'|êkṣaṇam
Citrasena|śiraḥ kāyād apāharata Pāṇḍavaḥ.
sa papāta rath'|ôpasthe divā|kara|sama|dyutiḥ
10.20 Citrasenaṃ viśastaṃ tu dṛṣṭvā tatra mahā|rathāḥ
sādhu|vāda|svanāṃś cakruḥ siṃha|nādāṃś ca puṣkalān.
viśastaṃ bhrātaraṃ dṛṣṭvā Karṇa|putrau mahā|rathau
Suṣeṇaḥ Satyasenaś ca muñcantau vividhāñ śarān.
tato 'bhyadhāvatāṃ tūrṇaṃ Pāṇḍavaṃ rathināṃ varam
jighāṃsantau yathā nāgaṃ vyāghrau rājan mahā|vane.

were also eager to kill the other, intent on finding their opponent's weaknesses.

It was Chitra·sena, however, who pierced Nákula's bow at the handle with a sharp, copper, spear-headed arrow, great king. Without wavering, Chitra·sena then struck his bowless opponent on the forehead with three gold-feathered and stone-whetted shafts. With his sharp arrows he then sent Nákula's horses to their death and felled Nákula's standard and charioteer with three shafts each.

Nákula looked glorious, Your Majesty, like a mountain 10.15
with three peaks, when those three arrows stood on his forehead, fired by the arms of his enemy.

Deprived of his bow and chariot, heroic Nákula then took up his sword and shield and leaped down from his vehicle, like a lion from a mountaintop. Chitra·sena showered Nákula with arrows as he charged forward on foot. But fleet-footed Nákula soaked them up with his shield. Tireless and resourceful in his fighting, mighty-armed Nákula then ran up to Chitra·sena's chariot and climbed up onto it, while the entire army looked on. The Pándava then struck off Chitra·sena's head from his body, along with its earrings, crown, fine nose and handsome long eyes. Chitra·sena fell onto the chariot platform, radiant as the sun.

At the sight of Chitra·sena's slaughter, the great warriors 10.20
on the battlefield applauded and shouted numerous lion-roars. But the mighty warriors Sushéna and Satya·sena—those sons of Karna—fired volleys of arrows when they saw that their brother had been slain. Like tigers eager to kill an elephant in a large forest, O king, they swiftly charged against the Pándava, that best of charioteers. Like clouds

tāv abhyadhāvatāṃ tīkṣṇau dvāv apy enaṃ mahā|ratham
śar'|âughān samyag asyantau jīmūtau salilaṃ yathā.
sa śaraiḥ sarvato viddhaḥ prahṛṣṭa iva Pāṇḍavaḥ
anyat kārmukam ādāya ratham āruhya vegavān
atiṣṭhata raṇe vīraḥ kruddha|rūpa iv' Ântakaḥ.

10.25 tasya tau bhrātarau rājañ śaraiḥ sannata|parvabhiḥ
rathaṃ viśakalī|kartuṃ samārabdhau viśāṃ pate.
tataḥ prahasya Nakulaś caturbhiś caturo raṇe
jaghāna niśitair bāṇaiḥ Satyasenasya vājinaḥ.
tataḥ sandhāya nārācaṃ rukma|puṅkhaṃ śilā|śitam
dhanuś ciccheda rāj'|êndra Satyasenasya Pāṇḍavaḥ.
ath' ânyaṃ ratham āsthāya dhanur ādāya c' âparam
Satyasenaḥ Suṣeṇaś ca Pāṇḍavaṃ paryadhāvatām.

avidhyat tāv a|sambhrānto Mādrī|putraḥ pratāpavān
dvābhyāṃ dvābhyāṃ mahā|rāja śarābhyāṃ raṇa|mūrdhani.
10.30 Suṣeṇas tu tataḥ kruddhaḥ Pāṇḍavasya mahad dhanuḥ
ciccheda prahasan yuddhe kṣura|preṇa mahā|rathaḥ.

ath' ânyad dhanur ādāya Nakulaḥ krodha|mūrcchitaḥ
Suṣeṇaṃ pañcabhir viddhvā dhvajam ekena cicchide.
Satyasenasya ca dhanur hast'|âvāpaṃ ca māriṣa
ciccheda tarasā yuddhe tata uccukruśur janāḥ.

ath' ânyad dhanur ādāya vega|ghnaṃ bhāra|sādhanam
śaraiḥ saṃchādayām āsa samantāt Pāṇḍu|nandanam.
sannivārya tu tān bāṇān Nakulaḥ para|vīra|hā
Satyasenaṃ Suṣeṇaṃ ca dvābhyāṃ dvābhyām avidhyata.
10.35 tāv enaṃ pratyavidhyetāṃ pṛthak pṛthag a|jihma|gaiḥ

pouring rain, the two men violently rushed against that mighty warrior, firing torrents of shafts directly at him. But although pierced by arrows on every side, the swift Pándava took up another bow with seeming joy and ascended a chariot. Looking like wrathful Death, the hero then took up position in battle.

The two brothers then began to destroy Nákula's chariot 10.25
with their straight arrows, O lord of the people. With a laugh, however, Nákula killed Satya·sena's four horses on the battlefield with four sharp arrows. The Pándava then strung an iron shaft—gold-feathered and stone-whetted—and sliced through Satya·sena's bow, king of kings. Satya·sena, however, mounted a different chariot and, taking up another bow, charged with Sushéna against the Pándava.

Without flinching, the powerful son of Madri pierced them with two arrows each at the front of the battle, great
king. Enraged, the mighty warrior Sushéna then cut through 10.30
the Pándava's mighty bow with a razor-edged arrow, laughing as he fought.

Senseless with fury, Nákula took up another bow and, after piercing Sushéna with five arrows, he cut through his banner with one more. He then swiftly pierced Satya·sena's bow and hand-guard in the battle, at which point the people cried out loud, my lord.

Grabbing another effective, swift-killing bow, Satya·sena covered the son of Pandu with arrows on all sides. But Nákula, that slayer of enemy heroes, warded off their arrows and pierced Satya·sena and Sushéna with two shafts each.
They in turn shot him separately with their straight-flying 10.35
shafts and wounded Nákula's charioteer with their sharp

sārathiṃ c' âsya rāj'|êndra śitair vivyadhatuḥ śaraiḥ.
satyaseno rath'|ēṣāṃ tu Nakulasya dhanus tathā
pṛthak śarābhyāṃ ciccheda kṛta|hastaḥ pratāpavān.

sa rathe 'tirathas tiṣṭhan ratha|śaktiṃ parāmṛśat
svarṇa|daṇḍām a|kuṇṭh'|âgrāṃ taila|dhautāṃ su|nirmalām.
lelihānām iva vibho nāga|kanyāṃ mahā|viṣām
samudyamya ca cikṣepa Satyasenasya saṃyuge.
sā tasya hṛdayaṃ saṃkhye bibheda śatadhā nṛ|pa.
sa papāta rathād bhūmiṃ gata|sattvo 'lpa|cetanaḥ.

10.40 bhrātaraṃ nihataṃ dṛṣṭvā Suṣeṇaḥ krodha|mūrchitaḥ
abhyavarṣac charais tūrṇaṃ pādātaṃ Pāṇḍu|nandanam.
caturbhiś caturo vāhān dhvajaṃ chittvā ca pañcabhiḥ
tribhir vai sārathiṃ hatvā Karṇa|putro nanāda ha.

Nakulaṃ virathaṃ dṛṣṭvā Draupadeyo mahā|ratham
Sutasomo 'bhidudrāva parīpsan pitaraṃ raṇe.
tato 'dhiruhya Nakulaḥ Sutasomasya taṃ ratham
śuśubhe Bharata|śreṣṭho giri|stha iva kesarī.
anyat kārmukam ādāya Suṣeṇaṃ samayodhayat
tāv ubhau śara|varṣābhyāṃ samāsādya paras|param
paras|para|vadhe yatnaṃ cakratuḥ su|mahā|rathau.

arrows, king of kings. Dexterous and mighty Satya·sena then individually cut through Nákula's bow and chariot-pole with his shafts.

While standing on his chariot, the mighty warrior Nákula then seized his chariot-spear, which was gold-shafted, sharp-pointed, cleansed with oil and completely unstained. Wielding that spear, which resembled a poisonous young snake licking its tongue, he hurled it at Satya·sena in battle, my lord. The spear split his heart into a hundred pieces in the battle, Your Majesty, and Satya·sena fell from his chariot onto the ground, lifeless and unconscious.

On seeing his brother's slaughter, Sushéna became sense- 10.40
less with rage and, while the son of Pandu was on foot, he swiftly showered him with arrows. Piercing Nákula's four horses with four arrows and his banner with five more, the son of Karna killed Nákula's charioteer with three shafts and then rejoiced.

When Suta·soma, the son of Dráupadi, saw that Nákula had lost his chariot, he charged against the great warrior Sushéna in order to help his father in battle. Nákula, that best of Bharatas, then climbed onto Suta·soma's chariot. He looked magnificent, like a lion standing on a mountain. Taking up another bow, he fought against Sushéna, whereupon the two extremely mighty charioteers attacked one another with showers of arrows, each trying to kill the other.

10.45 Suṣeṇas tu tataḥ kruddhaḥ Pāṇḍavaṃ viśikhais tribhiḥ
Sutasomaṃ tu viṃśatyā bāhvor urasi c' ârpayat.
tataḥ kruddho mahā|rāja Nakulaḥ para|vīra|hā
śarais tasya diśaḥ sarvāś chādayām āsa vīryavān.
tato gṛhītvā tīkṣṇ'|âgram ardha|candraṃ su|tejanam
su|vegavantaṃ cikṣepa Karṇa|putrāya saṃyuge.
tasya tena śiraḥ kāyāj jahāra nṛ|pa|sattama
paśyatāṃ sarva|sainyānāṃ; tad adbhutam iv' âbhavat.
sa hataḥ prāpatad rājan Nakulena mah"|ātmanā
nadī|vegād iv' ārugṇas tīra|jaḥ pāda|po mahān.
10.50 Karṇa|putra|vadhaṃ dṛṣṭvā Nakulasya ca vikramam
pradudrāva bhayāt senā tāvakī Bharata'|rṣabha.
tāṃ tu senāṃ mahā|rāja Madra|rājaḥ pratāpavān
apālayad raṇe śūraḥ senā|patir arin|damaḥ.
vibhīs tasthau mahā|rāja vyavasthāpya ca vāhinīm
siṃha|nādaṃ bhṛśaṃ kṛtvā dhanuḥ|śabdaṃ ca dāruṇam.
tāvakāḥ samare rājan rakṣitā dṛḍha|dhanvanā
pratyudyayur arātīṃs te samantād vigata|vyathāḥ.
Madra|rājaṃ mah"|êṣv|āsaṃ parivārya samantataḥ
sthitā rājan mahā|senā yoddhu|kāmā samantataḥ.
10.55 Sātyakir Bhīmasenaś ca Mādrī|putrau ca Pāṇḍavau
Yudhiṣṭhiraṃ puraskṛtya hrī|niṣevam arin|damam.
parivārya raṇe vīrāḥ siṃha|nādaṃ pracakrire
bāṇa|śaṅkha|ravāṃs tīvrān kṣveḍāṃś ca vividhā dadhuḥ.
tath" âiva tāvakāḥ sarve Madr'|âdhipatim añjasā
parivārya su|saṃrabdhāḥ punar yoddhum arocayan.

Sushéna furiously struck the Pándava with three arrows 10.45
and hit Suta·soma with twenty on his chest and arms. Enraged, powerful Nákula, that slayer of enemy heroes, then quickly enveloped every direction with his shafts, O mighty king. Grabbing a fine-edged, well-sharpened arrow with a semi-circular head, he shot it with great speed at the son of Karna in battle. Under the eyes of all the troops, he struck off Sushéna's head from his body with that arrow, best of kings. It was like a miracle. Killed by great-spirited Nákula, Sushéna fell down, Your Majesty, like a tall tree on a bank that has been broken by the force of a river.

On seeing Nákula's courage and the death of Karna's 10.50
son, your army fled in fear, bull of the Bharatas. But the bold king of the Madras—that heroic general who tames his enemies—protected your army on the battlefield, Your Majesty. Rallying the army, he stood there fearlessly, making loud lion-roars and twanging his bow terribly. Their fears dispelled and protected by Shalya with his strong bow, your troops advanced forward on every side against the enemy in battle, O king. Eager for war, the great army rallied around that great archer, the king of the Madras, and took up position on every side, Your Majesty.

Sátyaki, Bhima·sena and the two Pándava sons of Madri 10.55
stood behind modest Yudhi·shthira, that tamer of enemies. Surrounding him in battle, the heroes shouted lion-roars and made piercing noises of various kinds with their arrows and conches. In the same way, all your troops swiftly grouped around the lord of the Madras and once more longed for war, filled as they were with immense fury.

tataḥ pravavṛte yuddhaṃ bhīrūṇāṃ bhaya|vardhanam
tāvakānāṃ pareṣāṃ ca mṛtyuṃ kṛtvā nivartanam,
yathā dev'|âsuraṃ yuddhaṃ pūrvam āsīd viśāṃ pate
a|bhītānāṃ tathā rājan Yama|rāṣṭra|vivardhanam.
10.60 tataḥ kapi|dhvajo rājan hatvā Saṃśaptakān raṇe
abhyadravata tāṃ senāṃ Kauravīṃ Pāṇḍu|nandanaḥ.
tath" âiva Pāṇḍavāḥ sarve Dhṛṣṭadyumna|puro|gamāḥ
abhyadhāvanta tāṃ senāṃ visṛjantaḥ śitāñ śarān.
Pāṇḍavair avakīrṇānāṃ saṃmohaḥ samajāyata;
na ca jajñus tv anīkāni diśo vā vidiśas tathā.
āpūryamāṇā niśitaiḥ śaraiḥ Pāṇḍava|coditaiḥ
hata|pravīrā vidhvastā kīryamāṇā samantataḥ.

Kauravy avadhyata camūḥ Pāṇḍu|putrair mahā|rathaiḥ.
tath" âiva Pāṇḍavaṃ sainyaṃ śarai rājan samantataḥ
raṇe 'hanyata putrais te śataśo 'tha sahasraśaḥ.
10.65 te sene bhṛśa|saṃtapte vadhyamāne paras|param
vyākule samapadyetāṃ varṣāsu saritāv iva
āviveśa tatas tīvraṃ tāvakānāṃ mahad bhayam
Pāṇḍavānāṃ ca rāj'|êndra tathā|bhūte mah"|āhave.

Resolving to die rather than flee, your troops and the enemy then fought a battle that was terrifying for the timid. It was like a battle in the past between the gods and demons and it filled Yama's kingdom with fearless men, O lord of the people.

After monkey-bannered Árjuna had killed the Samshá- 10.60
ptakas in battle, that delight of Pandu then attacked the Káurava troops, O king. Likewise, under the leadership of Dhrishta·dyumna, all the Pándavas attacked the Káurava army, firing sharp arrows as they did so. Confusion arose among the Káurava troops as they were scattered by the Pándavas: the regiments were unable even to make out either the major or the minor directions. Enveloped by the sharp arrows that the Pándavas fired, they fell apart and dispersed on all sides, their heroes slain.

The sons of Pandu—those great warriors—slaughtered the Káurava army. And in the same way, your sons killed hundreds and thousands of Pándava troops everywhere in the battle with their arrows.

As they massacred each other in their violent fury, the 10.65
armies became churned up like rivers in the rainy season. A great and intense fear then overtook your troops and the Pándavas in that huge battle, king of kings.

11–17
SHALYA'S DEATH

SAÑJAYA uvāca:

11.1 TASMIN VILULITE sainye vadhyamāne paras|param
dravamāṇeṣu yodheṣu vidravatsu ca dantiṣu,
kūjatāṃ stanatāṃ c' âiva padātīnāṃ mah"|āhave
nihateṣu mahā|rāja hayeṣu bahudhā tadā,
prakṣaye dāruṇe ghore saṃhāre sarva|dehinām
nānā|śastra|samāvāye vyatiṣakta|ratha|dvi|pe,
harṣaṇe yuddha|śauṇḍānāṃ bhīrūṇāṃ bhaya|vardhane
gāhamāneṣu yodheṣu paras|para|vadh'|âiṣiṣu,
11.5 prāṇ'|ādāne mahā|ghore vartamāne duro|dare
saṃgrāme ghora|rūpe tu Yama|rāṣṭra|vivardhane,
Pāṇḍavās tāvakaṃ sainyaṃ vyadhaman niśitaiḥ śaraiḥ;
tath" âiva tāvakā yodhā jaghnuḥ Pāṇḍava|sainikān.
tasmiṃs tathā vartamāne yuddhe bhīru|bhay'|āvahe
pūrv'|âhṇe c' âpi saṃprāpte bhās|kar'|ôdayanaṃ prati,
labdha|lakṣāḥ pare rājan rakṣitās tu mah"|ātmanā
ayodhayaṃs tava balaṃ mṛtyuṃ kṛtvā nivartanam.
balibhiḥ Pāṇḍavair dṛptair labdha|lakṣaiḥ prahāribhiḥ
Kauravy asīdat pṛtanā mṛg" îv' âgni|samākulā.
11.10 tāṃ dṛṣṭvā sīdatīṃ senāṃ paṅke gām iva dur|balām
ujjihīrṣus tadā Śalyaḥ prāyāt Pāṇḍu|sutān prati.
Madra|rājaḥ su|saṃkruddho gṛhītvā dhanur uttamam
abhyadravata saṃgrāme Pāṇḍavān ātatāyinaḥ.
Pāṇḍavā api bhū|pāla samare jita|kāśinaḥ
Madra|rājaṃ samāsādya bibhidur niśitaiḥ śaraiḥ.

SÁNJAYA said:

THE TROOPS slaughtered each other in their turmoil. 11.1
Soldiers fled and elephants ran away. Infantrymen screamed and groaned in that great battle, while horses were killed in droves, great king. A horrific carnage set in, and there was a terrible massacre of every embodied creature. Weapons of various kinds clashed together, and elephants became enmeshed with chariots. Those who were intoxicated with battle bristled with joy, while those who were timid were filled with fear. Warriors charged forward in their eagerness to kill each other.

During this terrible game of killing—this awful battle 11.5
which swelled Yama's kingdom—the Pándavas scattered your soldiers with their sharp arrows, and your warriors likewise killed the Pándava troops. During this battle, which was waged at the beginning of the day at sunrise, and which filled the timid with fear, the enemy fought against your army under the protection of heroic Yudhi·shthira, hitting their marks and preferring death to flight, O king. Like a doe disturbed by fire, the Káurava army became overwhelmed by the strong and proud attacking Pándavas, who always hit their marks.

When Shalya saw that his army was weakening, like a 11.10
cow sinking feebly in mud, he attacked the sons of Pandu in order to save his men. Filled with great fury, the king of the Madras took up an excellent bow and charged against the Pándava archers in battle. But the Pándavas—those conquerors in battle—confronted the king of the Madras and pierced him with their sharp arrows, O protector of the earth. The king of the Madras, that great warrior,

tataḥ śara|śatais tīkṣṇair Madra|rājo mahā|rathaḥ
ardayām āsa tāṃ senāṃ Dharma|rājasya paśyataḥ.
prādur āsan nimittāni nānā|rūpāṇy anekaśaḥ.
cacāla śabdaṃ kurvāṇā mahī c' âpi sa|parvatā.
11.15 sa|daṇḍa|śūlā dīpt'|âgrā dīryamāṇāḥ samantataḥ
ulkā bhūmiṃ divaḥ petur āhatya ravi|maṇḍalam.
mṛgāś ca mahiṣāś c' âpi pakṣiṇaś ca viśāṃ pate
apasavyaṃ tadā cakruḥ senāṃ te bahuśo nṛpa.
bhṛgu|sūnu|dharā|putrau śaśi|jena samanvitau
caramaṃ Pāṇḍu|putrāṇāṃ purastāt sarva|bhū|bhujām.
śastr'|âgreṣv abhavaj jvālā netrāṇy āhatya varṣatī
śiraḥsv alīyanta bhṛśaṃ kāk'|ôlūkāś ca ketuṣu.
tatas tad yuddham atyugram abhavat saṅgha|cāriṇām.
tathā sarvāṇy anīkāni saṃnipatya jan'|âdhipa
abhyayuḥ Kauravā rājan Pāṇḍavānām anīkinīm.
11.20 Śalyas tu śara|varṣeṇa varṣann iva sahasra|dṛk
abhyavarṣata dharm'|ātmā Kuntī|putraṃ Yudhiṣṭhiram.
Bhīmasenaṃ śaraiś c' âpi rukma|puṅkhaiḥ śilā|śitaiḥ
Draupadeyāṃs tathā sarvān Mādrī|putrau ca Pāṇḍavau,
Dhṛṣṭadyumnaṃ ca Śaineyaṃ Śikhaṇḍinam ath' âpi ca
ek'|âikaṃ daśabhir bāṇair vivyādha sa mahā|balaḥ.
tato 'sṛjad bāṇa|varṣaṃ gharm'|ânte Maghavān iva.
tataḥ Prabhadrakā rājan Somakāś ca sahasraśaḥ
patitāḥ pātyamānāś ca dṛśyante Śalya|sāyakaiḥ.
bhramarāṇām iva vrātāḥ śalabhānām iva vrajāḥ
hrādinya iva meghebhyaḥ Śalyasya nyapatañ śarāḥ.
11.25 dvi|radās tura|gāś c' ārtāḥ pattayo rathinas tathā
Śalyasya bāṇair apatan babhramur vyanadaṃs tathā.

then tormented their army with hundreds of sharp arrows, even while the King of Righteousness looked on.

All kinds of bad omens then appeared. The earth and mountains groaned and trembled. Fire-tipped meteors— 11.15
along with sticks and spears—fell from the sky to the earth, crashing on all sides after striking the sun's sphere. Droves of deer, buffaloes and birds moved to the left of your army, lord of the people. In conjunction with Mercury, Venus and Mars stood behind the sons of Pandu and in front of all your kings. Dripping flames appeared on the tips of the troops' weapons, dazzling their eyes, while flocks of crows and owls clung to their heads and banners.

There was then a truly terrible battle between the hordes of troops. Gathering all their divisions, the Káuravas attacked the army of the Pándavas, Your Majesty. Righteous 11.20
Shalya rained showers of arrows upon Yudhi·shthira, the son of Kunti, as if he were thousand-eyed Indra pouring rain. With his gold-shafted, stone-sharpened arrows, the mighty hero pierced Bhima·sena, all the sons of Dráupadi, the two Pándava sons of Madri, Dhrishta·dyumna, the grandson of Shini,* and Shikhándin—all of them with ten darts each. Like Mághavat pouring rain at the end of the summer, Shalya fired a shower of arrows.

We then saw thousands of Prabhádrakas and Sómakas either killed or being killed by Shalya's arrows, Your Majesty. Like swarms of bees or hordes of locusts, Shalya's arrows fell like thunderbolts from the clouds. Elephants, horses, 11.25
infantrymen and charioteers fell down, wandered around or screamed out loud, plagued by Shalya's shafts. As if possessed by fury and courage, the mighty lord of the Madras

āviṣṭa iva Madr'|ēśo manyunā pauruṣeṇa ca
prācchādayad arīn saṃkhye kāla|sṛṣṭa iv' Ântakaḥ
vinardamāno Madr'|ēśo megha|hrādo mahā|balaḥ.

sā vadhyamānā Śalyena Pāṇḍavānām anīkinī
a|jāta|śatruṃ Kaunteyam abhyadhāvad Yudhiṣṭhiram.
tāṃ saṃmardya tataḥ saṃkhye laghu|hastaḥ śitaiḥ śaraiḥ
bāṇa|varṣeṇa mahatā Yudhiṣṭhiram atāḍayat.
tam āpatantaṃ patty|aśvaiḥ kruddho rājā Yudhiṣṭhiraḥ
avārayac charais tīkṣṇair mahā|dvi|pam iv' âṅkuśaiḥ.
11.30 tasya Śalyaḥ śaraṃ ghoraṃ mumoc' āśī|viṣ'|ôpamam.
sa nirbhidya mah"|ātmānaṃ vegen' âbhyapatac ca gām.

tato Vṛkodaraḥ kruddhaḥ Śalyaṃ vivyādha saptabhiḥ
pañcabhiḥ Sahadevas tu Nakulo daśabhiḥ śaraiḥ.
Draupadeyāś ca śatru|ghnaṃ śūram Ārtāyaniṃ śaraiḥ
abhyavarṣan mahā|rāja meghā iva mahī|dharam.
tato dṛṣṭvā vāryamāṇaṃ Śalyaṃ Pārthaiḥ samantataḥ
Kṛtavarmā Kṛpaś c' âiva saṃkruddhāv abhyadhāvatām
Ulūkaś ca mahā|vīryaḥ Śakuniś c' âpi Saubalaḥ.
samāgamy' âtha śanakair Aśvatthāmā mahā|balaḥ
tava putrāś ca kārtsnyena jugupuḥ Śalyam āhave.
11.35 Bhīmasenaṃ tribhir viddhvā Kṛtavarmā śilī|mukhaiḥ
bāṇa|varṣeṇa mahatā kruddha|rūpam avārayat.
Dhṛṣṭadyumnaṃ tataḥ kruddho bāṇa|varṣair apīḍayat.
Draupadeyāṃś ca Śakunir yamau ca Drauṇir abhyayāt.
Duryodhano yudhāṃ śreṣṭha āhave Keśav'|Ârjunau
samabhyayād ugra|tejāḥ śaraiś c' âpy ahanad balī.

enveloped his enemies in battle, like Death let loose by Time, roaring like thunder as he did so.

As they were slaughtered by Shalya, the Pándava forces fled to Yudhi·shthira, the son of Kunti, who has no adversary. But Shalya—agile with his hands—pounded them in battle with his sharp darts and pummeled Yudhi·shthira with a huge shower of arrows. With his own sharp arrows, however, Yudhi·shthira angrily held Shalya back as he attacked with his foot soldiers and horses, just as a huge
elephant is restrained by hooks. Shalya then released a terri- 11.30
ble arrow against Yudhi·shthira, which was like a poisonous snake. The arrow pierced the hero and then swiftly lodged in the earth.

Enraged, Vrikódara then pierced Shalya with seven arrows, while Saha·deva struck him with five and Nákula with ten. Like clouds pouring rain on the earth, the sons of Dráupadi also showered heroic and enemy-killing Artáyani with their arrows, great king.

When Krita·varman and Kripa saw that Shalya was being contained by the Parthas on all sides, they angrily charged forward, as did fervent Ulúka and Shákuni, the son of Súbala. Mighty Ashva·tthaman and your sons also gradually joined them and protected Shalya in battle in every way.

Krita·varman pierced wrathful-looking Bhima·sena with 11.35
three darts and held him back with a huge torrent of shafts. In his rage, he then pounded Dhrishta·dyumna with showers of arrows. Shákuni attacked the sons of Dráupadi, while Ashva·tthaman, the son of Drona, attacked the twins. Powerful Dur·yódhana—that champion of warriors—assailed

evaṃ dvandva|śatāny āsaṃs tvadīyānāṃ paraiḥ saha
ghora|rūpāṇi citrāṇi tatra tatra viśāṃ pate.

ṛkṣa|varṇāñ jaghān' âśvān Bhojo Bhīmasya saṃyuge.
so 'vatīrya rath'|ôpasthādd hat'|âśvaḥ Pāṇḍu|nandanaḥ
kālo daṇḍam iv' ôdyamya gadā|pāṇir ayudhyata.

11.40 pramukhe Sahadevasya jaghān' âśvān sa Madra|rāṭ
tataḥ Śalyasya tanayaṃ Sahadevo 'sinā 'vadhīt.

Gautamaḥ punar ācāryo Dhṛṣṭadyumnam ayodhayat
a|saṃbhrāntam a|saṃbhrānto yatnavān yatnavattaram.

Draupadeyāṃs tathā vīrān ek'|âikaṃ daśabhiḥ śaraiḥ
aviddhyad ācārya|suto n' âtikruddhaḥ hasann iva.
punaś ca Bhīmasenasya jaghān' âśvāṃs tath" āhave.
so 'vatīrya rathāt tūrṇaṃ hat'|âśvaḥ Pāṇḍu|nandanaḥ
kālo daṇḍam iv' ôdyamya gadāṃ kruddho mahā|balaḥ,
pothayām āsa tura|gān rathaṃ ca Kṛtavarmaṇaḥ.
Kṛtavarmā tv avaplutya rathāt tasmād apākramat.

11.45 Śalyo 'pi rājan saṃkruddho nighnan Somaka|Pāṇḍavān
punar eva śitair bāṇair Yudhiṣṭhiram apīḍayat.
tasya Bhīmo raṇe kruddhaḥ saṃdaśya daśana|cchadaṃ
vināśāy' âbhisandhāya gadām ādatta vīryavān,
Yama|daṇḍa|pratīkāśāṃ kāla|rātrim iv' ôdyatām
gaja|vāji|manuṣyāṇāṃ deh'|ânta|karaṇīm ati,

Késhava and Árjuna in battle with fierce vigor and struck them with his arrows.

In this way, lord of the people, hundreds of contests took place all over the battlefield between your troops and the enemy; they were both beautiful and awful to look at.

The Bhojan Krita·varman killed Bhima's horses in battle, which were the colour of bears. At his horses' death, that delight of Pandu descended from his chariot platform and fought, mace in hand, like Time wielding his staff.

The king of the Madras killed Saha·deva's horses right 11.40
in front of him, but Saha·deva slew Shalya's son with his sword.

That teacher, the grandson of Gótama, fought once more against Dhrishta·dyumna; neither of the heroes faltered and both applied every effort.

Ashva·tthaman, that son of a teacher, who was not yet excessively angry,* seemed to laugh as he pierced the heroic sons of Dráupadi with ten arrows each. He then once again killed Bhima·sena's horses in battle. At the death of his horses, the mighty son of Pandu descended quickly from his chariot and wielded his mace, like Time brandishing his staff. He then pummeled Krita·varman's horses and chariot. But Krita·varman jumped down from his chariot and fled.

Shalya furiously slaughtered the Sómakas and Pánda- 11.45
vas and once more pounded Yudhi·shthira with his sharp arrows, Your Majesty. Filled with rage toward Shalya and biting his lips, fervent Bhima took up his mace in the battle, aiming it at his opponent in order to kill him. The mace that Bhima wielded was like the staff of Yama or the night of Time. Annihilating the bodies of elephants, horses and

hema|paṭṭa|parikṣiptām ulkām prajvalitām iva
śaikyāṃ vyālīm iv' âtyugrāṃ vajra|kalpām ayo|mayīm,
candan'|âguru|paṅk'|âktāṃ pramadām īpsitām iva
vasā|medo|'sra|digdh'|âṅgīṃ jihvāṃ Vaivasvatīm iva,
11.50 paṭu|ghaṇṭā|śata|ravāṃ Vāsavīm aśanīm iva
nirmukt'|āśī|viṣ'|ākārāṃ pṛktāṃ gaja|madair api,
trāsinīṃ ripu|sainyānāṃ sva|sainya|pariharṣiṇīm
manuṣya|loke vikhyātāṃ giri|śṛṅga|vidāriṇīm.
yayā Kailāsa|bhavane Mah"|ēśvara|sakhaṃ balī
āhvayām āsa yuddhāya Bhīmaseno mahā|balaḥ,
yayā māyā|mayān dṛptān su|bahūn Dhana|d'|ālaye
jaghāna Guhyakān kruddho mandar'|ârthe mahā|balaḥ
nivāryamāṇo bahubhir Draupadyāḥ priyam āsthitaḥ.
tāṃ vajra|maṇi|ratn'|âugha|kalmāṣāṃ vajra|gauravām
samudyamya mahā|bāhuḥ Śalyam abhyapatad raṇe.
11.55 gadayā yuddha|kuśalas tayā dāruṇa|nādayā
pothayām āsa Śalyasya caturo 'śvān mahā|javān.
tataḥ Śalyo raṇe kruddhaḥ pīne vakṣasi tomaram
nicakhāna nadan vīro. varma bhittvā 'sya so 'bhyayāt.
Vṛkodaras tv a|saṃbhrāntas tam ev' ôddhṛtya tomaram
yantāraṃ Madrarājasya nirbibheda tato hṛdi.
sa bhinna|varmā rudhiraṃ vaman vitrasta|mānasaḥ

men, it was wrapped in gold cloth and looked like a blazing meteor. Slinged and made of iron, it was like a thunderbolt or a vicious she-snake. Just as a desirable young woman is smeared with sandalwood, aloe and mud, so that mace's body was greased with marrow, fat and blood, as if it were the tongue of Vivásvat's son.* Screeching like a hundred shrill 11.50
bells, it resembled Vásava's thunderbolt. It looked like a poisonous snake that had shed its skin and was covered with elephant secretions. A terror to enemy troops, it brought joy to its allies. Renowned throughout the human world, it could tear through a mountain peak.

With this mace, powerful and mighty Bhima·sena once challenged Kubéra, the friend of Mahéshvara, to fight in the realm of Kailása. With this mace, wrathful Bhima once destroyed numerous proud Gúhyakas, despite their powers of illusion, in order to acquire *mándara* flowers in the realm of wealth-giving Kubéra; although obstructed by many, he fulfilled his favor to Dráupadi.*

Wielding that mace, which was heavy as a thunderbolt and speckled with an abundance of diamonds, jewels and gems, mighty-armed Bhima charged against Shalya in battle.

Skilled at fighting, he crushed Shalya's four swift horses 11.55
with that terrible-sounding mace. But heroic Shalya, who was filled with battle-fury, hurled a lance against Bhima's broad chest, roaring as he did so. Piercing Bhima's armor, the lance penetrated him. Vrikódara, however, did not waver but extracted that same lance and used it to impale the king of the Madras' charioteer in the chest. The lance cut through the charioteer's armor, and he fell down head first, vomiting blood, wretched and deranged. The king of the Madras then

papāt' âbhimukho dīno. Madra|rājas tv apākramat.
kṛta|pratikṛtaṃ dṛṣṭvā Śalyo vismita|mānasaḥ
gadām āśritya dharm'|ātmā pratyamitram avaikṣata.
11.60 tataḥ su|manasaḥ Pārthā Bhīmasenam apūjayan
tad dṛṣṭvā karma saṃgrāme ghoram a|kliṣṭa|karmaṇaḥ.

SAÑJAYA uvāca:

12.1 PATITAṂ PREKṢYA yantāraṃ Śalyaḥ sarv'|âyasīṃ gadām
ādāya tarasā rājaṃs tasthau girir iv' â|calaḥ.
taṃ dīptam iva kāl'|âgniṃ pāśa|hastam iv' Ântakam
sa|śṛṅgam iva Kailāsaṃ sa|vajram iva Vāsavam,
sa|śūlam iva hary|akṣaṃ vane mattam iva dvi|pam
javen' âbhyapatad Bhīmaḥ pragṛhya mahatīṃ gadām.
tataḥ śaṅkha|praṇādaś ca tūryāṇāṃ ca sahasraśaḥ
siṃha|nādaś ca saṃjajñe śūrāṇāṃ harṣa|vardhanaḥ.
12.5 prekṣantaḥ sarvatas tau hi yodhā yodha|mahā|dvi|pau
tāvakāś c' âpare c' âiva «sādhu sādhv ity» apūjayan.
na hi Madr'|âdhipād anyo Rāmād vā Yadu|nandanāt
soḍhum utsahate vegaṃ Bhīmasenasya saṃyuge.
tathā Madr'|âdhipasy' âpi gadā|vegaṃ mah"|ātmanaḥ
soḍhum utsahate n' ânyo yodho yudhi Vṛkodarāt.
tau vṛṣāv iva nardantau maṇḍalāni viceratuḥ
āvalgitau gadā|hastau Madra|rāja|Vṛkodarau.
maṇḍal'|āvarta|mārgeṣu gadā|viharaṇeṣu ca
nirviśeṣam abhūd yuddhaṃ tayoḥ puruṣa|siṃhayoḥ.
12.10 tapta|hema|mayaiḥ śubhrair babhūva bhaya|vardhanī
agni|jvālair iv' ābaddhā paṭṭaiḥ Śalyasya sā gadā.

retreated. Seeing Bhima's counter-action, righteous Shalya took up his mace and glowered at his enemy in dismay.

After seeing his terrible feat in battle, the Parthas then 11.60
joyfully honored tireless Bhima·sena.

SÁNJAYA said:

YOUR MAJESTY, when Shalya saw that his charioteer had 12.1
fallen, he quickly took up his mace, which was entirely made of iron, and stood still like an immovable mountain. Bhima, however, grabbed his own huge mace and charged against Shalya, who looked like the blazing fire of Time, like Death holding his noose, like mountain-peaked Kailása, like thunderbolt-wielding Vásava, like yellow-eyed Shiva bearing his trident, or like a frenzied elephant in a forest.

Thousands of conches and musical instruments then blared out loud, and there was the sound of lion-roars,
bringing joy to the heroes. On every side, troops from both 12.5
your army and the enemy watched those warriors, who were like mighty elephants, and applauded them, shouting: "Marvelous! Marvelous!" For, apart from the king of the Madras—or Rama, that delight of the Yadus—no one could withstand Bhima·sena's force in battle. Likewise, apart from Vrikódara, no warrior could withstand the power of the heroic king of the Madras' mace in battle. Bellowing like bulls, Vrikódara and the king of the Madras circled around each other, both of them jumping in the air and brandishing their maces. Nothing separated the human lions in their contest—neither the way that they circled each other nor
the way that they wielded their maces. Shalya's terrifying 12.10
mace was wrapped in glittering cloths that were made of

tath" âiva carato mārgān maṇḍaleṣu mah"|ātmanaḥ
vidyud|abhra|pratīkāśā Bhīmasya śuśubhe gadā.

tāḍitā Madra|rājena Bhīmasya gadayā gadā
dahyamān" êva khe rājan sā 'sṛjat pāvak'|ârciṣaḥ.
tathā Bhīmena Śalyasya tāḍitā gadayā gadā
aṅgāra|varṣaṃ mumuce; tad adbhutam iv' âbhavat.
dantair iva mahā|nāgau śṛṅgair iva maha"|ṛṣabhau
tottrair iva tad" ânyonyaṃ gad"|âgrābhyāṃ nijaghnatuḥ.
12.15 tau gad"|âbhihatair gātraiḥ kṣaṇena rudhir'|ôkṣitau
prekṣaṇīyatarāv āstāṃ puṣpitāv iva kiṃśukau.

gadayā Madra|rājasya savya|dakṣiṇam āhataḥ
Bhīmaseno mahā|bāhur na cacāl' â|calo yathā.
tathā Bhīma|gadā|vegais tāḍyamāno muhur muhuḥ
Śalyo na vivyathe rājan dantin" êva mahā|giriḥ.
śuśruve dikṣu sarvāsu tayoḥ puruṣa|siṃhayoḥ
gadā|nipāta|saṃhrādo vajrayor iva niḥsvanaḥ.

nivṛtya tu mahā|vīryau samucchrita|mahā|gadau
punar antara|mārga|sthau maṇḍalāni viceratuḥ.
12.20 ath' âbhyetya padāny aṣṭau sannipāto 'bhavat tayoḥ
udyamya loha|daṇḍābhyām ati|mānuṣa|karmaṇoḥ.
pothayantau tad" ânyonyaṃ maṇḍalāni viceratuḥ
kriyā|viśeṣaṃ kṛtinau darśayām āsatus tadā.

refined gold and looked like fire flames. Similarly, the mace of heroic Bhima shone like a lightning cloud, as he moved around in circles.

When Bhima's mace was struck by the king of the Madras' mace, it released sparks of fire into the sky, as if it were ablaze. In the same way, when Shalya's mace was struck by Bhima's mace, it released a shower of burning coals, as if a miracle had occurred. Like mighty elephants striking each other with their tusks or great bulls hitting each other with their horns, they beat one another with the tips of their maces, as if they were using goads. They instantly became 12.15
drenched in blood from pounding each other's limbs with their maces; as a result, they looked even more handsome, just like a pair of flowering *kim·shuka* trees.

Although mighty-armed Bhima·sena was struck on his left and right side by the king of the Madras' mace, he remained unmoved, like an unshakable mountain. Similarly, Your Majesty, although Shalya was pummeled again and again by blows from Bhima's mace, he did not flinch, just as when a huge mountain is struck by an elephant. The noise made by the blows of these human lions' maces was heard in every direction, just like the sound of thunderbolts.

Although the powerful warriors retreated for a while, they once again raised their maces and circled each other closely. Advancing eight steps, those two men—who performed 12.20
feats that were beyond human—confronted one another, wielding their iron clubs. Pummeling each other, they continued to move around in circles and expertly displayed their excellent skill. Brandishing their terrifying maces, which were like peaked summits, the warriors struck each other

ath' ôdyamya gade ghore sa|śṛṅgāv iva parvatau
tāv ājaghnatur anyonyaṃ bhūmi|kaṃpe yathā 'calau.
kriyā|viśeṣaṃ kṛtinau raṇa|bhūmi|tale 'calau.

tau paras|para|saṃrambhād gadābhyāṃ su|bhṛś'|āhatau
yugapat petatur vīrāv ubhāv Indra|dhvajāv iva.
ubhayoḥ senayor vīrās tadā hā|hā|kṛt" âbhavan,*
bhṛśaṃ marmaṇy abhihatāv ubhāv āstāṃ su|vihvalau.

12.25 tataḥ sva|ratham āropya Madrāṇām ṛṣabhaṃ raṇe
apovāha Kṛpaḥ Śalyaṃ tūrṇam āyodhanād atha.
kṣībavad vihvalatvāt tu nimeṣāt punar utthitaḥ
Bhīmaseno gadā|pāṇiḥ samāhvayata Madra|pam.

tatas tu tāvakāḥ śūrā nānā|śastra|samāyutāḥ
nānā|vāditra|śabdena Pāṇḍu|senām ayodhayan.
bhujāv ucchritya śastraṃ ca śabdena mahatā tataḥ
abhyadravan mahā|rāja Duryodhana|purogamāḥ.
tad anīkam abhiprekṣya tatas te Pāṇḍu|nandanāḥ
prayayuḥ siṃha|nādena Duryodhana|puro|gamān.

12.30 teṣām āpatatāṃ tūrṇaṃ putras te Bharata'|ṛṣabha
prāsena Cekitānaṃ vai vivyādha hṛdaye bhṛśam.
sa papāta rath'|ôpasthe tava putreṇa tāḍitaḥ
rudhir'|âugha|pariklinnaḥ praviśya vipulaṃ tamaḥ.

Cekitānaṃ hataṃ dṛṣṭvā Pāṇḍaveyā mahā|rathāḥ
a|saktam abhyavarṣanta śara|varṣāṇi bhāgaśaḥ.
tāvakānām anīkeṣu Pāṇḍavā jita|kāśinaḥ
vyacaranta mahā|rāja prekṣaṇīyāḥ samantataḥ.

like mountains clashing in an earthquake. Both men were expert in specialized skills and both were unshakable on the battlefield.

Like Indra's banners, the two heroes then fell down simultaneously, both of them heavily wounded by the violence their maces had inflicted on each other. The heroes of both armies cried out in distress and, severely wounded in their vital organs, the two warriors became extremely bewildered.

Kripa then climbed onto his chariot on the battlefield and 12.25
quickly took Shalya, that bull of the Madras, away from the conflict. As if drunk with giddiness, Bhima·sena stood up again in the blink of an eye and challenged the lord of the Madras, mace in hand.

Amid the sound of various musical instruments, your heroic troops then fought against Pandu's army, armed with different types of weapons. Raising their arms and wielding their weapons, they charged forward with a loud shout, led by Dur·yódhana. When they saw that army, the sons of Pandu advanced forward with a lion-roar against your troops, who were led by Dur·yódhana.

As the Pándavas swiftly charged forward, your son pierced 12.30
Chekitána deeply in the heart with a lance, bull of the Bharatas. Soaked in pools of blood, Chekitána entered a great darkness and fell onto his chariot platform, struck down by your son.

On seeing that Chekitána was dead, the great Pándava warriors rained continuous showers of arrows, one after the other. The conquering Pándavas were beautiful in every way as they rampaged through your troops' divisions, great king.

Kṛpaś ca Kṛtavarmā ca Saubalaś ca mahā|rathaḥ
ayodhayan Dharma|rājaṃ Madra|rāja|puraskṛtāḥ.
12.35 Bhāradvājasya hantāraṃ bhūri|vīrya|parākramam
Duryodhano mahā|rāja Dhṛṣṭadyumnam ayodhayat.
tri|sāhasrā rathā rājaṃs tava putreṇa coditāḥ
ayodhayanta Vijayaṃ Droṇa|putra|puraskṛtāḥ.
vijaye dhṛta|saṃkalpāḥ samare tyakta|jīvitāḥ
prāviśaṃs tāvakā rājan haṃsā iva mahat saraḥ.

tato yuddham abhūd ghoraṃ paras|para|vadh'|âiṣiṇām
anyonya|vadha|saṃyuktam anyonya|prīti|vardhanam.
tasmin pravṛtte saṃgrāme rājan vīra|vara|kṣaye
anilen' ēritaṃ ghoram uttasthau pārthivaṃ rajaḥ.
12.40 śravaṇān nāma|dheyānāṃ Pāṇḍavānāṃ ca kīrtanāt
paras|paraṃ vijānīmo yad ayudhyann a|bhītavat.
tad rajaḥ puruṣa|vyāghra śoṇitena praśāmitam
diśaś ca vimalā jātās tasmiṃs tamasi śāmite.

tathā pravṛtte saṃgrāme ghora|rūpe bhayānake
tāvakānāṃ pareṣāṃ ca n' āsīt kaś cit parāṅ|mukhaḥ.
Brahma|loka|parā bhūtvā prārthayanto jayaṃ yudhi
su|yuddhena parākrāntā narāḥ svargam abhīpsavaḥ.
bhartṛ|piṇḍa|vimokṣ'|ârthaṃ bhartṛ|kārya|viniścitāḥ
svarga|saṃsakta|manaso yodhā yuyudhire tadā.
12.45 nānā|rūpāṇi śastrāṇi visṛjanto mahā|rathāḥ
anyonyam abhigarjantaḥ praharantaḥ paras|param,
«hata vidhyata gṛhṇīta praharadhvaṃ nikṛntata
iti» sma vācaḥ śrūyante tava teṣāṃ ca vai bale.

Under the leadership of the king of the Madras, Kripa, Krita·varman and the son of Súbala—that mighty warrior—then fought against the King of Righteousness. Dur·yó- 12.35
dhana battled with Dhrishta·dyumna, Your Majesty, that immensely powerful and courageous killer of the son of Bharad·vaja.* Urged on by your son and led by the son of Drona, three thousand warriors fought against Víjaya,* Your Majesty. Firm in their resolve to win victory and ready to sacrifice their lives in battle, your troops advanced forward, like swans entering a huge lake, O king.

In their eagerness to destroy each other, there was then a terrible battle of mutual carnage, which inspired both sides with delight. During this battle, in which excellent heroes were slaughtered, a horrific dust of earth arose, swirled up by the wind. It was only from hearing names and from 12.40
people shouting about the Pándavas that we could discern each other as the troops fearlessly fought on. Blood then made the dust settle, and the directions became clear when the darkness dissipated, O tiger among men.

During that horrific and terrifying battle, not one of your troops or the enemy turned their backs. Intent on the Brahma world and desiring victory in war, the men showed their courage through virtuous battle, eager as they were for heaven. Dedicated to their duty to their ancestors and with their minds fixed on heaven, the warriors fought in order to give food to their forefathers. As the great warriors 12.45
hurled their various weapons, hitting and growling at each other, one could hear men from both your army and theirs shouting: "Kill! Shoot! Seize! Strike! Hack!"

tataḥ Śalyo mahā|rāja Dharma|putraṃ Yudhiṣṭhiram
vivyādha niśitair bāṇair hantu|kāmo mahā|ratham.
tasya Pārtho mahā|rāja nārācān vai catur|daśa
marmāṇy uddiśya marma|jño nicakhāna hasann iva.
āvārya Pāṇḍavaṃ bāṇair hantu|kāmo mahā|balaḥ
vivyādha samare kruddho bahubhiḥ kaṅka|patribhiḥ.
12.50 atha bhūyo mahā|rāja śareṇ' ānata|parvaṇā
Yudhiṣṭhiraṃ samājaghne sarva|sainyasya paśyataḥ.
dharma|rājo 'pi saṃkruddho Madra|rājaṃ mahā|yaśāḥ
vivyādha niśitair bāṇaiḥ kaṅka|barhiṇa|vājitaiḥ.

Candrasenaṃ ca saptatyā sūtaṃ ca navabhiḥ śaraiḥ
Drumasenaṃ catuḥ|ṣaṣṭyā nijaghāna mahā|rathaḥ.
cakra|rakṣe hate Śalyaḥ Pāṇḍavena mah"|ātmanā
nijaghāna tato rājaṃś Cedīn vai pañca|viṃśatim.
Sātyakiṃ pañca|viṃśatyā Bhīmasenaṃ ca pañcabhiḥ
Mādrī|putrau śaten' ājau vivyādha niśitaiḥ śaraiḥ.
12.55 evaṃ vicaratas tasya saṃgrāme rāja|sattama
saṃpraiṣayac chitān Pārthaḥ śarān āśī|viṣ'|ôpamān.
dhvaj'|âgraṃ c' âsya samare Kuntī|putro Yudhiṣṭhiraḥ
pramukhe vartamānasya bhallen' âpāharad rathāt.
Pāṇḍu|putreṇa vai tasya ketuṃ chinnaṃ mah"|ātmanā
nipatantam apaśyāma giri|śṛṅgam iv' āhatam.

Shalya then pierced Yudhi·shthira the son of Righteousness with his sharp arrows, desiring to kill that great warrior, great king. The son of Pritha, however, aimed at Shalya's vital organs—knowing as he did a man's mortal points—and seemed to laugh as he fired fourteen arrows at him. Filled with battle-fury and eager to kill Yudhi·shthira, mighty Shalya warded off the Pándava and shot him with numerous heron-feathered shafts. He then once again, Your Majesty, 12.50
struck Yudhi·shthira with a straight arrow, even while the whole army was looking on. The glorious King of Righteousness, however, furiously pierced the king of the Madras with his sharp arrows, which were feathered with heron and peacock plumes.

The great warrior Yudhi·shthira then shot Chandra·sena with seventy arrows, as well as Druma·sena with sixty-four and Shalya's charioteer with nine. When his chariot-wheel protectors were killed by the great-spirited Pándava in this way, Shalya slaughtered twenty-five of the Chedis, Your Majesty. He then pierced Sátyaki in battle with twenty-five sharp arrows, as well as Bhima·sena with five and the sons of Madri with a hundred. While Shalya was thus 12.55
rampaging in battle, the son of Pritha fired sharp arrows at him, which were like poisonous snakes, best of kings. With a spear-headed shaft, Yudhi·shthira, the son of Kunti, then chopped off the top of the standard from Shalya's chariot as his opponent stood in front of him. We watched Shalya's banner fall down like a razed mountain summit, cut down by the great-spirited son of Pandu.

dhvajaṃ nipatitaṃ dṛṣṭvā Pāṇḍavaṃ ca vyavasthitam
saṃkruddho Madra|rājo 'bhūc chara|varṣaṃ mumoca ha.
Śalyaḥ sāyaka|varṣeṇa Parjanya iva vṛṣṭimān
abhyavarṣad a|mey'|ātmā kṣatriyān kṣatriya'|ṛṣabhaḥ.
12.60 Sātyakiṃ Bhīmasenaṃ ca Mādrī|putrau ca Pāṇḍavau
ek'|âikaṃ pañcabhir viddhvā Yudhiṣṭhiram apīḍayat.
tato bāṇa|mayaṃ jālaṃ vitataṃ Pāṇḍav'|ôrasi
apaśyāma mahā|rāja megha|jālam iv' ôdgatam.
tasya Śalyo raṇe kruddhaḥ śaraiḥ saṃnata|parvabhiḥ
diśaḥ saṃchādayām āsa pradiśaś ca mahā|rathaḥ.
tato Yudhiṣṭhiro rājā bāṇa|jālena pīḍitaḥ
babhūva hata|vikrānto Jambho Vṛtra|haṇā yathā.

SAÑJAYA uvāca:

13.1 PĪḌITE DHARMA|rāje tu Madra|rājena māriṣa
Sātyakir Bhīmasenaś ca Mādrī|putrau ca Pāṇḍavau
parivārya rathaiḥ Śalyaṃ pīḍayām āsur āhave.
tam ekaṃ bahubhir dṛṣṭvā pīḍyamānaṃ mahā|rathaiḥ
sādhu|vādo mahāñ jajñe, siddhāś c' āsan praharṣitāḥ
«āścaryam ity» abhāṣanta munayaś c' âpi saṃgatāḥ.
Bhīmaseno raṇe Śalyaṃ śalya|bhūtaṃ parākrame
ekena viddhvā bāṇena punar vivyādha saptabhiḥ.
Sātyakiś ca śaten' âinaṃ Dharma|putra|parīpsayā
Madr'|ēśvaram avākīrya siṃha|nādam ath' ânadat.
13.5 Nakulaḥ pañcabhiś c' âinaṃ Sahadevaś ca pañcabhiḥ
viddhvā taṃ tu punas tūrṇaṃ tato vivyādha saptabhiḥ.

When the king of the Madras saw that his banner had fallen and that the Pándava was holding his ground, he released a shower of arrows in his fury. Like rain-pouring Parjánya,* Shalya—that bull-like warrior of limitless spirit—rained a shower of arrows over the fighters. He then bom- 12.60
barded Sátyaki, Bhima·sena, the two Pándava sons of Madri, and Yudhi·shthira, piercing them with five shafts each.

We then saw a web of arrows rise like a mass of clouds and cover the Pándava's chest, great king. In his fury at Yudhi·shthira, Shalya—that mighty warrior—enveloped the major and minor directions with his straight shafts on the battlefield. Besieged by this web of arrows, King Yudhi·shthira then lost his courage, just as Jambha did when he was attacked by the slayer of Vritra.*

SÁNJAYA said:

MY LORD, WHEN the ruler of the Madras was besieging the 13.1
King of Righteousness, Sátyaki, Bhima·sena and the two Pándava sons of Madri surrounded Shalya with their chariots and attacked him in battle. There was a great cheer at the sight of these mighty charioteers oppressing Shalya, many against one. The *siddhas* were joyful and the assembled ascetics declared that it was wonderful.

Bhima·sena wounded Shalya in battle with one arrow and then pierced him with seven more, even though Shalya was a very spear in his prowess.* Desiring to rescue the son of Righteousness, Sátyaki covered the lord of the Madras
with a hundred arrows and then roared a lion-roar. Nákula 13.5
pierced Shalya with five arrows, while Saha·deva shot him

sa tu śūro raṇe yattaḥ pīḍitas tair mahā|rathaiḥ
vikṛṣya kārmukaṃ ghoraṃ vega|ghnaṃ bhāra|sādhanam.
Sātyakiṃ pañca|viṃśatyā Śalyo vivyādha māriṣa
Bhīmasenaṃ tu saptatyā Nakulaṃ saptabhis tathā.
tataḥ sa|viśikhaṃ cāpaṃ Sahadevasya dhanvinaḥ
chittvā bhallena samare vivyādh' âinaṃ tri|saptabhiḥ.
Sahadevas tu samare mātulaṃ bhūri|varcasam
sa|jyam anyad dhanuḥ kṛtvā pañcabhiḥ samatāḍayat
śarair āśī|viṣ'|ākārair jvalaj jvalana|sannibhaiḥ.
13.10 sārathiṃ c' âsya samare śareṇ' ānata|parvaṇā
vivyādha bhṛśa|saṃkruddhas taṃ vai bhūyas tribhiḥ śaraiḥ.

Bhīmasenas tu saptatyā Sātyakir navabhiḥ śaraiḥ
dharma|rājas tathā ṣaṣṭyā gātre Śalyaṃ samārpayat.
tataḥ Śalyo mahā|rāja nirviddhas tair mahā|rathaiḥ
susrāva rudhiraṃ gātrair gairikaṃ parvato yathā.
tāṃś ca sarvān mah"|êṣv|āsān pañcabhiḥ pañcabhiḥ śaraiḥ
vivyādha tarasā rājaṃs; tad adbhutam iv' âbhavat.
tato 'pareṇa bhallena Dharma|putrasya māriṣa
dhanuś ciccheda samare sa|jyaṃ sa su|mahā|rathaḥ.
13.15 ath' ânyad dhanur ādāya Dharma|putro Yudhiṣṭhiraḥ
s'|âśva|sūta|dhvaja|rathaṃ Śalyaṃ prācchādayac charaiḥ.
sa cchādyamānaḥ samare Dharma|putrasya sāyakaiḥ
Yudhiṣṭhiram ath' âvidhyad daśabhir niśitaiḥ śaraiḥ.

with five shafts and then instantly pierced him with seven more.

But although harassed by these great warriors, heroic Shalya remained intent on battle and drew his fast-slaying bow, which was dreadful and effective. He pierced Sátyaki with twenty-five arrows, Bhima·sena with seventy and Nákula with seven, my lord. With a spear-headed shaft, Shalya then cut through Saha·deva's arrow-bearing bow and pierced that archer in battle with three volleys of seven darts each. Saha·deva, however, strung another bow and, with five arrows that resembled poisonous snakes and that blazed like flames, he struck his supremely glorious uncle in battle. Filled with 13.10
violent anger, he shot Shalya's charioteer in battle with a straight arrow and then again with three more shafts.

Bhima·sena then hit Shalya with seventy arrows, while Sátyaki struck him with nine, and the King of Righteousness shot him with sixty in the leg. Blood poured from Shalya's limbs when he was wounded by those great warriors, like a mountain flowing streams of red chalk. Shalya, however, swiftly pierced all those great archers with five arrows each, Your Majesty; it was like a miracle. With another spear-headed shaft, my lord, that extremely mighty warrior then cut through the strung bow of the son of Righteousness in battle. But Yudhi·shthira, the son of Righteousness, took 13.15
up another bow and covered Shalya with arrows, as well as his horses, charioteer and chariot. But although engulfed in battle by the arrows of the son of Righteousness, Shalya pierced Yudhi·shthira with ten sharp darts.

Sātyakis tu tataḥ kruddho Dharma|putre śar'|ârdite
Madrāṇām adhipaṃ śūraṃ śarair vivyādha pañcabhiḥ.
sa Sātyakeḥ praciccheda kṣura|preṇa mahad dhanuḥ
Bhīmasena|mukhāṃs tāṃś ca tribhis tribhir atāḍayat.
tasya kruddho mahā|rāja Sātyakiḥ satya|vikramaḥ
tomaraṃ preṣayām āsa svarṇa|daṇḍaṃ mahā|dhanam.
13.20 Bhīmaseno 'tha nārācaṃ jvalantam iva panna|gam
Nakulaḥ samare śaktiṃ Sahadevo gadāṃ śubhām
dharma|rājaḥ śataghnīṃ ca jighāṃsuḥ Śalyam āhave.

tān āpatata ev' āśu pañcānāṃ vai bhuja|cyutān
vārayām āsa samare śastra|saṅghān sa Madra|rāṭ.
Sātyaki|prahitaṃ Śalyo bhallaiś ciccheda tomaram
Bhīmena prahitaṃ c' âpi śaraṃ kanaka|bhūṣaṇam.
dvidhā ciccheda samare kṛta|hastaḥ pratāpavān
Nakula|preṣitāṃ śaktiṃ hema|daṇḍāṃ bhay'|āvahām,
gadāṃ ca Sahadevena śar'|âughaiḥ samavārayat
śarābhyāṃ ca śataghnīṃ tāṃ rājñaś ciccheda Bhārata.
13.25 paśyatāṃ Pāṇḍu|putrāṇāṃ siṃha|nādaṃ nanāda ca.

n' âmṛṣyat tatra Śaineyaḥ śatror vijayam āhave.
ath' ânyad dhanur ādāya Sātyakiḥ krodha|mūrchitaḥ
dvābhyāṃ Madr'|ēśvaraṃ viddhvā sārathiṃ ca tribhiḥ śaraiḥ.

tataḥ Śalyo raṇe rājan sarvāṃs tān daśabhiḥ śaraiḥ
vivyādha bhṛśa|saṃkruddhas tottrair iva mahā|dvi|pān.
te vāryamāṇāḥ samare Madra|rājñā mahā|rathāḥ

When the son of Righteousness was being plagued by Shalya's arrows, Sátyaki furiously wounded the heroic king of the Madras with five shafts. Shalya, however, cut through Sátyaki's huge bow with a razor-edged arrow and pounded the warriors that were being led by Bhima·sena with three arrows each. Furious at Shalya, Sátyaki—whose strength lies in truth—hurled a lance, which was gold-staffed and costly.
Bhima·sena also fired an iron arrow at Shalya, which looked 13.20
like a blazing serpent, while Nákula launched a javelin in the battle and Saha·deva threw a glistening mace. The King of Righteousness also released a *shata·ghni* missile, eager as he was to kill Shalya in battle.

The king of the Madras, however, repelled these hordes of weapons that were launched by the five warriors and that were flying swiftly toward him on the battlefield. With his spear-headed arrows, Shalya sliced through the lance that Sátyaki hurled and through the gold-adorned shaft that Bhima fired. In that battle, the mighty warrior also dexterously split in two the terrifying, gold-staffed javelin that Nákula threw, and thwarted Saha·deva's mace with torrents of arrows, as he did King Yudhi·shthira's *shata·ghni* missile
with his shafts. Under the eyes of Pandu's sons, he then 13.25
roared a lion-roar, descendant of Bharata.

Sátyaki, the descendant of Shini, could not bear his enemy's victory in that battle. Senseless with rage, he took up another bow and pierced the lord of the Madras with two arrows and Shalya's charioteer with three.

Filled with violent fury, Shalya then wounded all his opponents with ten arrows in battle, Your Majesty, as if he were piercing mighty elephants with barbs. Repelled by the

na śekuḥ saṃmukhe sthātuṃ tasya śatru|niṣūdanāḥ.

tato Duryodhano rājā dṛṣṭvā Śalyasya vikramam
nihatān Pāṇḍavān mene Pañcālān atha Sṛñjayān.

13.30 tato rājan mahā|bāhur Bhīmasenaḥ pratāpavān
saṃtyajya manasā prāṇān Madr'|âdhipam ayodhayat.
Nakulaḥ Sahadevaś ca Sātyakiś ca mahā|rathaḥ
parivārya tadā Śalyaṃ samantād vyakirañ śaraiḥ.
sa caturbhir mah"|êṣv|āsaiḥ Pāṇḍavānāṃ mahā|rathaiḥ
vṛtas tān yodhayām āsa Madra|rājaḥ pratāpavān.
tasya Dharma|suto rājan kṣura|preṇa mah"|āhave
cakra|rakṣaṃ jaghān' āśu Madra|rājasya pārthivaḥ.
tasmiṃs tu nihate śūre cakra|rakṣe mahā|rathe
Madra|rājo 'pi balavān sainikān āvṛṇoc charaiḥ.

13.35 samāvṛtāṃs tatas tāṃs tu rājan vīkṣya sva|sainikān
cintayām āsa samare Dharma|putro Yudhiṣṭhiraḥ:

«kathaṃ nūnaṃ bhavet satyaṃ tan Mādhava|vaco mahat?
na hi kruddho raṇe rājā kṣapayeta balaṃ mama!»

tataḥ sa|ratha|nāg'|âśvāḥ Pāṇḍavāḥ Pāṇḍu|pūrva|ja
Madra|rājaṃ samāseduḥ pīḍayantaḥ samantataḥ.
nānā|śastr'|âugha|bahulāṃ śastra|vṛṣṭiṃ samudyatāṃ
vyadhamat samare rājā mah"|âbhrāṇ' îva Mārutaḥ.

king of the Madras in battle, the great warriors were unable to hold their ground before him, enemy-slayers though they were.

When he saw Shalya's prowess, King Dur·yódhana considered the Pándavas, Panchálas and Srínjayas to be dead.
But great-armed, mighty Bhima·sena then began to fight 13.30
against the king of the Madras, Your Majesty, after mentally sacrificing his life. Nákula, Saha·deva and the great warrior Sátyaki also surrounded Shalya and sprayed him on all sides with arrows. But although encompassed by those four great archers and mighty warriors of the Pándavas, the glorious king of the Madras battled against them. In that great battle, Your Majesty, the royal son of Righteousness quickly killed the king of the Madras' chariot-wheel protector with a razor-edged arrow. At the death of his wheel-protector—who was a heroic and great warrior—the powerful king of
the Madras covered the enemy troops with his shafts. On 13.35
seeing his troops enveloped by shafts, Yudhi·shthira, the son of Righteousness, had this thought during the battle, Your Majesty:

"How can the great words of Mádhava come true? I pray that this furious king does not destroy my army in battle!"

Then, O brother of Pandu, the Pándavas attacked the king of the Madras with their chariots, elephants and horses, pressing him on all sides. But just as the wind gods disperse great clouds, so the king scattered in battle the shower of weapons that his opponents raised against him, even though it was thick with hordes of different arms.

tataḥ kanaka|puṅkhāṃ tāṃ Śalya|kṣiptāṃ viyad|gatām
śara|vṛṣṭim apaśyāma śalabhānām iv' āyatim.
13.40 te śarā Madra|rājena preṣitā raṇa|mūrdhani
saṃpatantaḥ sma dṛśyante śalabhānāṃ vrajā iva.
Madra|rāja|dhanur|muktaiḥ śaraiḥ kanaka|bhūṣaṇaiḥ
nirantaram iv' ākāśaṃ saṃbabhūva jan'|âdhipa.
na Pāṇḍavānāṃ n' âsmākaṃ tatra kaś cid vyadṛśyata
bāṇ'|ândha|kāre mahati kṛte tatra mah"|āhave.
Madra|rājena balinā lāghavāc chara|vṛṣṭibhiḥ
cālyamānaṃ tu taṃ dṛṣṭvā Pāṇḍavānāṃ bal'|ârṇavam
vismayaṃ paramaṃ jagmur deva|gandharva|dānavāḥ.
sa tu tān sarvato yatnāc charaiḥ saṃpīḍya māriṣa
dharma|rājam avacchādya siṃhavad vyanadan muhuḥ.
13.45 te cchannāḥ samare tena Pāṇḍavānāṃ mahā|rathāḥ
n' âśaknuvaṃs tadā yuddhe pratyudyātuṃ mahā|ratham.
dharma|rāja|puro|gās tu Bhīmasena|mukhā rathāḥ
na jahuḥ samare śūraṃ Śalyam āhava|śobhinam.

SAÑJAYA uvāca:

14.1 ARJUNO DRAUṆINĀ viddho yuddhe bahubhir āyasaiḥ
tasya c' ânucaraiḥ śūrais Trigartānāṃ mahā|rathaiḥ.
Drauṇiṃ vivyādha samare
tribhir eva śilī|mukhaiḥ
tath" êtarān mah"|êṣv|āsān
dvābhyāṃ dvābhyāṃ Dhanañjayaḥ;
bhūyaś c' âiva mahā|rāja śara|varṣair avākirat.

We then saw a shower of gold-feathered arrows moving through the air like a flight of locusts, fired by Shalya. The 13.40
arrows that he released could be seen flying into the front of the battle like a swarm of locusts. The sky became entirely filled with the gold-adorned arrows that the king of the Madras fired from his bow, O lord of the people. Not one of the Pándavas or our troops were able to be seen when that vast darkness of arrows descended during that great battle.

The gods, *gandhárvas* and *dánavas* were filled with the highest wonder when they saw the mighty king of the Madras deftly shake the mass of the Pándava army with his showers of arrows.* Vigorously pounding the enemy on every side, my lord, Shalya enshrouded the King of Righteousness with shafts, roaring repeatedly like a lion.

Enveloped by Shalya in battle, the mighty warriors of the 13.45
Pándavas were unable to attack the great hero in that war. Nevertheless, led by the King of Righteousness and with Bhima·sena at their head, the warriors did not flee from heroic Shalya, who so adorned the battlefield.

SÁNJAYA said:

THE SON OF DRONA and his heroic followers, the mighty 14.1
warriors of the Tri·gartas, wounded Árjuna in battle with several iron arrows. Dhanan·jaya, however, pierced Drona's son on the battlefield with three stone-tipped shafts and shot the other great archers with two arrows each. He then once more sprayed them with showers of shafts, great king.

śara|kaṇṭakitās te tu tāvakā Bharata'|rṣabha
na jahuḥ Pārthaṃ āsādya tāḍyamānāḥ śitaiḥ śaraiḥ.
Arjunaṃ ratha|vaṃśena Droṇa|putra|puro|gamāḥ
ayodhayanta samare parivārya mahā|rathāḥ.
14.5 tais tu kṣiptāḥ śarā rājan kārtasvara|vibhūṣitāḥ
Arjunasya rath'|ôpasthaṃ pūrayām āsur añjasā.
tathā Kṛṣṇau mah"|êṣv|āsau vṛṣabhau sarva|dhanvinām
śarair vīkṣya vitunn'|âṅgau prahṛṣṭā yuddha|dur|madāḥ.

kūbaraṃ ratha|cakrāṇi īṣā yoktrāṇi vai vibho
yugaṃ c' âiv' ânukarṣaṃ ca śara|bhūtam abhūt tadā.
n' âitādṛśaṃ dṛṣṭa|pūrvaṃ rājan n' âiva ca naḥ śrutam
yādṛśaṃ tatra Pārthasya tāvakāḥ saṃpracakrire.

sa rathaḥ sarvato bhāti citra|puṅkhaiḥ śitaiḥ śaraiḥ
ulkā|śataiḥ saṃpradīptaṃ vimānam iva bhū|tale.
14.10 tato 'rjuno mahā|rāja śaraiḥ saṃnata|parvabhiḥ
avākirat tāṃ pṛtanāṃ megho vṛṣṭy" êva parvatam.
te vadhyamānāḥ samare Pārtha|nām'|âṅkitaiḥ śaraiḥ
Pārtha|bhūtam amanyanta prekṣamāṇās tathā|vidham.

kop'|ôddhūta|śara|jvālo dhanuḥ|śabd'|ânilo mahān
sainy'|êndhanaṃ dadāh' āśu tāvakaṃ Pārtha|pāvakaḥ.
cakrāṇāṃ patatāṃ c' âpi yugānāṃ ca dharā|tale
tūṇīrāṇāṃ patākānāṃ dhvajānāṃ ca rathaiḥ saha,
īṣāṇām anukarṣāṇāṃ tri|veṇūnāṃ ca Bhārata
akṣāṇām atha yoktrāṇāṃ pratodānāṃ ca sarvaśaḥ,

Although bristling with arrows and pummeled by sharp darts, your troops did not flee from the son of Pritha once they had attacked him, bull of the Bharatas. Led by Drona's son, the great warriors surrounded Árjuna with a column of chariots and fought him in battle. Difficult to conquer in war, they fired gold-adorned arrows, which swiftly filled 14.5
up Árjuna's chariot platform, and rejoiced at seeing the lacerated bodies of the two Krishnas—those great archers and bulls among all bowmen.

The shaft, wheels, pole, thongs, yoke and axle-tree of Árjuna's chariot all turned into arrows, my lord. Never before had we seen or heard anything like what your troops did to the son of Pritha, Your Majesty.

The chariot appeared radiant in every way as a result of those sharp arrows with their many-colored feathers; it looked like a celestial palace that had descended to the earth, blazing with a hundred lamps.

Then, great king, Árjuna covered the battalion with his 14.10
straight arrows, like a cloud pouring rain on a mountain. Slaughtered by arrows that were branded with the Partha's name, the troops thought, as they looked around them, that their very surroundings had become Pritha's son.

The son of Pritha was like a vast fire that swiftly consumed the kindling of your army; his arrows were flames that were fueled by anger and the twang of his bow was the wind. In the Partha's chariot-tracks, one could see heaps of wheels, yokes, quivers, flags, banners and chariots that had fallen to the ground. Everywhere, descendant of Bharata, there were mounds of chariot-poles, axle-trees, pole-joints,*

14.15 śirasāṃ patatāṃ c' âpi kuṇḍal'|ôṣṇīṣa|dhāriṇām
bhujānāṃ ca mahā|bhāga skandhānāṃ ca samantataḥ,
chattrāṇāṃ vyajanaiḥ sārdhaṃ mukuṭānāṃ ca rāśayaḥ
samadṛśyanta Pārthasya ratha|mārgeṣu Bhārata.
tataḥ kruddhasya Pārthasya ratha|mārge viśāṃ pate
a|gamya|rūpā pṛthivī māṃsa|śoṇita|kardamā.
bhīrūṇāṃ trāsa|jananī śūrāṇāṃ harṣa|vardhanī
babhūva Bharata|śreṣṭha Rudrasy' ākrīḍanaṃ yathā.

hatvā tu samare Pārthaḥ sahasre dve paran|tapaḥ
rathānāṃ sa|varūthānāṃ vidhūmo 'gnir iva jvalan.
14.20 yathā hi bhagavān Agnir jagad dagdhvā car'|âcaram
vidhūmo dṛśyate rājaṃs tathā Pārtho Dhanañjayaḥ.

Drauṇis tu samare dṛṣṭvā Pāṇḍavasya parākramam
rathen' âtipatākena Pāṇḍavaṃ pratyavārayat.
tāv ubhau puruṣa|vyāghrau tāv ubhāv dhanvināṃ varau
samīyatus tad" ânyonyaṃ paraspara|vadh'|âiṣiṇau.
tayor āsīn mahā|rāja bāṇa|varṣaṃ su|dāruṇam
jīmūtayor yathā vṛṣṭis tap'|ânte Bharata'|rṣabha.
anyonya|spardhinau tau tu śaraiḥ saṃnata|parvabhiḥ
tatakṣatus tad" ânyonyaṃ śṛṅgābhyāṃ vṛṣabhāv iva.
14.25 tayor yuddhaṃ mahā|rāja ciraṃ samam iv' âbhavat
śastrāṇāṃ saṃgamaś c' âiva ghoras tatr' âbhavat punaḥ.

tato 'rjunaṃ dvādaśabhī rukma|puṅkhaiḥ su|tejanaiḥ
Vāsudevaṃ ca daśabhir Drauṇir vivyādha Bhārata.
tataḥ praharṣād Bībhatsur vyākṣipad Gāṇḍivaṃ dhanuḥ
mānayitvā muhūrtaṃ tu guru|putraṃ mah"|āhave.
vy|aśva|sūta|rathaṃ cakre Savyasācī paran|tapaḥ

shafts, axles, thongs, and whips. Piled up on every side, illustrious king, there were fallen heads—still wearing their earrings and turbans—as well as limbs, shoulders, parasols, fans and crowns. In the chariot tracks of the enraged son of Pritha, the earth became inaccessible, O lord of the people, mixed as it was with flesh, blood and mire. Filling heroes with joy and the timid with fear, it seemed like Rudra's playground, O best of Bharatas. 14.15

After destroying two thousand armored chariots in battle, the enemy-slaying Partha resembled a fire that blazed without smoke. Indeed Dhanan·jaya, the son of Pritha, looked 14.20
like divine and smokeless Agni after he has incinerated the universe with all its moving and unmoving creatures.

When the son of Drona saw the Pándava's prowess in battle, he tried to restrain him with his many-flagged chariot. The two tiger-like men and excellent archers attacked one another, each eager to kill the other. The terrible shower of arrows that they fired was like rain pouring from clouds at the end of the summer, bull of the Bharatas. Competing against each other with their straight arrows, best of Bharatas, they tore into one another like bulls with horns. The 14.25
contest between the two men was long and seemed equal, and there was an awful and continuous clash of weapons, O mighty king.

The son of Drona then pierced Árjuna with twelve sharp, gold-feathered arrows and hit Vásu·deva with ten, descendant of Bharata. After showing his respects to the teacher's son for a while in that great battle, Bibhátsu fired his Gandíva bow with delight. Depriving Ashva·tthaman of his

mṛdu|pūrvaṃ tataś c' âinaṃ punaḥ punar atāḍayat.

hat'|âśve tu rathe tiṣṭhan Droṇa|putras tv ayo|mayam
musalaṃ Pāṇḍu|putrāya cikṣepa parigh'|ôpamam.
14.30 tam āpatantaṃ sahasā hema|paṭṭa|vibhūṣitam
ciccheda saptadhā vīraḥ Pārthaḥ śatru|nibarhaṇaḥ.

sa cchinnaṃ musalaṃ dṛṣṭvā Drauṇiḥ parama|kopanaḥ
ādade parighaṃ ghoraṃ nag'|êndra|śikhar'|ôpamam
cikṣepa c' âiva Pārthāya Drauṇir yuddha|viśāradaḥ.
tam antakam iva kruddhaṃ parighaṃ prekṣya Pāṇḍavaḥ
Arjunas tvarito jaghne pañcabhiḥ sāyak'|ôttamaiḥ.
sa cchinnaḥ patito bhūmau Pārtha|bāṇair mah"|āhave
dārayan pṛthiv"|îndrāṇāṃ manāṃs' îva ca Bhārata.

tato 'parais tribhir bhallair Drauṇiṃ vivyādha Pāṇḍavaḥ.
so 'tividdho balavatā Pārthena su|mah"|ātmanā
n' âkampata tadā Drauṇiḥ pauruṣe sve vyavasthitaḥ.
14.35 Surathaṃ ca tato rājan Bhāradvājaṃ mahā|ratham
avākirac chara|vrātaiḥ sarva|kṣatrasya paśyataḥ.
tatas tu Suratho 'py ājau Pañcālānāṃ mahā|rathaḥ
rathena megha|ghoṣeṇa Drauṇim ev' âbhyadhāvata.
vikarṣan vai dhanuḥ śreṣṭhaṃ sarva|bhāra|sahaṃ dṛḍham
jvalan'|āśī|viṣa|nibhaiḥ śaraiś c' âinam avākirat.

horses, charioteer and chariot, enemy-destroying Savya·sachin effortlessly* pounded him again and again.

Standing on his horseless chariot, the son of Drona hurled an iron club at the son of Pandu, which was like an iron bar. As the club swiftly flew toward him, decorated with gold 14.30
cloth, the heroic son of Pritha, that destroyer of enemies, sliced it into seven pieces.

Filled with intense rage at seeing his severed club, the son of Drona picked up a terrifying mace, which resembled the peak of the king of mountains, and hurled it at the son of Pritha, skilled as he was in warfare. But when Árjuna, the son of Pandu, saw that mace, which looked like wrathful Death, he quickly destroyed it with five of his best arrows. The mace fell to the ground, cut down by the Partha's arrows in that great battle; as it did so, it seemed to tear apart the hearts of the Káurava kings, descendant of Bharata.

The Pándava then pierced the son of Drona with three spear-headed arrows. But although badly wounded by the mighty and great-spirited son of Pritha, the son of Drona did not flinch and stood by his courage. Under the eyes of 14.35
all the warriors, he then covered Súratha, that great hero and descendant of Bharad·vaja, with swarms of arrows. Súratha, that great warrior of the Panchálas, then attacked the son of Drona in battle with his thundering chariot. Drawing his excellent bow, which was strong and able to bear every strain, he pelted him with arrows that looked like blazing, poisonous snakes.

Suratham vīkṣya saṃkruddham āpatantaṃ mahā|ratham
cukopa samare Drauṇir daṇḍ'|āhata iv' ôra|gaḥ.
tri|śikhāṃ bhru|kuṭīṃ kṛtvā sṛkkiṇī parisaṃlihan
udvīkṣya Surathaṃ roṣād dhanur|jyām avasṛjya ca
mumoca tīkṣṇaṃ nārācaṃ Yama|daṇḍ'|ôpama|dyutim.
14.40 sa tasya hṛdayaṃ bhittvā praviveś' âtivegitaḥ
Śakr'|âśanir iv' ôtsṛṣṭo vidārya dharaṇī|talam.
tataḥ sa patito bhūmau nārācena samāhataḥ
vajreṇa ca yathā śṛṅgaṃ parvatasya vidīryataḥ.
tasmin vinihate vīre Droṇa|putraḥ pratāpavān
āruroha rathaṃ tūrṇaṃ tam eva rathināṃ varaḥ.

tataḥ sajjo mahā|rāja Drauṇir āhava|dur|madaḥ
Arjunaṃ yodhayām āsa Saṃśaptaka|vṛto raṇe.
tatra yuddhaṃ mahac c' āsīd Arjunasya paraiḥ saha
madhyaṃ|dina|gate sūrye Yama|rāṣṭra|vivardhanam.
14.45 tatr' āścaryam apaśyāma dṛṣṭvā teṣāṃ parākramam
yad eko yugapad vīrān samayodhayad Arjunaḥ.
vimardaḥ su|mahān āsīd ekasya bahubhiḥ saha
Śata|krator yathā pūrvaṃ mahatyā daitya|senayā.

SAÑJAYA uvāca:

15.1 DURYODHANO mahā|rāja Dhṛṣṭadyumnaś ca Pārṣataḥ
cakratuḥ su|mahad yuddhaṃ śara|śakti|samākulam.
tayor āsan mahā|rāja śara|dhārāḥ sahasraśaḥ
ambu|dānāṃ yathā kāle jala|dhārāḥ samantataḥ.
rājā ca Pārṣataṃ viddhvā śaraiḥ pañcabhir āśu|gaiḥ

When he saw Súratha, that great warrior, rushing furiously toward him, the son of Drona became filled with rage on the battlefield, like a snake hit by a stick. Furrowing his forehead into three lines and licking the corners of his mouth, he glared at Súratha with anger. Letting go of his bowstring, he then released a sharp, iron arrow, which glistened like Yama's staff. The arrow tore through Súratha's 14.40
heart and entered the earth with great speed, splitting it like a thunderbolt hurled by Shakra. Struck by the arrow, Súratha fell to the ground, ripped apart like a mountain peak that has been smashed by a thunderbolt. At the death of that hero, the glorious son of Drona—that best of charioteers—then quickly climbed onto Súratha's chariot.

Armed and surrounded by the Samsháptakas, the invincible son of Drona then fought against Árjuna, Your Majesty. Under the midday sun, there was then a huge battle between Árjuna and his enemies, which swelled Yama's kingdom. As 14.45
we watched the courage of those men, it was a wonder for us to see how Árjuna simultaneously fought against all the heroes on his own. It was an enormous conflict of one man against many, just as in the past when Indra of a hundred sacrifices fought against the huge army of the demons.

SÁNJAYA said:

THEN, YOUR Majesty, Dur·yódhana and Dhrishta·dyu- 15.1
mna, the grandson of Príshata, fought a huge battle that teemed with arrows and spears. Both heroes, great king, fired thousands of streams of arrows, just as clouds pour torrents of rain in every direction in monsoon. With five swift arrows, King Dur·yódhana pierced the grandson of

Droṇa|hantāram ugr'|êṣuṃ punar vivyādha saptabhiḥ.
Dhṛṣṭadyumnas tu samare balavān dṛḍha|vikramaḥ
saptatyā viśikhānāṃ vai Duryodhanam apīḍayat.
15.5 pīḍitaṃ vīkṣya rājānaṃ sodaryā Bharata'|rṣabha
mahatyā senayā sārdhaṃ parivavruḥ sma Pārṣatam.
sa taiḥ parivṛtaḥ śūraḥ sarvato 'tirathair bhṛśam
vyacarat samare rājan darśayann astra|lāghavam.

Śikhaṇḍī Kṛtavarmāṇaṃ Gautamaṃ ca mahā|ratham
Prabhadrakaiḥ samāyukto yodhayām āsa dhanvinau.
tatr' âpi su|mahad yuddhaṃ ghora|rūpaṃ viśāṃ pate
prāṇān saṃtyajatāṃ yuddhe prāṇa|dyūt'|âbhidevane.

Śalyaḥ sāyaka|varṣāṇi vimuñcan sarvato|diśam
Pāṇḍavān pīḍayām āsa sa|Sātyaki|Vṛkodarān
15.10 tathā tau tu yamau yuddhe Yama|tulya|parākramau
yodhayām āsa rāj'|êndra vīryeṇ' âstra|balena ca.
Śalya|sāyaka|nunnānāṃ Pāṇḍavānāṃ mahā|mṛdhe
trātāraṃ n' âbhyagacchanta ke cit tatra mahā|rathāḥ.

tatas tu Nakulaḥ śūro Dharma|rāje prapīḍite
abhidudrāva vegena mātulaṃ mātṛ|nandanaḥ.
saṃchādya samare vīraṃ Nakulaḥ para|vīra|hā
vivyādha c' âinaṃ daśabhiḥ smayamānaḥ stan'|ântare,
sarva|pārasavair bāṇaiḥ karmāra|parimārjitaiḥ
svarṇa|puṅkhaiḥ śilā|dhautair dhanur|yantra|pracoditaiḥ.

Príshata—that slayer of Drona who fires fierce shafts—and then struck him again with seven more. But Dhrishta·dyumna—mighty and courageous in battle—bombarded Dur·yódhana with seventy arrows.

When they saw their king being attacked, Dur·yódhana's brothers surrounded the grandson of Príshata with a great force, bull of the Bharatas. But although completely surrounded on every side by those superior warriors, heroic Dhrishta·dyumna began to rampage in battle, Your Majesty, displaying his agility in weaponry. 15.5

With the support of the Prabhádrakas, Shikhándin then fought against two archers: Krita·varman and the great warrior Kripa, the descendant of Gótama. There, too, the battle was huge and terrible, lord of the people, as men sacrificed their lives in war. It was like a game of dice, in which life was the stake.

Firing showers of arrows in every direction, Shalya battered the Pándavas, including Sátyaki and Vrikódara. With 15.10
the force of his weaponry, O king of kings, he also vigorously fought against the Pándava twins, who were as strong as Yama in battle.* None of the great warriors among the Pándavas could find a protector, ravaged as the Pándavas were by Shalya's arrows in that great battle.

When the King of Righteousness was being assailed by Shalya, heroic Nákula—that delight of his mother—swiftly charged against his uncle. Covering the hero with arrows in battle, Nákula, that destroyer of enemy men, wounded Shalya with ten shafts in the center of his chest, smiling as he did so. Propelled by his bow, those gold-feathered and stone-cleansed shafts had been polished by a blacksmith and

15.15 Śalyas tu pīḍitas tena svasrīyeṇa mah"|ātmanā
Nakulaṃ pīḍayām āsa patribhir nata|parvabhiḥ.
tato Yudhiṣṭhiro rājā Bhīmaseno 'tha Sātyakiḥ
Sahadevaś ca Mādreyo Madra|rājam upādravan.
tān āpatata ev' āśu pūrayāṇān ratha|svanaiḥ
diśaś ca vidiśaś c' âiva kampayānāṃś ca medinīm
pratijagrāha samare senā|patir a|mitra|jit.
Yudhiṣṭhiraṃ tribhir viddhvā Bhīmasenaṃ ca pañcabhiḥ
Sātyakiṃ ca śaten' ājau Sahadevaṃ tribhiḥ śaraiḥ.
tatas tu sa|śaraṃ cāpaṃ Nakulasya mah"|ātmanaḥ
Madr'|ēśvaraḥ kṣura|preṇa tadā māriṣa cicchede.
tad aśīryata vicchinnaṃ dhanuḥ Śalyasya sāyakaiḥ.
15.20 ath' ânyad dhanur ādāya Mādrī|putro mahā|rathaḥ
Madra|rāja|rathaṃ tūrṇaṃ pūrayām āsa patribhiḥ.
Yudhiṣṭhiras tu Madr'|ēśaṃ Sahadevaś ca māriṣa
daśabhir daśabhir bāṇair urasy enam avidhyatām.
Bhīmasenas tu taṃ ṣaṣṭyā Sātyakir daśabhiḥ śaraiḥ
Madra|rājam abhidrutya jaghnatuḥ kaṅka|patribhiḥ.
Madra|rājas tataḥ kruddhaḥ Sātyakiṃ navabhiḥ śaraiḥ
vivyādha bhūyaḥ saptatyā śarāṇāṃ nata|parvaṇām.
ath' âsya sa|śaraṃ cāpaṃ muṣṭau ciccheda māriṣa
hayāṃś ca caturaḥ saṃkhye preṣayām āsa mṛtyave.
15.25 virathaṃ Sātyakiṃ dṛṣṭvā Madra|rājo mahā|rathaḥ
viśikhānāṃ śaten' âinam ājaghāna samantataḥ.
Mādrī|putrau ca saṃrabdhau Bhīmasenaṃ ca Pāṇḍavam

were entirely made of iron. But although besieged in this 15.15
way by his heroic nephew, Shalya bombarded Nákula with his straight arrows.

King Yudhi·shthira, Bhima·sena, Sátyaki and Saha·deva, the son of Madri, then charged against the king of the Madras. But, as they attacked swiftly, filling all the major and minor directions with the rumble of their chariots and making the earth tremble, Shalya—that enemy-conquering general—confronted them in battle. He pierced Yudhi·shthira with three arrows in battle, Bhima·sena with five, Sátyaki with a hundred and Saha·deva with three. Then, my lord, with a razor-edged arrow, the king of the Madras sliced through the shaft-bearing bow of heroic Nákula. The bow shattered, severed by Shalya's arrows.

But the son of Madri, that great warrior, took up another 15.20
bow and quickly filled the king of the Madras' chariot with arrows. Yudhi·shthira and Saha·deva also wounded the king of the Madras with ten arrows each in the chest, my lord. Charging against the king of the Madras, Bhima·sena too struck Shalya with sixty heron-feathered arrows, while Sátyaki hit him with ten.

Enraged, the king of the Madras pierced Sátyaki with nine arrows and then once more with seventy straight shafts. He then severed Sátyaki's arrow-bearing bow at the handle and sent his four horses to their death in the battle, my lord.
When the king of the Madras saw that Sátyaki was deprived 15.25
of his chariot, that great warrior struck him on all sides with a hundred shafts. He then wounded the two furious sons of Madri, the Pándava Bhima·sena, and Yudhi·shthira with ten arrows, descendant of Kuru.It was a wonder for us to see

Yudhiṣṭhiraṃ ca Kauravya vivyādha daśabhiḥ śaraiḥ.
tatr' âdbhutam apaśyāma Madra|rājasya pauruṣam
yad enaṃ sahitāḥ Pārthā n' âbhyavartanta saṃyuge.

ath' ânyaṃ ratham āsthāya Sātyakiḥ satya|vikramaḥ
pīḍitān Pāṇḍavān dṛṣṭvā Madra|rāja|vaśaṃ gatān
abhidudrāva vegena Madrāṇām adhipaṃ balāt.
āpatantaṃ rathaṃ tasya Śalyaḥ samiti|śobhanaḥ
pratyudyayau rathen' âiva matto mattam iva dvipam.
15.30 sa saṃnipātas tumulo babhūv' âdbhuta|darśanaḥ
Sātyakeś c' âiva śūrasya Madrāṇām adhipasya ca
yādṛśo vai purā vṛttaḥ Śambar'|â|mara|rājayoḥ.

Sātyakiḥ prekṣya samare Madra|rājam avasthitam
vivyādha daśabhir bāṇais «tiṣṭha tiṣṭh' êti» c' âbravīt.
Madra|rājas tu su|bhṛśaṃ viddhas tena mah"|ātmanā
Sātyakiṃ prativivyādha citra|puṅkhaiḥ śitaiḥ śaraiḥ.
tataḥ Pārthā mah"|êṣv|āsāḥ Sātvat'|âbhisṛtaṃ nṛ|pam
abhyavartan rathais tūrṇaṃ mātulaṃ vadha|kāṅkṣayā.

tata āsīt parāmardas tumulaḥ śoṇit'|ôdakaḥ
śūrāṇāṃ yudhyamānānāṃ siṃhānām iva nardatām.
15.35 teṣām āsīn mahā|rāja vyadhikṣepaḥ paras|param
siṃhānām āmiṣ'|ēpsūnāṃ kūjatām iva saṃyuge.
teṣāṃ bāṇa|sahasr'|âughair ākīrṇā vasu|dh" âbhavat
antar|ikṣaṃ ca sahasā bāṇa|bhūtam abhūt tadā.
śar'|ândha|kāraṃ sahasā kṛtaṃ tena samantataḥ

the courage of the king of the Madras, as, even collectively, the sons of Pritha were unable to overwhelm him.

Sátyaki—whose strength lies in truth—ascended another chariot. At the sight of the Pándavas being besieged and dominated by the king of the Madras, he charged with power and speed against the Madra lord. But Shalya, that ornament of councils, advanced with his own chariot against Sátyaki's charging vehicle, like one frenzied elephant confronting another. There was then a tumultuous conflict, 15.30
incredible to see, between heroic Sátyaki and the king of the Madras; it was like a battle in the past between Shámbara and the king of the gods.

Sátyaki glared at the king of the Madras as he stood his ground on the battlefield and pierced him with ten arrows, shouting: "Stay still! Stay still!" But although severely wounded by that hero, the king of the Madras shot Sátyaki back with his sharp arrows, which were adorned with many-colored feathers. Eager to kill their uncle, the sons of Pritha—great archers that they were—then swiftly attacked King Shalya with their chariots after he had been assailed by the Sátvata warrior.*

There was then a tumultuous carnage, in which blood flowed like water, as the heroes fought one another like roaring lions. They battled against one another like bellow- 15.35
ing lions that compete for meat in a fight, Your Majesty. The earth became strewn with heaps of thousands of the men's shafts, and the sky turned instantly into arrows. A sudden darkness arose on all sides because of the arrows that those heroes fired; it was as if a shadow had been cast from the clouds. The directions glowed with shimmering,

abhra|cchāy" êva saṃjajñe śarair muktair mah"|ātmabhiḥ.
tatra rājan śarair muktair nirmuktair iva panna|gaiḥ
svarṇa|puṅkhaiḥ prakāśadbhir vyarocanta diśas tadā.

tatr' âdbhutaṃ paraṃ cakre Śalyaḥ śatru|nibarhaṇaḥ
yad ekaḥ samare śūro yodhayām āsa vai bahūn.
15.40 Madra|rāja|bhuj'|ôtsṛṣṭaiḥ kaṅka|barhiṇa|vājitaiḥ
saṃpatadbhiḥ śarair ghorair avākīryata medinī.
tatra Śalya|rathaṃ rājan vicarantaṃ mah"|āhave
apaśyāma yathā pūrvaṃ Śakrasy' âsura|saṃkṣaye.

SAÑJAYA uvāca:

16.1 TATAḤ SAINYĀS tava vibho Madra|rāja|puraskṛtāḥ
punar abhyadravan Pārthān vegena mahatā raṇe.
pīḍitās tāvakāḥ sarve pradhāvanto raṇ'|ôtkaṭāḥ
kṣaṇena c' âiva Pārthāṃs te bahutvāt samaloḍayan.
te vadhyamānāḥ samare Pāṇḍavā n' âvatasthire
nivāryamāṇā Bhīmena paśyatoḥ Kṛṣṇayos tadā.

tato Dhanañjayaḥ kruddhaḥ Kṛpaṃ saha pad'|ânugaiḥ
avākirac char'|âugheṇa Kṛtavarmāṇam eva ca.
16.5 Śakuniṃ Sahadevas tu saha|sainyam avākirat
Nakulaḥ pārśvataḥ sthitvā Madra|rājam avaikṣata.
Draupadeyā nar'|êndrāṃś ca bhūyiṣṭhān samavārayan
Droṇa|putraṃ ca Pāñcālyaḥ Śikhaṇḍī samavārayat.
Bhīmasenas tu rājānaṃ gadā|pāṇir avārayat
Śalyaṃ tu saha sainyena Kuntī|putro Yudhiṣṭhiraḥ.

gold-feathered shafts, which were released like snakes that had shed their skin, Your Majesty.

Shalya, that destroyer of enemies, then performed another wonder as he heroically fought in battle, one against many. The earth was covered with the terrifying, hurtling 15.40
arrows that the king of the Madras fired and that were heron- and peacock-feathered. We watched Shalya's chariot rampage in that great war, Your Majesty, just as Shakra's chariot did in the past in his battle against the demons.

SÁNJAYA said:

THEN, MY LORD, your troops once again charged with 16.1
great force against Pritha's sons in battle, led by the king of the Madras. Although they were under attack, your men all rushed forward—drunk with war—and, by the strength of their numbers, instantly threw the Parthas into disarray. The two Krishnas watched as the Pándava soldiers were unable to hold their ground as they were slaughtered in battle, even though Bhima tried to restrain them.

Enraged, Dhanan·jaya then covered Krita·varman, Kripa and Kripa's followers with a swarm of arrows. Saha·deva 16.5
pelted Shákuni and his troops, while Nákula stood at Saha·deva's flank and glared at the king of the Madras. The sons of Dráupadi held off numerous kings, while the Panchála hero Shikhándin restrained the son of Drona. Brandishing his mace, Bhima·sena warded off King Dur·yódhana, while Yudhi·shthira, the son of Kunti, repelled Shalya and his army.

tataḥ samabhavat sainyaṃ saṃsaktaṃ tatra tatra ha
tāvakānāṃ pareṣāṃ ca saṃgrāmeṣv a|nivartinām.
tatra paśyāmy ahaṃ karma Śalyasy' âtimahad raṇe
yad ekaḥ sarva|sainyāni Pāṇḍavānām ayodhayat.
16.10 vyadṛśyata tadā Śalyo Yudhiṣṭhira|samīpataḥ
raṇe candramaso 'bhyāśe śanaiś|cara iva grahaḥ.
pīḍayitvā tu rājānaṃ śarair āśī|viṣ'|ôpamaiḥ
abhyadhāvat punar Bhīmaṃ śara|varṣair avākirat.
tasya tal lāghavaṃ dṛṣṭvā tath" âiva ca kṛt'|âstratām
apūjayann anīkāni pareṣāṃ tāvakāni ca.

pīḍyamānās tu Śalyena Pāṇḍavā bhṛśa|vikṣatāḥ
prādravanta raṇaṃ hitvā krośamāne Yudhiṣṭhire.
vadhyamāneṣv anīkeṣu Madra|rājena Pāṇḍavaḥ
a|marṣa|vaśam āpanno dharma|rājo Yudhiṣṭhiraḥ.
tataḥ pauruṣam āsthāya Madra|rājam atāḍayat.
16.15 jayo v" âstu vadho v" êti kṛta|buddhir mahā|rathaḥ
samāhūy' âbravīt sarvān bhrātṝn Kṛṣṇaṃ ca Mādhavam:

«Bhīṣmo Droṇaś ca Karṇaś ca ye c' ânye pṛthivī|kṣitaḥ
Kaurav'|ârthe parākrāntāḥ saṃgrāme nidhanaṃ gatāḥ.
yathā|bhāgaṃ yath"|ôtsāhaṃ bhavantaḥ kṛta|pauruṣāḥ.
bhāgo 'vaśiṣṭa eko 'yaṃ mama Śalyo mahā|rathaḥ.

so 'ham adya yudhā jetum āśaṃse Madrak'|âdhipam
tatra yan mānasaṃ mahyaṃ tat sarvaṃ nigadāmi vaḥ.

All over the battlefield, your army and the enemy troops engaged in war, neither side willing to flee the conflict. I then saw Shalya perform an enormous feat in battle, as he alone fought against all the Pándava troops. Standing 16.10
close to Yudhi·shthira on the battlefield, Shalya resembled the planet Saturn near the moon. Bombarding King Yudhi·shthira with shafts that were like poisonous snakes, he charged forward again and covered Bhima with showers of arrows. At the sight of Shalya's agility and his dexterity with weapons, your troops and the enemy both applauded him.

Pounded by Shalya, the heavily wounded Pándava troops ran away and fled the battlefield, despite Yudhi·shthira's shouts. As his troops were slaughtered by the king of the Madras, the King of Righteousness—that Pándava Yudhi·shthira—became overwhelmed with fury. Applying his courage, he began to besiege the king of the Madras. De- 16.15
termined to win victory or die, the great warrior then summoned all his brothers, as well as Krishna, the Mádhava, and said:

"Bhishma, Drona, Karna and other kings have all shown their valor for the Káuravas' cause and have died in battle. You, too, have shown your courage, each according to your share and with your individual vigor. Mine is the one share that remains. That share is the great warrior Shalya.

Today I aim to kill the king of the Madras in battle! Let me tell you everything that I have in mind for the task.

cakra|rakṣāv imau vīrau mama Mādravatī|sutau
a|jeyau Vāsaven' âpi samare śūra|saṃmatau.

16.20 sādhv imau mātulaṃ yuddhe kṣatra|dharma|puraskṛtau
mad|arthe pratiyudhyetāṃ mān'|ârhau satya|saṃgarau!
māṃ vā Śalyo raṇe hantā
tam v" âhaṃ! bhadram astu vaḥ!
iti satyām imāṃ vāṇīṃ
loka|vīrā nibodhata!

yotsye 'haṃ mātulen' âdya kṣātra|dharmeṇa pārthivāḥ
svam aṃśaṃ abhisandhāya vijayāy' êtarāya ca.
tasya me 'py adhikaṃ śastraṃ sarv'|ôpakaraṇāni ca
saṃsajjantu rathe kṣipraṃ śāstravad ratha|yojakāḥ.
Śaineyo dakṣiṇaṃ cakraṃ Dhṛṣṭadyumnas tath" ôttaram.
pṛṣṭha|gopo bhavatv adya mama Pārtho Dhanañjayaḥ.

16.25 puraḥ|saro mam' âdy' âstu Bhīmaḥ śastra|bhṛtāṃ varaḥ
evam abhyadhikaḥ Śalyād bhaviṣyāmi mahā|mṛdhe!»
evam uktās cakrus tadā sarve rājñaḥ priy'|âiṣiṇaḥ.
tataḥ praharṣaḥ sainyānāṃ punar āsīt tadā mṛdhe
Pañcālānāṃ Somakānāṃ Matsyānāṃ ca viśeṣataḥ.
pratijñāṃ tāṃ tadā rājā kṛtvā Madr'|ēśaṃ abhyayāt.
tataḥ śaṅkhāṃś ca bherīś ca śataśaś c' âiva puṣkalān
avādayanta Pañcālāḥ siṃha|nādāṃś ca nedire.

The two heroic sons of Mádravati will protect my chariot wheels. Even Vásava could not defeat them in battle, such is their reckoning as heroes. Let these two good and 16.20
respectable men, who honor the warrior code and are true to their vows, fight against their uncle for my cause!

Either Shalya will kill me in battle or I will kill him. Blessings be to you! Listen to my words of truth, heroes of the world!

Today, O kings, I will attend to my own share, whether the result be victory or defeat, and I will fight against my uncle in accord with the warrior code.

Let the chariot-workers quickly and skillfully supply my chariot with more weapons and implements of every kind than Shalya has. Sátyaki, the grandson of Shini, should protect my right wheel and Dhrishta·dyumna my left. Dhanan·jaya, the son of Pritha, should today protect my rear
and Bhima, that best of warriors, should today fight in front 16.25
of me. In this way I will be superior to Shalya in the great battle!"

Addressed in this way and wishing to favor the king, they all did as they were instructed. The troops then once more became joyful in that battle, especially the Panchálas, Sómakas and Matsyas.

After King Yudhi·shthira had made this vow, he attacked the ruler of the Madras. At this, the Panchálas shouted lion-roars and played hundreds of loud conches and drums.

te 'bhyadhāvanta saṃrabdhā Madra|rājaṃ tarasvinaṃ
mahatā harṣa|jen' âtha nādena Kuru|puṅ|gavāḥ,
hrādena gaja|ghaṇṭānāṃ śaṅkhānāṃ ninadena ca
tūrya|śabdena mahatā nādayantaś ca medinīm.

16.30 tān pratyagṛhṇāt putras te Madra|rājaś ca vīryavān
mahā|meghān iva bahūñ śailāv ast'|ôdayāv ubhau.
Śalyas tu samara|ślāghī Dharma|rājam arin|damam
vavarṣa śara|varṣeṇa Śambaraṃ Maghavā iva.*
tath" âiva Kuru|rājo 'pi pragṛhya ruciraṃ dhanuḥ
Droṇ'|ôpadeśān vividhān darśayāno mahā|manāḥ.
vavarṣa śara|varṣāṇi citraṃ laghu ca su|ṣṭhu ca
na c' âsya vivaraṃ kaś cid dadarśa carato raṇe.

tāv ubhau vividhair bāṇais tatakṣāte paras|param
śārdūlāv āmiṣa|prepsū parākrāntāv iv' āhave.
16.35 Bhīmas tu tava putreṇa yuddha|śauṇḍena saṃgataḥ
Pāñcālyaḥ Sātyakiś c' âiva Mādrī|putrau ca Pāṇḍavau
Śakuni|pramukhān vīrān pratyagṛhṇan samantataḥ.
tad" āsīt tumulaṃ yuddhaṃ punar eva jay'|âiṣiṇām
tāvakānāṃ pareṣāṃ ca rājan dur|mantrite tava.

Duryodhanas tu Bhīmasya śareṇ' ānata|parvaṇā
cicched' ādiśya saṃgrāme dhvajaṃ hema|pariṣkṛtam.
sa kiṅkiṇīka|jālena mahatā cāru|darśanaḥ
papāta ruciraḥ saṃkhye Bhīmasenasya paśyataḥ.
punaś c' âsya dhanuś citraṃ gaja|rāja|kar'|ôpamam
kṣureṇa śita|dhāreṇa pracakarta nar'|âdhipaḥ.

The bull-like Kurus then furiously charged against the ardent king of the Madras with a great shout of joy. As they did so, they made the earth resound with the jangling of elephant-bells, the blare of conches, and the vast noise of musical instruments.

Your son and the mighty king of the Madras confronted 16.30
these men, like two mountains in the west and east blocking a mass of large clouds. Shalya, proud in battle, poured a shower of arrows over the enemy-taming King of Righteousness, just as Mághavat once did against Shámbara. Likewise, the king of the Kurus took up a beautiful bow and proudly displayed the various skills he had been taught by Drona. Nimbly and with ease, Dur·yódhana fired various showers of arrows and no one could find a weakness in him as he rampaged in battle.

Shalya and Yudhi·shthira tore into one another with numerous arrows, like brave tigers in a battle that are hungry for meat. Bhima fought against your son, who was drunk 16.35
with war, while the Panchálan Sátyaki and the two Pándava sons of Madri confronted on every side the heroes that were led by Shákuni. Because of your bad advice, Your Majesty, your troops and the enemy once again engaged in a turbulent battle, both sides eager for victory.

In that battle, Dur·yódhana aimed at Bhima's gilded banner and split it with a straight arrow. Under Bhima·sena's very eyes, the beautiful, glistening banner fell in the battle, adorned with a large mesh of bells. With a sharp, razor-edged arrow, the king also sliced through Bhima's splendid bow, which resembled an elephant's trunk. But although his 16.40
bow was severed, ardent Bhima strode forward and pierced

16.40 sa cchinna|dhanvā tejasvī ratha|śaktyā sutaṃ tava
bibhed' ôrasi vikramya; sa rath'|ôpastha āviśat.
tasmin moham anuprāpte punar eva Vṛkodaraḥ
yantur eva śiraḥ kāyāt kṣura|preṇ' âharat tadā.
hata|sūtā hayās tasya ratham ādāya Bhārata
vyadravanta diśo rājan. hā|hā|kāras tad" âbhavat.
tam abhyadhāvat trāṇ'|ârthaṃ Droṇa|putro mahā|rathaḥ
Kṛpaś ca Kṛtavarmā ca putraṃ te 'pi parīpsavaḥ.
tasmin vilulite sainye trastās tasya pad'|ânugāḥ.
Gāṇḍīva|dhanvā visphārya dhanus tān ahanac charaiḥ.
16.45 Yudhiṣṭhiras tu Madr'|ēśam abhyadhāvad a|marṣitaḥ
svayaṃ sannodayann aśvān danta|varṇān mano|javān.
tatr' āścaryam apaśyāma Kuntī|putre Yudhiṣṭhire
purā bhūtvā mṛdur dānto yat tadā dāruṇo 'bhavat.
vivṛt'|âkṣaś ca Kaunteyo vepamānaś ca manyunā
ciccheda yodhān niśitaiḥ śaraiḥ śata|sahasraśaḥ.
yāṃ yāṃ pratyudyayau senāṃ
tāṃ tāṃ jyeṣṭhaḥ sa Pāṇḍavaḥ
śarair apātayad rājan
girīn vajrair iv' ôttamaiḥ.
s'|âśva|sūta|dhvaja|rathān rathinaḥ pātayan bahūn
akrīḍad eko balavān pavanas toya|dān iva.
16.50 s'|âśv'|ārohāṃś ca tura|gān pattīṃś c' âiva sahasradhā
vyapothayata saṃgrāme kruddho Rudraḥ paśūn iva.

your son in the chest with his chariot-spear. Dur·yódhana then collapsed on his chariot platform.

While Dur·yódhana was unconscious, Vrikódara then also chopped off the head of Dur·yódhana's charioteer with a razor-edged arrow. At the death of their charioteer, Dur·yódhana's horses fled in every direction, taking the chariot with them, descendant of Bharata. Your soldiers then cried out in distress, Your Majesty.

Kripa, Krita·varman and the son of Drona—that great warrior—then chased after the chariot in order to save it and rescue your son. Dur·yódhana's army fell into disarray and his followers became terrified. The bearer of the Gandíva then drew his bow and began to annihilate the troops with his arrows.

Driving on his horses by himself—which were white as 16.45
ivory and swift as thought—Yudhi·shthira then attacked the king of the Madras in a frenzy. It was a wonder to see Yudhi·shthira, the son of Kunti, become so brutal when previously he had been so mild and restrained. Rolling his eyes and shaking with fury, the son of Kunti gored your soldiers with hundreds and thousands of sharp arrows. With his shafts, the eldest son of Pandu brought down every regiment that he attacked, as if he were toppling mountains with massive thunderbolts. Destroying hordes of charioteers, steeds, drivers, banners and chariots, mighty Yudhi·shthira played with his enemies on his own, like the wind
plays with clouds. Like Rudra destroying creatures in a rage, 16.50
so he pummeled thousands of horses, cavalrymen and foot soldiers in battle.

śūnyam āyodhanaṃ kṛtvā śara|varṣaiḥ samantataḥ
abhyadravata Madr'|ēśaṃ «tiṣṭha Śaly' êti» c' âbravīt.
tasya tac caritaṃ dṛṣṭvā saṃgrāme bhīma|karmaṇaḥ
vitresus tāvakāḥ sarve. Śalyas tv enaṃ samabhyayāt.

tatas tau bhṛśa|saṃkruddhau pradhmāya salil'|ôdbhavau
samāhūya tad" ânyonyaṃ bhartsayantau samīyatuḥ.

Śalyas tu śara|varṣeṇa pīḍayām āsa Pāṇḍavam.
Madra|rājaṃ tu Kaunteyaḥ śara|varṣair avākirat.
16.55 adṛśyetāṃ tadā rājan kaṅka|patribhir ācitau
udbhinna|rudhirau śūrau Madra|rāja|Yudhiṣṭhirau.
puṣpitau śuśubhāte vai vasante kiṃśukau yathā
dīpyamānau mah"|ātmānau prāṇa|dyūtena dur|madau.

dṛṣṭvā sarvāṇi sainyāni n' âdhyavasyaṃs tayor jayam.
hatvā Madr'|âdhipaṃ Pārtho bhokṣyate 'dya vasun|dharām,
Śalyo vā Pāṇḍavaṃ hatvā dadyād Duryodhanāya gām
it' îva niścayo n' âbhūd yodhānāṃ tatra Bhārata.

pradakṣiṇam abhūt sarvaṃ Dharma|rājasya yudhyataḥ.
tataḥ śara|śataṃ Śalyo mumoc' âtha Yudhiṣṭhire
dhanuś c' âsya śit'|âgreṇa bāṇena nirakṛntata.
16.60 so 'nyat kārmukam ādāya Śalyaṃ śara|śatais tribhiḥ
avidhyat kārmukaṃ c' âsya kṣureṇa nirakṛntata.
ath' âsya nijaghān' âśvāṃś caturo nata|parvabhiḥ

After he had emptied the entire battlefield with his showers of arrows, Yudhi·shthira attacked the king of the Madras, shouting, "Stay still, Shalya!" Your troops all became terrified when they saw the awful feats that Yudhi·shthira performed in battle. Shalya, however, attacked Yudhi·shthira.

Filled with violent rage, the two heroes blew their conch shells and challenged one another. They then clashed, abusing each other as they did so.

Shalya bombarded the Pándava with a shower of arrows. But the son of Kunti enveloped the king of the Madras
with showers of shafts. The king of the Madras and Yu- 16.55
dhi·shthira—both of them heroes—were seen covered with heron-feathered arrows and spurting blood. Invincible in that contest for life, those radiant heroes looked as glorious as flowering *kim·shuka* trees in the spring.

As the soldiers all watched, none of them could determine which warrior would win. None could decide, descendant of Bharata, whether the son of Pritha would kill the king of the Madras and enjoy the earth that day, or whether Shalya would kill the Pándava and hand over the earth to Dur·yódhana.

Everyone stood to the left of the King of Righteousness as he fought.

Shalya then fired a hundred shafts at Yudhi·shthira and
sliced through his bow with a sharp-pointed arrow. Yudhi· 16.60
shthira, however, took up another bow, pierced Shalya with three hundred shafts, and then cut through Shalya's bow with a razor-tipped arrow. With his straight shafts, he then killed Shalya's four horses and slaughtered both of Shalya's

dvābhyām atiśit'|âgrābhyām ubhau tu pārṣṇi|sārathī.
tato 'sya dīpyamānena pītena niśitena ca
pramukhe vartamānasya bhallen' âpāharad dhvajam.
tataḥ prabhagnaṃ tat sainyaṃ
Dauryodhanam arin|dama.
tato Madr'|âdhipaṃ Drauṇir
abhyadhāvat tathā|kṛtam
āropya c' âinaṃ sva|rathe
tvaramāṇaḥ pradudruve.
muhūrtam iva tau gatvā nardamāne Yudhiṣṭhire
sthitvā tato Madra|patir anyaṃ syandanam āsthitaḥ.
16.65 vidhivat kalpitaṃ śubhraṃ mah"|âmbu|da|ninādinam
sajja|yantr'|ôpakaraṇaṃ dviṣatāṃ loma|harṣaṇam.

SAÑJAYA UVĀCA:

17.1 ATH' ÂNYAD dhanur ādāya balavān vegavattaram
Yudhiṣṭhiraṃ Madra|patir bhittvā siṃha iv' ânadat.
tataḥ sa śara|varṣeṇa Parjanya iva vṛṣṭi|mān
abhyavarṣad a|mey'|ātmā kṣatriyaṃ kṣatriya'|rṣabhaḥ.
Sātyakiṃ daśabhir viddhvā Bhīmasenaṃ tribhiḥ śaraiḥ
Sahadevaṃ tribhir viddhvā Yudhiṣṭhiram apīḍayat.
tāṃs tān anyān mah"|êṣv|āsān s'|âśvān sa|ratha|kūbarān
ardayām āsa viśikhair ulkābhir iva kuñjarān.
17.5 kuñjarān kuñjar'|ārohān aśvān aśva|prayāyinaḥ
rathāṃś ca rathibhiḥ sārdhaṃ jaghāna rathināṃ varaḥ.
bāhūṃś ciccheda tarasā s'|āyudhān ketanāni ca.
cakāra ca mahīṃ yodhais tīrṇāṃ vedīṃ kuśair iva.

rear-charioteers with two very sharp-pointed arrows. While Shalya was standing in front of him, Yudhi·shthira then struck down his banner with a copper, spear-headed arrow, which glistened and was sharp.

Dur·yódhana's army then broke up, tamer of enemies. At this, the son of Drona rushed toward the king of the Madras and, taking him onto his own chariot, swiftly sped away. After they had driven for only a while, Yudhi·shthira roared out loud. The ruler of the Madras then stopped and climbed onto another chariot. Expertly built and equipped 16.65
with every type of implement, the splendid chariot roared like a great thundercloud, bringing horror to its enemies.

SÁNJAYA said:

THE MIGHTY lord of the Madras then took up another, 17.1
swifter bow and roared like a lion after piercing Yudhi·shthira. Like Parjánya pouring rain, that bull of the kshatriyas—infinite in spirit—rained a shower of arrows over the warrior. Wounding Sátyaki with ten arrows and Bhima·sena with three, he pierced Saha·deva with three more and bombarded Yudhi·shthira. As if he were tormenting elephants with firebrands, Shalya then besieged various other archers, horses and chariot-shafts with his arrows.

Elephants and elephant-riders, horses and horsemen, 17.5
chariots and chariot-drivers were all slaughtered by that best of charioteers. With speed, Shalya sliced through arms that wielded weapons and through banners, too. As if strewing an altar with *kusha* grass, he covered the earth with soldiers.

tathā tam ari|sainyāni ghnantaṃ mṛtyum iv' Ântakam
parivavrur bhṛśaṃ kruddhāḥ Pāṇḍu|Pañcāla|Somakāḥ.
taṃ Bhīmasenaś ca Śineś ca naptā
Mādryāś ca putrau puruṣa|pravīrau
samāgataṃ bhīma|balena rājñā
paryāpur anyonyam ath' āhvayantaḥ.
tatas tu śūrāḥ samare nar'|êndra
nar'|ēśvaraṃ prāpya yudhāṃ variṣṭham
āvārya c' âinaṃ samare nṛ|vīrā
jaghnuḥ śaraiḥ patribhir ugra|vegaiḥ.
17.10 saṃrakṣito Bhīmasenena rājā
Mādrī|sutābhyām atha Mādhavena
Madr'|âdhipaṃ patribhir ugra|vegaiḥ
stan'|ântare Dharma|suto nijaghne.
tato raṇe tāvakānāṃ rath'|âughāḥ
samīkṣya Madr'|âdhipatiṃ śar'|ārtam
paryāvavruḥ pravarās te su|sajjā
Duryodhanasy' ânumate purastāt.
tato drutaṃ Madra|jan'|âdhipo raṇe
Yudhiṣṭhiraṃ saptabhir abhyaviddhyat.
taṃ c' âpi Pārtho navabhiḥ pṛṣatkair
vivyādha rājaṃs tumule mah"|ātmā.
ā|karṇa|pūrṇ'|āyata|saṃprayuktaiḥ
śarais tadā saṃyati taila|dhautaiḥ
anyonyam ācchādayatāṃ mahā|rathau
Madr'|âdhipaś c' âpi Yudhiṣṭhiraś ca.
tatas tu tūrṇaṃ samare mahā|rathau
paras|parasy' ântaram īkṣamāṇau
śarair bhṛśaṃ vivyadhatur nṛp'|ôttamau
mahā|balau śatrubhir a|pradhṛṣyau.
17.15 tayor dhanur|jyā|tala|niḥsvano mahān

Filled with violent fury, the Pandus, Panchálas and Só-makas then surrounded Shalya as he annihilated the enemy troops like life-ending Death. Summoning each other, Bhima·sena, the grandson of Shini, and the sons of Madri—those two heroes among men—confronted Shalya as he fought against the terrifyingly powerful King Yudhi·shthira.

Approaching in battle that king of men and champion of warriors, the valiant heroes surrounded Shalya and struck him with feathered arrows that flew with fierce velocity, O lord of the people. Protected by Bhima·sena, Mádhava* 17.10
and the sons of Madri, the royal son of Righteousness then shot the king of the Madras in the center of the chest with his fierce-flying arrows. But on seeing that the king of the Madras was being plagued by arrows in battle, the fine and well-equipped hordes of warriors in your army followed Dur·yódhana's command by grouping in front of him.

The king of the Madras then quickly shot Yudhi·shthira with seven arrows in battle. In the mayhem, Your Majesty, the heroic son of Pritha pierced Shalya back with nine shafts.

The king of the Madras and Yudhi·shthira—both of them great warriors—then covered each other in battle with arrows that were cleansed with oil and that were fired from bows stretched and drawn as far as the ear. Searching for each other's weaknesses in that battle, those great warriors and best of men swiftly and violently wounded one another with swarms of arrows, mighty as they were and unable to be defeated by their enemies.

When those great-spirited warriors—the ruler of the Ma- 17.15
dras and the hero of the Pandus—showered each other with

mah"|êndra|vajr'|âśani|tulya|niḥsvanaḥ
paras|paraṃ bāṇa|gaṇair mah"|ātmanoḥ
pravarṣator Madra|pa|Pāṇḍu|vīrayoḥ.
tau ceratur vyāghra|śiśu|prakāśau
mahā|vaneṣv āmiṣa|gṛddhināv iva.
viṣāṇinau nāga|varāv iv' ôbhau
tatakṣatuḥ saṃyati jāta|darpau.
tatas tu Madr'|âdhipatir mah"|ātmā
Yudhiṣṭhiraṃ bhīma|balaṃ prasahya
vivyādha vīraṃ hṛdaye 'tivegaṃ
śareṇa sūry'|âgni|sama|prabheṇa.
tato 'tividdho 'tha Yudhiṣṭhiro 'pi
su|saṃprayuktena śareṇa rājan
jaghāna Madr'|âdhipatiṃ mah"|ātmā
mudaṃ ca lebhe ṛṣabhaḥ Kurūṇām.
tato muhūrtād iva pārthiv'|êndro
labdhvā saṃjñāṃ krodha|saṃrakta|netraḥ
śatena Pārthaṃ tvarito jaghāna
sahasra|netra|pratima|prabhāvaḥ.
17.20 tvaraṃs tato Dharma|suto mah"|ātmā
Śalyasya kopān navabhiḥ pṛṣatkaiḥ
bhittvā hy uras tapanīyaṃ ca varma
jaghāna ṣaḍbhis tv aparaiḥ pṛṣatkaiḥ.
tatas tu Madr'|âdhipatiḥ prakṛṣṭaṃ
dhanur vikṛṣya vyasṛjat pṛṣatkān
dvābhyāṃ śarābhyāṃ ca tath" âiva rājñaś
ciccheda cāpaṃ Kuru|puṅ|gavasya.

hordes of arrows, a huge noise, like the sound of great Indra's thunderbolts, reverberated from their bowstrings and the palms of their hands. They charged around like young tigers in a forest greedy for meat. Like two mighty tusked elephants, they lacerated each other, brimming with battle-pride.

Then, with an arrow that glowed like the fire of the sun, the great-spirited king of the Madras violently pierced heroic Yudhi·shthira in the heart, fierce though he was and terrifying in his power.

Although badly wounded, great-spirited Yudhi·shthira—that bull of the Kurus—struck the king of the Madras with a well-fired arrow and rejoiced, Your Majesty.

After only a moment, Shalya—that king of the earth—regained consciousness. Then, with a strength that rivaled that of thousand-eyed Indra, he swiftly hit the son of Partha with a hundred shafts, his eyes bloodshot with fury.
Enraged, the heroic son of Righteousness instantly pierced 17.20
Shalya's chest with nine arrows and struck his gold armor with six more.

The lord of the Madras then drew his excellent bow and fired his arrows. With two of them, he sliced through the bow of the royal bull of the Kurus.

navaṃ tato 'nyat samare pragṛhya
rājā dhanur ghorataraṃ mah"|ātmā
Śalyaṃ tu vivyādha śaraiḥ samantād
yathā Mah"|êndro Namuciṃ śit'|âgraiḥ.
tatas tu Śalyo navabhiḥ pṛṣatkair
Bhīmasya rājñaś ca Yudhiṣṭhirasya
nikṛtya raukme paṭu|varmaṇī tayor
vidārayām āsa bhujau mah"|ātmā.
tato 'pareṇa jvalan'|ârka|tejasā
kṣureṇa rājño dhanur unmamātha.
Kṛpaś ca tasy' âiva jaghāna sūtaṃ
ṣaḍbhiḥ śaraiḥ so 'bhimukhaḥ papāta.
17.25 Madr'|âdhipaś c' âpi Yudhiṣṭhirasya
śaraiś caturbhir nijaghāna vāhān.
vāhāṃś ca hatvā vyakaron mah"|ātmā
yodha|kṣayaṃ Dharma|sutasya rājñaḥ.
tathā kṛte rājani Bhīmaseno
Madr'|âdhipasy' āśu tato mah"|ātmā
chittvā dhanur vegavatā śareṇa
dvābhyām avidhyat su|bhṛśaṃ nar'|êndram.
tath" âpareṇ' âsya jahāra yantuḥ
kāyāc chiraḥ saṃnahanīya|madhyāt.
jaghāna c' âśvāṃś caturaḥ su|śīghraṃ
tathā bhṛśaṃ kupito Bhīmasenaḥ.
tam agra|ṇīḥ sarva|dhanur|dharāṇām
ekaṃ carantaṃ samare 'tivegam
Bhīmaḥ śatena vyakirac charāṇāṃ
Mādrī|putraḥ Sahadevas tath" âiva.

But great-spirited king Yudhi·shthira took up a new, more terrifying bow in the battle and pierced Shalya on every side with sharp-pointed arrows, just as great Indra did against Námuchi.

With nine shafts, however, heroic Shalya cut through the strong, gold armor of both Bhima and King Yudhi·shthira and then lacerated their arms. He then destroyed King Yudhi·shthira's bow with another razor-tipped arrow, which blazed like the burning sun.

Kripa then killed Yudhi·shthira's charioteer with six shafts;
the charioteer fell down face first. And the king of the Ma- 17.25
dras also slew Yudhi·shthira's horses with four arrows. After slaughtering those horses, heroic Shalya started to massacre the troops of the royal son of Righteousness.

When King Yudhi·shthira was in this peril, great-spirited Bhima·sena quickly cut through the king of the Madras' bow with a swift arrow and severely wounded that king of men with two more. With another he chopped off the head of Shalya's charioteer, whose torso was covered in armor. Filled with violent anger, Bhima·sena then swiftly killed Shalya's four horses. Together with Saha·deva, the son of Madri, Bhima—that champion of all archers—then sprayed Shalya with a hundred arrows as he fiercely rampaged on his own in battle.

taiḥ sāyakair mohitaṃ vīkṣya Śalyaṃ
Bhīmaḥ śarair asya cakarta varma.
sa Bhīmasenena nikṛtta|varmā
Madr'|âdhipaś carma sahasra|tāram
17.30 pragṛhya khaḍgaṃ ca rathān mah"|ātmā
praskandya Kuntī|sutam abhyadhāvat.
chittvā rath'|ēṣāṃ Nakulasya so 'tha
Yudhiṣṭhiraṃ bhīma|balo 'bhyadhāvat.
taṃ c' âpi rājānam ath' ôtpatantaṃ
kruddhaṃ yath" âiv' Ântakam āpatantam
Dhṛṣṭadyumno Draupadeyāḥ Śikhaṇḍī
Śineś ca naptā sahasā parīyuḥ.
ath' âsya carm' â|pratimaṃ nyakṛntad
Bhīmo mah"|ātmā navabhiḥ pṛṣatkaiḥ
khaḍgaṃ ca bhallair nicakarta muṣṭau
nadan prahṛṣṭas tava sainya|madhye.
tat karma Bhīmasya samīkṣya hṛṣṭās
te Pāṇḍavānāṃ pravarā rath'|âughāḥ.
nādaṃ ca cakrur bhṛśam utsmayantaḥ
śaṅkhāṃś ca dadhmuḥ śaśi|saṃnikāśān.
ten' âtha śabdena vibhīṣaṇena
tav' âbhitaptaṃ balam a|pradhṛṣyam
kāṃ|dig|bhūtaṃ rudhireṇ' ôkṣit'|âṅgaṃ
visaṃjña|kalpaṃ ca tathā viṣaṇṇam.
17.35 sa Madra|rājaḥ sahasā vikīrṇo
Bhīm'|âgra|gaiḥ Pāṇḍava|yodha|mukhyaiḥ
Yudhiṣṭhirasy' âbhimukhaṃ javena
siṃho yathā mṛga|hetoḥ prayātaḥ.
sa dharma|rājo nihat'|âśva|sūtaḥ
krodhena dīpto jvalana|prakāśaḥ

On seeing that Shalya was stunned by those arrows, Bhima sliced off Shalya's armor with his shafts. But although stripped of his armor, the heroic king of the Madras took up his sword and thousand-starred shield, leaped down 17.30
from his chariot, and attacked the son of Kunti. Slicing through Nákula's chariot-shaft, he charged against Yudhi·shthira with terrifying power. At this, Dhrishta·dyumna, the sons of Dráupadi, Shikhándin and the grandson of Shini suddenly surrounded the king as he furiously rose up, charging forward like Death.

With nine arrows heroic Bhima then cut through Shalya's unparalleled shield and, with his spear-headed shafts, he joyfully chopped off Shalya's sword at the hilt, roaring as he did so in the middle of your army.

Seeing Bhima's feat, hordes of excellent warriors among the Pándavas rejoiced. Laughing, they shouted loud lion-roars and blew their moon-like conches. Your invincible army became distressed at this terrible noise. Despondent and almost lifeless, they fled, their bodies soaked with blood.

17.35
But although violently besieged by these eminent Pándava warriors that were led by Bhima, the king of the Madras swiftly advanced toward Yudhi·shthira, like a lion chasing a deer.

The King of Righteousness, who had lost his horses and chariot-driver, blazed furiously like a fire. When he saw the lord of the Madras, he swiftly attacked his enemy

dṛṣṭvā ca Madr'|âdhipatiṃ sma tūrṇaṃ
samabhyadhāvat tam ariṃ balena.
Govinda|vākyaṃ tvaritaṃ vicintya
dadhre matiṃ Śalya|vināśanāya
sa dharma|rājo nihat'|âśva|sūto
rathe tiṣṭhañ śaktim ev' âbhyakāṅkṣat.
tac c' âpi Śalyasya niśamya karma
mah"|ātmano bhāgam ath' âvaśiṣṭam
kṛtvā manaḥ Śalya|vadhe mah"|ātmā
yath"|ôktam Indr'|âvara|jasya cakre.
sa dharma|rājo maṇi|hema|daṇḍāṃ
jagrāha śaktiṃ kanaka|prakāśām.
netre ca dīpte sahasā vivṛtya
Madr'|âdhipaṃ kruddhamanā niraikṣat.
17.40 nirīkṣito 'sau nara|deva rājñā
pūt'|ātmanā nirhṛta|kalmaṣeṇa
āsīn na yad bhasmasān Madra|rājas
tad adbhutaṃ me pratibhāti rājan.
tatas tu śaktiṃ rucir'|ôgra|daṇḍāṃ
maṇi|pravek'|ôjjvalitāṃ pradīptām
cikṣepa vegāt su|bhṛśaṃ mah"|ātmā
Madr'|âdhipāya pravaraḥ Kurūṇām.
dīptām ath' âināṃ prahitāṃ balena
sa|visphuliṅgāṃ sahasā patantīm
praikṣanta sarve Kuravaḥ sametā
divo yug'|ânte mahatīm iv' ôlkām.
tāṃ kāla|rātrīm iva pāśa|hastāṃ
Yamasya dhātrīm iva c' ôgra|rūpām
sa Brahma|daṇḍa|pratimām a|moghāṃ
sasarja yatto yudhi dharma|rājaḥ.

with force. After quickly pondering Go·vinda's words, the King of Righteousness—although stripped of his horses and driver—set his mind on Shalya's destruction and searched for a spear as he stood on his chariot.

Witnessing the actions of heroic Shalya and recalling that this man was his remaining share, great-spirited Yu·dhi·shthira set his heart on killing Shalya and did as Indra's brother* had advised. The King of Righteousness took up a spear which was bright as gold and which had a shaft that was covered with gold and jewels. In his rage, he fervently rolled his blazing eyes and glared at the king of the Madras.
It seemed a miracle to me, Your Majesty, that the king of 17.40
the Madras did not turn into ash when he was stared at by King Yudhi·shthira, who is pure and stainless.

With immense strength, the heroic champion of the Kurus then swiftly hurled that gleaming spear at the king of the Madras. The spear blazed with fine jewels and its shaft was radiant and fierce. All the assembled Kurus watched as that blazing spear was hurled with force and flew violently forward, letting off sparks, like a vast meteor in the sky at the end of an era.

The spear that was vigorously hurled by the King of Righteousness in that battle resembled the noose-bearing night of Time or the hideous nurse of Yama. As unerring as Brahma's staff, it was worshipped diligently by the sons of Pandu with incense, garlands, high chairs, food and water.

gandha|srag|agry'|āsana|pāna|bhojanair
abhyarcitāṃ Pāṇḍu|sutaiḥ prayatnāt
sāṃvartak'|âgni|pratimāṃ jvalantīṃ
kṛtyām atharv'|âṅgirasīm iv' ôgrām,
17.45 Īśāna|hetoḥ pratinirmitāṃ tāṃ
Tvaṣṭrā ripūṇām asu|deha|bhakṣyām
bhūmy|antar|ikṣ'|ādi|jal'|āśayāni
prasahya bhūtāni nihantum īśām,
ghaṇṭā|patākā|maṇi|vajra|nālāṃ
vaiḍūrya|citrāṃ tapanīya|daṇḍām
Tvaṣṭrā prayatnān niyamena kḷptāṃ
Brahma|dviṣām anta|karīm a|moghām,
bala|prayatnād adhirūḍha|vegāṃ
mantraiś ca ghorair abhimantrya yatnāt
sasarja mārgeṇa ca tāṃ vareṇa
vadhāya Madr'|âdhipates tadānīm.
«hato 'si pāp' êty» abhigarjamāno
Rudro 'ndhakāy' ânta|karaṃ yath" êṣum
prasārya bāhuṃ su|dṛḍhaṃ su|pāṇiṃ
krodhena nṛtyann iva dharma|rājaḥ.
tāṃ sarva|śaktyā prahitāṃ su|śaktiṃ
Yudhiṣṭhireṇ' â|prativārya|vīryām
pratigrahāy' âbhinanarda Śalyaḥ
samyagg|hutām agnir iv' ājya|dhārām.
17.50 sā tasya marmāṇi vidārya śubhram
uro viśālaṃ ca tath" âiva bhittvā
viveśa gāṃ toyam iv' â|prasaktā
yaśo viśālaṃ nṛ|pater vahantī.

It blazed like a fire at the dissolution of the cosmos and was as fierce as a rite from the Athárva Veda. Created by Tva- 17.45
shtri* for Ishána,* it consumed the lives and bodies of its enemies. Capable of completely annihilating every creature that lives in the earth, sky or water, its handle was adorned with bells, banners, jewels and diamonds. Gold-staffed, it glittered with lapis lazuli. It was forged by Tvashtri with care and skill and it destroyed Brahma's enemies unfailingly. After diligently consecrating this spear with terrifying mantras, Yudhi·shthira hurled it along the best line of flight in order to kill the king of the Madras, furnishing it with speed through a mighty effort. As he stretched out his strong, fine-handed arm, the King of Righteousness seemed to dance in his rage as he shouted: "You are dead, sinner!" He was like Rudra firing an arrow to kill Ándhaka.*

Like a fire receiving a libation of ghee that has been properly sacrificed, Shalya roared as he received the mighty spear that Yudhi·shthira hurled with all his might, unstoppable in its momentum.

The spear tore through Shalya's vital organs, ripping apart 17.50
his handsome, broad chest. Unable to be stopped, it entered the earth as if it were water, taking with it the wide fame of the king.

nās"|âkṣi|karṇ'|āsya|viniḥsṛtena
prasyandatā ca vraṇa|saṃbhavena
saṃsikta|gātro rudhireṇa so 'bhūt
Krauñco yathā Skanda|hato mah"|âdriḥ.
prasārya bāhū ca rathād gato gāṃ
saṃchinna|marmā Kuru|nandanena
mah"|êndra|vāha|pratimo mah"|ātmā
vajr'|āhataṃ śṛṅgam iv' â|calasya.
bāhū prasāry' âbhimukho dharma|rājasya Madra|rāṭ
tato nipatito bhūmāv Indra|dhvaja iv' ôcchritaḥ.
sa tathā bhinna|sarv'|âṅgo rudhireṇa samukṣitaḥ
pratyudgata iva premṇā bhūmyāṃ sa nara|puṅ|gavaḥ
priyayā kāntayā kāntaḥ patamāna iv' ôrasi.
17.55 ciraṃ bhuktvā vasumatīṃ priyāṃ kāntām iva prabhuḥ
sarvair aṅgaiḥ samāśliṣya prasupta iva so 'bhavat.
dharmye dharm'|ātmanā yuddhe nihato Dharma|sūnunā
samyagg|huta iva sv|iṣṭaḥ praśānto 'gnir iv' âdhvare.
śaktyā vibhinna|hṛdayaṃ vipraviddh'|āyudha|dhvajam
saṃśāntam api Madr'|ēśaṃ lakṣmīr n' âiva vimuñcati.

* * *

tato Yudhiṣṭhiraś cāpam ādāy' Êndra|dhanuṣ|prabham
vyadhamad dviṣataḥ saṃkhye kha|ga|rāḍ iva panna|gān.
dehāṃś su|niśitair bhallai ripūṇāṃ nāśayat kṣaṇāt.

Shalya's body became soaked with blood that flowed from his wound and that poured out of his nose, eyes, ears and mouth. He looked like the great mountain Krauncha when it was struck by Skanda.*

Pierced by the descendant of Kuru in his vital organs, that hero—who was like great Indra's elephant—stretched out his arms and fell from his chariot onto the ground, like a mountain peak hit by a thunderbolt. Stretching out his arms, the king of the Madras dropped to the earth in front of the King of Righteousness, like a lofty banner of Indra.

Drenched in blood and with every part of his body shattered, it was as if that bull among men had gone to greet the earth out of love, like a lover falling onto the breast
of his dear beloved. The king seemed asleep, as if he were 17.55
embracing the earth with all his limbs after he had enjoyed her like a dear beloved for a long period of time.

Slain in honorable battle by the virtuous son of Righteousness, Shalya resembled a sacrificial fire that is extinguished after it has received proper oblations and offerings.

Even though he was lifeless—his heart pierced by the spear and his weapons and standard scattered—the king of the Madras did not lose any of his beauty.

* * *

Taking up a bow that looked like a rainbow, Yudhi·shthira began to annihilate his enemies in battle, like the king of the birds slaughtering snakes. With his well-sharpened, spear-headed arrows, he destroyed the bodies of his enemies in an instant.

tataḥ Pārthasya bāṇ'|âughair āvṛtāḥ sainikās tava
nimīlit'|âkṣāḥ kṣiṇvanto bhṛśam anyonyam arditāḥ
kṣaranto rudhiraṃ dehair vipann'|āyudha|jīvitāḥ.

17.60 tataḥ Śalye nipatite Madra|rāj'|ânujo yuvā
bhrātus tulyo guṇaiḥ sarvai rathī Pāṇḍavam abhyayāt.
vivyādha ca nara|śreṣṭho nārācair bahubhis tvaran
hatasy' âpacitiṃ bhrātuś cikīrṣur yuddha|dur|madaḥ.

taṃ vivyādh' āśu|gaiḥ ṣaḍbhir dharma|rājas tvarann iva
kārmukaṃ c' âsya ciccheda kṣurābhyāṃ dhvajam eva ca.
tato 'sya dīpyamānena su|dṛḍhena śitena ca
pramukhe vartamānasya bhallen' âpāharac chiraḥ.
sa|kuṇḍalaṃ tad dadṛśe patamānaṃ śiro rathāt
puṇya|kṣayam anuprāpya patan svargād iva cyutaḥ.

17.65 tasy' âpakṛṣṭa|śīrṣaṃ tu śarīraṃ patitaṃ rathāt
rudhireṇ' âvasikt'|âṅgaṃ dṛṣṭvā sainyam abhajyata.
vicitra|kavace tasmin hate Madra|nṛ|p'|ânuje
hā|hā|kāraṃ prakurvāṇāḥ Kuravo 'bhipradudruvuḥ.
Śaly'|ânujaṃ hataṃ dṛṣṭvā tāvakās tyakta|jīvitāḥ
vitresuḥ Pāṇḍava|bhayād rajo|dhvastās tadā bhṛśam.

Routed by the hordes of shafts that were fired by the son of Pritha, your troops began to injure each other badly, closing their eyes in distress. Pouring blood from their bodies, they lost their weapons and their lives.

At Shalya's death, however, the youthful brother of the 17.60
king of the Madras—to whom he was equal in every virtue—charged against the Pándava on his chariot. As he sped forward, eager to honor his dead brother and difficult to defeat in battle, that best of men pierced Yudhi·shthira with several arrows.

But the King of Righteousness quickly wounded him back with six arrows and cut through his bow and banner with razor-tipped shafts. With a gleaming spear-headed arrow, which was strong and sharp, Yudhi·shthira then struck off his head as he stood before him. Just as a falling deity tumbles from heaven when it reaches the end of its merit, so his head was seen falling from the chariot, still wearing its earrings.

Your troops broke up when they saw the warrior's head- 17.65
less body falling from the chariot, his limbs spattered with blood. When the younger brother of the king of the Madras was killed in his glistening armor, the Kurus ran away, crying out in distress. Seeing the death of Shalya's younger brother, your soldiers, who were completely covered with dust, gave up their lives and became terrified in their fear of the Pándava.

tāṃs tathā bhajyamānāṃs tu Kauravān Bharata'|rṣabha
Śiner naptā kiran bāṇair abhyavartata Sātyakiḥ.
tam āyāntaṃ mah"|êṣv|āsam duṣ|prasahyaṃ dur|āsadam
Hārdikyas tvarito rājan pratyagṛhṇād a|bhītavat.
17.70 tau sametau mah"|ātmānau Vārṣṇeyau vara|vājinau
Hārdikyaḥ Sātyakiś c' âiva siṃhāv iva bal'|ôtkaṭau.
iṣubhir vimal'|ābhāsaiś chādayantau paras|param
arcirbhir iva sūryasya divā|kara|sama|prabhau.
cāpa|mārga|bal'|ôddhūtān mārgaṇān Vṛṣṇi|siṃhayoḥ
ākāśa|gān apaśyāma pataṅgān iva śīghra|gān.

Sātyakiṃ daśabhir viddhvā hayāṃś c' âsya tribhiḥ śaraiḥ
cāpam ekena ciccheda Hārdikyo nata|parvaṇā.
tan nikṛttaṃ dhanuḥ śreṣṭham apāsya Śini|puṅgavaḥ
anyad ādatta vegena vegavattaram āyudham.
17.75 tad ādāya dhanuḥ śreṣṭhaṃ variṣṭhaḥ sarva|dhanvinām
Hārdikyaṃ daśabhir bāṇaiḥ pratyavidhyat stan'|ântare.
tato rathaṃ yug'|ēṣāṃ ca cchittvā bhallaiḥ su|saṃyataiḥ
aśvāṃs tasy' âvadhīt tūrṇam ubhau ca pārṣṇi|sārathī.
tatas taṃ virathaṃ dṛṣṭvā Kṛpaḥ Śāradvataḥ prabho
apovāha tataḥ kṣipraṃ ratham āropya vīryavān.

Madra|rāje hate rājan virathe Kṛtavarmaṇi
Duryodhana|balaṃ sarvaṃ punar āsīt parāṅ|mukham.
tat pare n' ânvabudhyanta sainyena rajasā vṛte
balaṃ tu hata|bhūyiṣṭhaṃ tat tad" āsīt parāṅ|mukham
17.80 tato muhūrtāt te 'paśyan rajo bhaumaṃ samutthitam

Then, bull of the Bharatas, Sátyaki, the descendant of Shini, attacked the Káuravas as they dispersed, spraying them with his arrows. But Krita·varman, the son of Hrídika, quickly and fearlessly countered the great archer as he charged forward, irresistible and hard to confront, Your
Majesty. Sátyaki and the son of Hrídika clashed together 17.70
like lions of immense strength, both of them descendants of Vrishni and both of them heroes with excellent horses. Their splendor was like that of the sun as they covered each other with arrows that gleamed radiantly like sun rays. We watched as the Vrishni lions powerfully fired arrows from their bows, which swiftly flew through the air like bees.

The son of Hrídika wounded Sátyaki with ten arrows and his horses with three, and then cut through Sátyaki's bow with a single, straight shaft. The bull of the Shinis discarded that excellent, severed bow and quickly took up
another, swifter weapon. Taking up that fine bow, Sátyaki, 17.75
that best of archers, wounded the son of Hrídika in the middle of the chest with ten darts. With his well-directed arrows, he then cut through the son of Hrídika's yoke-shaft and swiftly killed his horses and rear-drivers. Seeing that Krita·varman had lost his chariot, lord Kripa, the mighty son of Sharádvat, took him onto his own chariot and drove him away quickly.

After the king of the Madras had been killed and Krita·varman stripped of his chariot, all of Dur·yódhana's army again took flight. The enemy was unable to be seen because of the dust that arose from the army, and most of the soldiers
were killed as they retreated. After a while, however, the 17.80

vividhaiḥ śoṇita|srāvaiḥ praśāntaṃ puruṣa'|rṣabha.

tato Duryodhano dṛṣṭvā bhagnaṃ sva|balam antikāt
javen' āpatataḥ Pārthān ekaḥ sarvān avārayat.
Pāṇḍavān sa|rathān dṛṣṭvā Dhṛṣṭadyumnaṃ ca Pārṣatam
Ānartaṃ ca dur|ādharṣaṃ śitair bāṇair avārayat.
taṃ pare n' âbhyavartanta martyā mṛtyum iv' āgatam.

ath' ânyaṃ ratham āsthāya Hārdikyo 'pi nyavartata.
tato Yudhiṣṭhiro rājā tvaramāṇo mahā|rathaḥ
caturbhir nijaghān' âśvān patribhiḥ Kṛtavarmaṇaḥ
vivyādha Gautamaṃ c' âpi ṣaḍbhir bhallaiḥ su|tejanaiḥ.
17.85 Aśvatthāmā tato rājñā hat'|âśvaṃ virathīkṛtam
tam apovāha Hārdikyaṃ sva|rathena Yudhiṣṭhirāt.
tataḥ Śāradvataḥ ṣaḍbhiḥ pratyaviddhyad Yudhiṣṭhiram
vivyādha c' âśvān niśitais tasy' âṣṭābhiḥ śilī|mukhaiḥ.

evam etan mahā|rāja yuddha|śeṣam avartata
tava dur|mantrite rājan saha putrasya Bhārata.

tasmin mah"|êṣv|āsa|vare viśaste
saṃgrāma|madhye Kuru|puṅ|gavena
pārthāḥ sametāḥ parama|prahṛṣṭāḥ
śaṅkhān pradadhmur hatam īkṣya Śalyam.
Yudhiṣṭhiraṃ ca praśaśaṃsur ājau
purā kṛte Vṛtra|vadhe yath" Êndram
cakruś ca nānā|vidha|vādya|śabdān
ninādayanto vasu|dhāṃ sametāḥ.

troops watched as the billowing dust of earth became settled by numerous spurts of blood, O bull of men.

When Dur·yódhana saw from nearby that his army was breaking up, he quickly charged against the Parthas and held all of them back on his own. Seeing the Pándavas on their chariots, as well as Dhrishta·dyumna, that grandson of Príshata, and Sátyaki, the dangerous leader of the Anártas, he restrained them with his sharp arrows. Just as mortals are unable to conquer death when it arrives, so the enemy was unable to withstand Dur·yódhana.

The son of Hrídika then climbed onto another chariot and returned to battle. But King Yudhi·shthira, that great warrior, instantly slayed Krita·varman's horses with four feathered arrows and wounded Kripa, the grandson of Gótama, with six well-sharpened, spear-headed shafts.
When the king had destroyed the son of Hrídika's horses 17.85
and chariot, Ashva·tthaman drove Krita·varman away from Yudhi·shthira in his own vehicle. Kripa, the son of Sharádvat, then shot Yudhi·shthira with six shafts and pierced his horses wih eight sharpened arrows.

Owing to the bad policy of you and your son, the rest of the battle continued in this way, O great king and descendant of Bharata.

When the bull of the Kurus slaughtered that champion of great archers in the middle of the battle, the assembled Parthas were filled with joy and blew their conches at the sight of Shalya's death. Just as Indra was praised in the past when he killed Vritra, so the assembled heroes praised Yudhi·shthira in battle and made the earth resound with the blare of various musical instruments.

18–29
THE KÁURAVAS DESTROYED

SAÑJAYA uvāca:

18.1 ŚALYE 'THA nihate rājan Madra|rāja|pad'|ânugāḥ
rathāḥ sapta|śatā vīrā niryayur mahato balāt.
Duryodhanas tu dvi|radam āruhy' âcala|sannibham
chattreṇa dhriyamāṇena vījyamānaś ca cāmaraiḥ
«na gantavyaṃ na gantavyam iti» Madrān avārayat.

Duryodhanena te vīrā vāryamāṇāḥ punaḥ punaḥ
Yudhiṣṭhiraṃ jighāṃsantaḥ Pāṇḍūnāṃ prāviśan balam.
te tu śūrā mahā|rāja kṛta|cittāś ca yodhane
dhanuḥ|śabdaṃ mahat kṛtvā sah' âyudhyanta Pāṇḍavaiḥ.
18.5 śrutvā ca nihataṃ Śalyaṃ Dharma|putraṃ ca pīḍitam
Madra|rāja|priye yuktair Madrakāṇāṃ mahā|rathaiḥ,
ājagāma tataḥ Pārtho Gāṇḍīvaṃ vikṣipan dhanuḥ
pūrayan ratha|ghoṣeṇa diśaḥ sarvā mahā|rathaḥ.

tato 'rjunaś ca Bhīmaś ca Mādrī|putrau ca Pāṇḍavau
Sātyakiś ca nara|vyāghro Draupadeyāś ca sarvaśaḥ
Dhṛṣṭadyumnaḥ Śikhaṇḍī ca Pañcālāḥ saha Somakaiḥ
Yudhiṣṭhiraṃ parīpsantaḥ samantāt paryavārayan.

te samantāt parivṛtāḥ Pāṇḍavāḥ puruṣa'|rṣabhāḥ
kṣobhayanti sma tāṃ senāṃ makarāḥ sāgaraṃ yathā
vṛkṣān iva mahā|vātāḥ kampayanti sma tāvakān.
18.10 puro|vātena Gaṅg" êva kṣobhyamānā mahā|nadī
akṣobhyata tadā rājan Pāṇḍūnāṃ dhvajinī tataḥ.

SÁNJAYA said:

AFTER SHALYA'S DEATH, Your Majesty, the heroic followers of the king of the Madras—numbering seven hundred warriors—charged forward with great force. But Dur·yódhana climbed onto a mountain-like elephant and, while he was being fanned with yak tails under a raised umbrella, he restrained the Madras, shouting, "Stop the advance! Stop the advance!" 18.1

Although Dur·yódhana repeatedly tried to restrain the heroes, they penetrated the army of the Pandus in their desire to kill Yudhi·shthira. Making a huge noise with their bows and intent on war, the heroes battled against the Pándavas, O great king.

When Árjuna, the son of Pritha, heard that Shalya was 18.5
dead and that the son of Righteousness was being besieged by the Mádraka heroes, who were devoted to the king of the Madras, that great warrior advanced forward, stretching his Gandíva bow and filling every direction with the sound of his chariot.

Árjuna, Bhima, the two Pándava sons of Madri, Sátyaki—that tiger among men—and all the sons of Dráupadi, as well as Dhrishta·dyumna, Shikhándin, the Panchálas and the Sómakas then surrounded Yudhi·shthira on every side, eager to rescue him.

Surrounding Yudhi·shthira on all sides, the Pándavas—those bulls among men—threw your army into confusion like *mákaras* churning up the ocean, and shook your troops
like great winds shaking trees. Just as the great river Ganga 18.10
is agitated by a stormy wind, so the army of Pandu's sons was stirred, Your Majesty.

praskandya senāṃ mahatīṃ mah"|ātmāno mahā|rathāḥ
bahavaś cukruśus tatra: «kva sa rājā Yudhiṣṭhiraḥ?
bhrātaro v" âsya te śūrā dṛśyante n' êha kena ca?
Dhṛṣṭadyumno 'tha Śaineyo Draupadeyāś ca sarvaśaḥ
Pañcālā vā mahā|vīryāḥ Śikhaṇḍī vā mahā|rathaḥ?»

evaṃ tān vādinaḥ śūrān Draupadeyā mahā|rathāḥ
abhyaghnan Yuyudhānaś ca Madra|rāja|pad'|ânugān.
cakrair vimathitāḥ ke cit ke cic chinnā mahā|dhvajaiḥ
te dṛśyante 'pi samare tāvakā nihatāḥ paraiḥ.
18.15 ālokya Pāṇḍavān yuddhe yodhā rājan samantataḥ
vāryamāṇā yayur vegāt putreṇa tava Bhārata.

Duryodhanaś ca tān vīrān vārayām āsa sāntvayan
na c' âsya śāsanaṃ ke cit tatra cakrur mahā|rathāḥ.
tato Gāndhāra|rājasya putraḥ Śakunir abravīt
Duryodhanaṃ mahā|rāja vacanaṃ vacana|kṣamaḥ:

ŚAKUNIR uvāca:

kiṃ naḥ saṃprekṣamāṇānāṃ
Madrāṇāṃ hanyate balam?
na yuktam etat samare
tvayi tiṣṭhati Bhārata.
sahitaiś c' âpi yoddhavyam ity eṣa samayaḥ kṛtaḥ.
atha kasmāt parān eva ghnato marṣayase nṛ|pa?

Attacking that great army, those numerous, heroic and mighty warriors of the Mádrakas shouted: "Where is king Yudhi·shthira? Why can we not see his heroic brothers here? What of Dhrishta·dyumna, the descendant of Shini, or all the sons of Dráupadi? Where are the powerful Panchálas and where is the great warrior Shikhándin?"

As they said these words, the heroic followers of the king of the Madras were killed by Yuyudhána* and those great warriors the sons of Dráupadi. Your troops were seen being slaughtered by the enemy in battle; some were crushed by
wheels, others were impaled by large banners. But when they 18.15
saw the Pándavas fighting in battle, warriors from every side of your army charged forward swiftly, even though your son tried to restrain them, descendant of Bharata.

Dur·yódhana tried to hold back the heroes with conciliatory words, but none of the great warriors obeyed him. Then Shákuni, the son of the king of Gandhára, addressed these words to Dur·yódhana, skilled as he was in speech, O great king:

SHÁKUNI said:

How can the army of the Madras be destroyed under our very eyes? It is not right for this to happen, descendant of Bharata, while you stand here in battle. We made a vow to fight together. How can you bear the enemy slaughtering your troops, Your Majesty?

DURYODHANA uvāca:

18.20 vāryamāṇā mayā pūrvaṃ n' âite cakrur vaco mama.
ete vinihatāḥ sarve praskannāḥ Pāṇḍu|vāhinīm.

ŚAKUNIR uvāca:

«na bhartuḥ śāsanaṃ vīrā raṇe kurvanty a|marṣitāḥ.
alaṃ kroddhum ath' âiteṣāṃ. n' âyaṃ kāla upekṣitum.
yāmaḥ sarve ca saṃbhūya sa|vāji|ratha|kuñjarāḥ
paritrātuṃ mah"|êṣv|āsān Madra|rāja|pad'|ânugān.
anyonyaṃ parirakṣāmo yatnena mahatā nṛ|pa!»
evaṃ sarve 'nusaṃcintya prayayur yatra sainikāḥ.

SAÑJAYA uvāca:

evam uktas tadā rājā balena mahatā vṛtaḥ
prayayau siṃha|nādena kampayann iva medinīṃ.
18.25 «hata vidhyata gṛhṇīta praharadhvaṃ nikṛntata
ity» āsīt tumulaḥ śabdas tava sainyasya Bhārata.
Pāṇḍavās tu raṇe dṛṣṭvā Madra|rāja|pad'|ânugān
sahitān abhyavartanta gulmam āsthāya madhyamam.
te muhūrtād raṇe vīrā hastā|hasti viśāṃ pate
nihatāḥ pratyadṛśyanta Madra|rāja|pad'|ânugāḥ.
tato naḥ saṃprayātānāṃ hata|Madrās tarasvinaḥ
hṛṣṭāḥ kilakilā|śabdam akurvan sahitāḥ pare.
utthitāni kabandhāni samadṛśyanta sarvaśaḥ.
papāta mahatī c' ôlkā madhyen' āditya|maṇḍalāt.
18.30 rathair bhagnair yug'|âkṣaiś ca nihataiś ca mahā|rathaiḥ
aśvair nipatitaiś c' âiva saṃchann" âbhūd vasun|dharā.

DUR·YÓDHANA replied:

I tried to restrain them beforehand, but they did not obey 18.20
me. All those who have attacked Pandu's army have died.

SHÁKUNI said:

"Heroes do not obey their commanders when they are frenzied in battle. Do not be angry with these men. This is not the time to be indifferent. Let us all unite and advance with our horses, elephants and chariots to save those great archers, the followers of the king of the Madras. Let us make a mighty effort to protect each other, Your Majesty!" In this way they all agreed and advanced toward the Madra troops.

SÁNJAYA said:

Addressed in this way, the king advanced forward, surrounded by a large force, and seemed to make the earth
quake with his lion-roar. Your troops made a cacophony of 18.25
noise, descendant of Bharata, as they shouted: "Kill! Gore! Seize! Strike! Hack!"

When the Pándavas saw the unified followers of the king of the Madras, they attacked them in battle with their central division. In an instant, lord of the people, the heroic followers of the king of the Madras were seen being killed in hand-to-hand combat. Then, as we advanced, the violent and united enemy jubilantly shouted cheers of joy at killing the Madras.

Headless bodies were seen rising on every side. A great
comet fell from the center of the sun's disk. The earth be- 18.30
came strewn with slaughtered warriors, fallen horses, and broken chariots, yokes and axles. Horses that were swift as the wind and still attached to their yokes could be seen

vātāyamānais tura|gair yug'|āsaktais tatas tataḥ
adṛśyanta mahā|rāja yodhās tatra raṇ'|âjire.
bhagna|cakrān rathān ke cid aharaṃs tura|gā raṇe
rath'|ârdhaṃ ke cid ādāya diśo daśa vibabhramuḥ;
tatra tatra vyadṛśyanta yoktraiḥ śliṣṭāḥ sma vājinaḥ.
rathinaḥ patamānāś ca dṛśyante sma nar'|ôttamāḥ
gaganāt pracyutāḥ siddhāḥ puṇyānām iva saṃkṣaye.
nihateṣu ca śūreṣu Madra|rāj'|ânugeṣu vai
asmān āpatataś c' âpi dṛṣṭvā Pārthā mahā|rathāḥ
abhyavartanta vegena jaya|gṛddhāḥ prahāriṇaḥ.
18.35 bāṇa|śabda|ravān kṛtvā vimiśrāñ śaṅkha|niḥsvanaiḥ
asmāṃs tu punar āsādya labdha|lakṣāḥ prahāriṇaḥ
śar'|âsanāni dhunvānāḥ siṃha|nādān pracukruśuḥ.
tato hatam abhiprekṣya Madra|rāja|balaṃ mahat
Madra|rājaṃ ca samare dṛṣṭvā śūraṃ nipātitam
Duryodhana|balaṃ sarvaṃ punar āsīt parāṅ|mukham.
vadhyamānaṃ mahā|rāja Pāṇḍavair jita|kāśibhiḥ
diśo bheje 'tha saṃbhrāntaṃ bhrāmitaṃ dṛḍha|dhanvibhiḥ.

SAÑJAYA UVĀCA:

19.1 PĀTITE YUDHI dur|dharṣe Madra|rāje mahā|rathe
tāvakās tava putrāś ca prāyaśo vimukh" âbhavan.*
vaṇijo nāvi bhinnāyāṃ yath" âgādhe 'plave 'rṇave
apāre pāram icchanto hate śūre mah"|ātmanā
Madra|rāje mahā|rāja vitrastāḥ śara|vikṣatāḥ
a|nāthā nātham icchanto mṛgāḥ siṃh'|ârditā iva.
vṛṣā yathā bhagna|śṛṅgāḥ śīrṇa|dantā yathā gajāḥ

hauling warriors here and there on the battlefield, mighty king. Some horses on the battlefield pulled chariots with broken wheels, others dragged half-chariots and wandered around in ten different directions; here and there horses were seen caught up in their reins. We saw charioteers—excellent men, Your Majesty—falling down like *siddhas* that tumble from the sky when their merit is used up.

After the slaughter of the king of the Madras' heroic followers, the attacking Parthas—those great warriors—charged against us with force when they saw us assailing
them, greedy as they were for victory. The sound of their 18.35
arrows mingled with the blare of their conches. Attacking us once more, those warriors, who always hit their marks, shook their bows and shouted out lion-roars.

When Dur·yódhana's troops saw that the mighty army of the king of the Madras had been destroyed and that the heroic king of the Madras had been slain in battle, they all once again turned their backs. Slaughtered by those mighty archers, the conquering Pándavas, they split off into various directions, Your Majesty, bewildered and confused.

SÁNJAYA said:

WHEN THAT GREAT warrior, the invincible king of the 19.1
Madras, was slain in battle, the majority of your troops and sons fled. When the heroic king of the Madras was slaughtered by great-spirited Yudhi·shthira, your soldiers were like traders who yearn for the further shore after they have been shipwrecked on the deep, raftless sea. Terrified and mangled by arrows, they yearned for a leader, leaderless as they were, and were like deer tormented by a lion, O

madhy'|âhne pratyapāyāma nirjit" â|jāta|śatrunā.

19.5 na sandhātum anīkāni na ca rājan parākrame
āsīd buddhir hate Śalye bhūyo yodhasya kasya cit.
Bhīṣme Droṇe ca nihate sūta|putre ca Bhārata
yad duḥkhaṃ tava yodhānāṃ bhayaṃ c' āsīd viśāṃ pate
tad bhayaṃ sa ca naḥ śoko bhūya ev' âbhyavartata.
nirāśāś ca jaye tasmin hate Śalye mahā|rathe
hata|pravīrā vidhvastā nikṛttāś ca śitaiḥ śaraiḥ
Madra|rāje hate rājan yodhās te prādravan bhayāt.
aśvān anye gajān anye rathān anye mahā|rathāḥ
āruhya java|saṃpannāḥ pādātāḥ prādravaṃs tathā.
dvi|sāhasrāś ca mātaṅgā giri|rūpāḥ prahāriṇaḥ
saṃprādravan hate Śalye aṅkuś'|âṅguṣṭha|noditāḥ.

19.10 te raṇād Bharata|śreṣṭha tāvakāḥ prādravan diśaḥ.
dhāvataś c' âpy apaśyāma śvasamānān śar'|āhatān
tān prabhagnān drutān dṛṣṭvā hat'|ôtsāhān parājitān
abhyavartanta Pañcālāḥ Pāṇḍavāś ca jay'|âiṣiṇaḥ.
bāṇa|śabda|ravāś c' âpi siṃha|nādāś ca puṣkalāḥ
śaṅkha|śabdaś ca śūrāṇāṃ dāruṇaḥ samapadyata.

dṛṣṭvā tu Kauravaṃ sainyaṃ bhaya|trastaṃ pravidrutam
anyonyaṃ samabhāṣanta Pañcālāḥ Pāṇḍavaiḥ saha:

great king. Like bulls with broken horns or elephants with shattered tusks, we fled at midday, defeated by Yudhi·shthira, who has no rival.

After Shalya's death, Your Majesty, it was once more the 19.5
case that none of your warriors had the resolve to rally the troops nor show prowess in battle. Once again, descendant of Bharata and lord of the people, we felt the same pain and fear that overtook your troops when Bhishma, Drona and the charioteer's son died. At the death of the great warrior Shalya, your soldiers lost all hope of victory and were ruined. With their heroes slaughtered and the king of the Madras dead, they fled in fear and were cut down by sharp arrows, O king. Great warriors and foot soldiers fled with speed—some climbed onto horses, others onto elephants and others onto chariots. After Shalya's death, two thousand violent elephants, the size of mountains, ran away, goaded by hooks and toes.

Your troops fled the battlefield in every direction, best of 19.10
Bharatas. We watched them as they ran away, panting and struck by arrows. Eager for victory, the Panchálas and Pándavas charged forward when they saw their enemy breaking up and fleeing, dejected in their defeat. Those heroes made a hideous noise of whizzing arrows, loud lion-roars and blaring conches.

When they saw the Káurava army fleeing and terrified with fear, the Panchálas and Pándavas said to each other:

«adya rājā satya|dhṛtir hat'|â|mitro Yudhiṣṭhiraḥ!
adya Duryodhano hīno dīptāyā nṛ|pati|śriyaḥ!
19.15 adya śrutvā hataṃ putraṃ Dhṛtarāṣṭro jan'|ēśvaraḥ
vihvalaḥ patito bhūmau kilbiṣaṃ pratipadyatām.
adya jānātu Kaunteyaṃ samarthaṃ sarva|dhanvinām.
ady' ātmānaṃ ca dur|medhā garhayiṣyati pāpa|kṛt.

adya Kṣattur vacaḥ satyaṃ smaratāṃ bruvato hitam.
adya|prabhṛti Pārthaṃ ca preṣya|bhūta iv' ācaran
vijānātu nṛ|po duḥkhaṃ yat prāptaṃ Pāṇḍu|nandanaiḥ.
adya Kṛṣṇasya māh"|ātmyaṃ vijānātu mahī|patiḥ!
ady' Ârjuna|dhanur|ghoṣaṃ ghoraṃ jānātu saṃyuge
astrāṇāṃ ca balaṃ sarvaṃ bāhvoś ca balam āhave!
adya jñāsyati Bhīmasya balaṃ ghoraṃ mah"|ātmanaḥ
hate Duryodhane yuddhe Śakreṇ' êv' âsure Bale.
19.20 yat kṛtaṃ Bhīmasenena Duḥśāsana|vadhe tadā
n' ânyaḥ kart" âsti loke 'smin ṛte Bhīmān mahā|balāt.

adya jyeṣṭhasya jānītāṃ Pāṇḍavasya parākramam
Madra|rājaṃ hataṃ śrutvā devair api su|duḥ|saham.
adya jñāsyati saṃgrāme Mādrī|putrau su|duḥ|sahau
nihate Saubale vīre Gāndhāreṣu ca sarvaśaḥ.

"On this day, King Yudhi·shthira, who holds fast to the truth, has conquered his enemies! On this day, Dur·yódhana has lost his glorious royal splendor! On this day let Dhri- 19.15
ta·rashtra feel anguish when he hears of his son's death and falls to the ground bewildered! On this day, let him learn that the son of Kunti is a match for every archer. On this day, that foolish sinner will reproach himself.

On this day, let him remember the true and beneficial words that were spoken by the Kshattri. From this day forward, by serving the son of Pritha like a slave, let King Dhrita·rashtra realize the suffering experienced by the sons of Pandu. On this day let that lord of the earth learn of the magnificence of Krishna! On this day let him understand the terrible sound of Árjuna's bow in battle, the full force of Árjuna's weapons, and the power of his arms in war! On this day, when Dur·yódhana dies in battle just as the demon Bali was slain by Shakra, Dhrita·rashtra will learn of
the terrible might of heroic Bhima! No one in the world 19.20
apart from mighty Bhima could do what Bhima·sena did when he killed Duhshásana.

On this day, let Dhrita·rashtra realize the bravery of the eldest Pándava when he hears that the king of the Madras is dead—difficult even for the gods to conquer. On this day, when the heroic son of Súbala and all the Gandháras are slaughtered, he will learn of the invincible sons of Madri in battle.

katham̩ jayo na teṣām̩ syād yeṣām̩ yoddhā Dhanañjayaḥ
Sātyakir Bhīmasenaś ca Dhṛṣṭadyumnaś ca Pārṣataḥ,
Draupadyās tanayāḥ pañca Mādrī|putrau ca Pāṇḍavau
Śikhaṇḍī ca mah"|êṣv|āso rājā c' âiva Yudhiṣṭhiraḥ?
19.25 yeṣām̩ ca jagatī|nātho nāthaḥ Kṛṣṇo Janārdanaḥ
katham̩ teṣām̩ jayo na syād yeṣām̩ dharmo vyapāśrayaḥ?
Bhīṣmam̩ Droṇam̩ ca Karṇam̩ ca Madra|rājānam eva ca
tath" ânyān nṛ|patīn vīrāñ śataśo 'tha sahasraśaḥ
ko 'nyaḥ śakto raṇe jetum ṛte Pārthād Yudhiṣṭhirāt
yasya nātho Hṛṣīkeśaḥ sadā satya|yaśo|nidhiḥ?»
ity evam̩ vadamānās te harṣeṇa mahatā yutāḥ
prabhagnām̩s tāvakān yodhān sam̩hṛṣṭāḥ pṛṣṭhato 'nvayuḥ.
Dhanañjayo rath'|ânīkam abhyavartata vīryavān
Mādrī|putrau ca Śakunim̩ Sātyakiś ca mahā|rathaḥ.
19.30 tān prekṣya dravataḥ sarvān Bhīmasena|bhay'|ârditān
Duryodhanas tadā sūtam abravīd vismayann iva:
«mām atikramate Pārtho dhanuṣ|pāṇim avasthitam.
jaghane sarva|sainyānām̩ mam' âśvān pratipādaya.
jaghane yudhyamānam̩ hi Kaunteyo mām̩ Dhanañjayaḥ
n' ôtsahed abhyatikrāntum̩ velām iva mah"|ôda|dhiḥ.
paśya sainyam̩ mahat sūta Pāṇḍavair samabhidrutam.
sainya|reṇum̩ samudbhūtam̩ paśyasv' âinam̩ samantataḥ.
sim̩ha|nādām̩ś ca bahuśaḥ śṛṇu ghorān bhay'|āvahān.
tasmād yāhi śanaiḥ sūta jaghanam̩ paripālaya.
19.35 mayi sthite ca samare niruddheṣu ca Pāṇḍuṣu
punar āvartate tūrṇam̩ māmakam̩ balam ojasā.»

How could the Pándavas not win when their warriors are Dhanan·jaya, Sátyaki, Bhima·sena, Dhrishta·dyumna the grandson of Príshata, the five sons of Dráupadi, the two Pándava sons of Madri, the archer Shikhándin and King Yu-
dhi·shthira? How could they not win when their refuge is 19.25
righteousness and when their leader is Krishna, Janárdana, the lord of the world? Who else but Yudhi·shthira, the son of Pritha, could defeat Bhishma, Drona, Karna, the king of the Madras, and the other hundreds and thousands of heroic kings in battle? Who else could do this when his lord is Hrishi·kesha, that perpetual resource of truth and glory?"

Saying these words with immense elation, they joyfully pursued your broken troops. Powerful Dhanan·jaya attacked their chariot division, while the sons of Madri and the great warrior Sátyaki attacked Shákuni.

When Dur·yódhana saw that his troops were fleeing and 19.30
distraught with fear of Bhima·sena, he said this to his charioteer, as if with a smile:

"The son of Pritha is overcoming me as I stand here with my bow. Drive my horses to the rear of all the troops. Dhanan·jaya, the son of Kunti, cannot overcome me if I fight in the rear, just as the ocean cannot pass the shore. Look, charioteer, at how my great army has been routed by the Pándavas. Look at the dust cloud that swirls everywhere because of my troops. Listen to the many lion-roars, terrible and fearful. Advance carefully, then, charioteer, and beware
of our rear. If I stand firm in battle and the sons of Pandu 19.35
are repelled, my army will soon return again with force."

tac chrutvā tava putrasya śūr'|ārya|sadṛśaṃ vacaḥ
sārathir hema|saṃchannāñ śanair aśvān acodayat.

gaj'|âśva|rathibhir hīnās tyakt'|ātmānaḥ padātayaḥ
eka|viṃśati|sāhasrāḥ saṃyugāy' âvatasthire.
nānā|deśa|samudbhūtā nānā|nagara|vāsinaḥ
avasthitās tadā yodhāḥ prārthayanto mahad yaśaḥ.

teṣām āpatatāṃ tatra saṃhṛṣṭānāṃ paras|param
saṃmardaḥ su|mahāñ jajñe ghora|rūpo bhayānakaḥ.
19.40 Bhīmasenas tadā rājan Dhṛṣṭadyumnaś ca Pārṣataḥ
balena catur|aṅgeṇa nānā|deśyān avārayat.
Bhīmam ev' âbhyavartanta raṇe 'nye tu padātayaḥ
prakṣveḍy' āsphoṭya saṃhṛṣṭā vīra|lokaṃ yiyāsavaḥ.
āsādya Bhīmasenaṃ tu saṃrabdhā yuddha|dur|madāḥ
Dhārtarāṣṭrā vinedur hi n' ânyāṃ c' âkathayan kathām.
parivārya raṇe Bhīmaṃ nijaghnus te samantataḥ.
sa vadhyamānaḥ samare padāti|gaṇa|saṃvṛtaḥ
na cacāla tataḥ sthānān Maināka iva parvataḥ.
te tu kruddhā mahā|rāja Pāṇḍavānāṃ mahā|ratham
nigrahītuṃ pravṛttā hi yodhāṃś c' ânyān avārayan.

19.45 akrudhyata raṇe Bhīmas tais tadā paryavasthitaiḥ.
so 'vatīrya rathāt tūrṇaṃ padātiḥ samavasthitaḥ.
jātarūpa|praticchannāṃ pragṛhya mahatīṃ gadām
avadhīt tāvakān yodhān daṇḍa|pāṇir iv' Ântakaḥ.
viprahīna|rath'|âśvāṃs tān avadhīt puruṣa'|rṣabhaḥ

When he heard your son's words—so appropriate for a heroic noble—the chariot-driver gently urged on his gold-decked horses.

Although they had lost their elephants, horses and charioteers, twenty-one thousand foot soldiers stood ready for war, willing to sacrifice their lives. Originating from different countries and stemming from different cities, the warriors stood there, eager for great glory.

As those troops rushed forward with joy, they collided against one another violently on the battlefield; it was frightening and terrible to see. Bhima·sena and Dhrishta·dyum- 19.40
na, the grandson of Príshata, repelled those men of diverse backgrounds with their fourfold army, Your Majesty. But other foot soldiers attacked Bhima in battle, shouting with joy and slapping their arms in their desire to reach the realm of the heroes. Dhrita·rashtra's troops—so difficult to defeat in battle—roared as they assailed Bhima in their rage. After that, they did not utter another sound. Surrounding Bhima in battle, they besieged him on all sides. But although under attack and surrounded by this contingent of foot soldiers in battle, Bhima did not move from his position; it was as if he were Mount Mainága. Enraged, the troops strove to subdue that mighty warrior of the Pándavas and repelled other fighters too, great king.

Bhima became filled with battle-fury when he was sur- 19.45
rounded by those men. Descending from his chariot, he took up position on foot. Seizing his immense, gold-covered mace, he began to annihilate your warriors, as if he were Death wielding his staff. That bull among men pounded and destroyed those twenty-one thousand foot soldiers, who

eka|viṃśati|sāhasrān padātīn samapothayat.
hatvā tat puruṣ'|ânīkaṃ Bhīmaḥ satya|parākramaḥ
Dhṛṣṭadyumnaṃ puraskṛtya na cirāt pratyadṛśyata.

pādātā nihatā bhūmau śiśyire rudhir'|ôkṣitāḥ
saṃbhagnā iva vātena karṇikārāḥ su|puṣpitāḥ.
19.50 nānā|śastra|samāyuktā nānā|kuṇḍala|dhāriṇaḥ
nānā|jātyā hatās tatra nānā|deśa|samāgatāḥ.
patākā|dhvaja|saṃchannaṃ padātīnāṃ mahad balam
nikṛttaṃ vibabhau raudraṃ ghora|rūpaṃ bhay'|āvaham.

Yudhiṣṭhira|puro|gāś ca saha|sainyā mahā|rathāḥ
abhyadhāvan mah"|ātmānaṃ putraṃ Duryodhanaṃ tava.
te sarve tāvakān dṛṣṭvā mah"|êṣv|āsān parāṅ|mukhān
n' âtyavartanta te putraṃ vel" êva makar'|ālayam.
tad adbhutam apaśyāma tava putrasya pauruṣam
yad ekaṃ sahitāḥ Pārthā na śekur ativartitum.
19.55 n' âtidūr'|âpayātaṃ tu kṛta|buddhiṃ palāyane
Duryodhanaḥ svakaṃ sainyam abravīd bhṛśa|vikṣatam:

«na taṃ deśaṃ prapaśyāmi pṛthivyāṃ parvateṣu vā
yatra yātān na vo hanyuḥ Pāṇḍavāḥ. kiṃ sṛtena vaḥ?
alpaṃ ca balam eteṣāṃ Kṛṣṇau ca bhṛśa|vikṣatau.
yadi sarve 'tra tiṣṭhāmo dhruvaṃ no vijayo bhavet.
viprayātāṃs tu vo bhinnān Pāṇḍavāḥ kṛta|vipriyāḥ
anusṛtya haniṣyanti. śreyān naḥ samare vadhaḥ.

had neither chariots nor horses. After massacring that contingent of men, Bhima—whose strength lies in truth—was soon seen standing behind Dhrishta·dyumna.

The foot soldiers lay dead on the ground, drenched in blood. They were like blossoming *karnikára* trees that had been toppled by the wind. Corpses now, the men were 19.50
armed with diverse weapons and wore various earrings; born into different castes, they had gathered together from different countries. Covered with flags and banners, that great massacred force of foot soldiers looked awful, hideous and terrifying.

Led by Yudhi·shthira, the great warriors and their troops then charged against your heroic son Dur·yódhana. But although they could all see your mighty archers fleeing, they could not get past your son, who was like a shore containing the ocean. We witnessed your son's incredible courage as the Parthas could not overcome him in battle, even though he was alone and they were united.

Dur·yódhana then addressed his army, which was heavily 19.55
wounded and intent on flight but not too far away:

"I can see no place on the earth or in the mountains where the Pándavas have not killed you when you have fled. What, then, is the point of fleeing? Their army is small and the two Krishnas are heavily wounded. If we all keep our position here, victory would certainly be ours. The sinful Pándavas will pursue you and kill you if you break up and flee. It is better for us to die in battle.

śṛṇvantu kṣatriyāḥ sarve yāvanto 'tra samāgatāḥ.
yadā śūraṃ ca bhīruṃ ca mārayaty antakaḥ sadā
ko nu mūḍho na yudhyeta puruṣaḥ kṣatriyo dhruvam?
19.60 śreyo no Bhīmasenasya kruddhasy' âbhimukhe sthitam.
sukhaḥ sāṃgrāmiko mṛtyuḥ kṣatra|dharmeṇa yudhyatām.
martyen' âvaśya|martavyaṃ gṛheṣv api kadā cana;
yudhyataḥ kṣatra|dharmeṇa mṛtyur eṣa sanātanaḥ.
hatv" êha sukham āpnoti, hataḥ pretya mahat phalam.
na yuddha|dharmāc chreyān vai
panthāḥ svargasya Kauravāḥ.
aciren' âiva tāl̃ lokān
hato yuddhe samaśnute.»

śrutvā tad vacanaṃ tasya pūjayitvā ca pārthivāḥ
punar ev' âbhyavartanta Pāṇḍavān ātatāyinaḥ.
tān āpatata ev' āśu vyūḍh'|ânīkāḥ prahāriṇaḥ
pratyudyayus tadā Pārthā jaya|gṛddhāḥ pramanyavaḥ.
19.65 Dhanañjayo rathen' ājāv abhyavartata vīryavān
viśrutaṃ triṣu lokeṣu vyākṣipan Gāṇḍīvaṃ dhanuḥ.
Mādrī|putrau ca Śakuniṃ Sātyakiś ca mahā|balaḥ
javen' âbhyapatan hṛṣṭā yattā vai tāvakaṃ balam.

SAÑJAYA uvāca:

20.1 SAṂNIVṚTTE jan'|âughe tu Śālvo mleccha|gaṇ'|âdhipaḥ
abhyavartata saṃkruddhaḥ Pāṇḍavānāṃ mahad balam.
āsthāya su|mahā|nāgaṃ prabhinnaṃ parvat'|ôpamam
dṛptam Airāvata|prakhyam a|mitra|gaṇa|mardanam,
yo 'sau mahān bhadra|kula|prasūtaḥ

Let every warrior assembled here listen. Since death always kills both heroes and cowards, what man would be so
stupid as not to fight if he is a committed warrior? It is better 19.60
for us to take a stand in front of furious Bhima·sena. Death in battle brings happiness to those who fight according to the warrior code.

Through force of necessity, mortals sometimes have to die in their houses; but death is perpetual for the man who fights according to the warrior code. If one kills, one attains happiness in this world, and if one dies, one attains great fruit in the next world. There is no better path to heaven, Káuravas, than the code of war. By dying in battle, a man very quickly obtains those realms."

Hearing Dur·yódhana's speech, the kings praised him and once again confronted the bow-drawing Pándavas. But the violent sons of Pritha—incensed and greedy for victory—drew up their divisions and rose against the Káuravas as they charged forward. Mighty Dhanan·jaya advanced 19.65
with his chariot in battle, stretching his Gandíva bow, which is famous throughout the three worlds. At the same time, the two sons of Madri and mighty Sátyaki zealously and swiftly rushed forward with joy against Shákuni and your army.

SÁNJAYA said:

WHEN THE MASS of the Káurava troops withdrew, Sha- 20.1
lva, the leader of the *mleccha* army, became enraged and attacked the mighty force of the Pándavas. He stood on top of a frenzied, rutting elephant, which resembled Airávata* itself. Enormous and looking like a mountain, it crushed

su|pūjito Dhārtarāṣṭreṇa nityam
su|kalpitaḥ śāstra|viniścaya|jñaiḥ
sad" ôpavāhyaḥ samareṣu rājan
tam āsthito rāja|varo babhūva
yath" ôdaya|sthaḥ savitā kṣap"|ânte.
sa tena nāga|pravareṇa rājann
abhyudyayau Pāṇḍu|sutān sametān
śitaiḥ pṛṣatkair vidadāra vegair
Mah"|êndra|vajra|pratimaiḥ su|ghoraiḥ.
20.5 tataḥ śarān vai sṛjato mahā|raṇe
yodhāṃś ca rājan nayato Yam'|ālayam
n' âsy' ântaraṃ dadṛśuḥ sve pare vā,
yathā purā vajra|dharasya daityāḥ
Airāvaṇa|sthasya camū|vimarde
daityāḥ purā Vāsavasy' êva rājan.
te Pāṇḍavāḥ Somakāḥ Sṛñjayāś ca
tam eka|nāgaṃ dadṛśuḥ samantāt
sahasraśo vai vicarantam ekaṃ
yathā Mah"|êndrasya gajaṃ samīpe.
saṃdrāvyamāṇaṃ tu balaṃ pareṣāṃ
parīta|kalpaṃ vibabhau samantataḥ.
n' âiv' âvatasthe samare bhṛśaṃ bhayād
vimṛdyamānaṃ tu paras|paraṃ tadā.
tataḥ prabhagnā sahasā mahā|camūḥ
sā Pāṇḍavī tena nar'|âdhipena
diśaś catasraḥ sahasā vidhāvitā
gaj'|êndra|vegaṃ tam a|pārayantī.

its enemy forces. A pedigree, the huge animal was continuously worshipped by the son of Dhrita·rashtra. It was well equipped by men who were experts in elephant-science and was always ridden into battle, Your Majesty. Standing on this elephant, that best of kings looked like the sun as it rises at dawn.

Shalva charged forward on this excellent elephant, O king, and pierced the assembled sons of Pandu with his swift, sharp arrows, which were as terrible as great Indra's thunderbolts. None of your troops or the enemy could see 20.5
a weakness in him as he fired his arrows in that great battle, sending warriors to Yama's realm. It was just as in the past, Your Majesty, when the *daityas* were unable to find any weakness in thunderbolt-wielding Vásava as he stood on his elephant Airávana and crushed the demons' army.

The Pándavas, Sómakas and Srínjayas watched that one, single elephant career everywhere before them as if it were a thousand animals, just as great Indra's elephant once did. The enemy troops looked almost possessed as they were put to flight in every direction. Brutally crushing each other in their fear, they were unable to stand their ground in battle. The great Pándava army then suddenly broke up, violently routed in all four directions by that king of men and impotent against the mighty elephant's force.

dṛṣṭvā ca tāṃ vegavatīṃ prabhagnāṃ
sarve tvadīyā yudhi yodha|mukhyāḥ
apūjayaṃs te tu nar'|âdhipaṃ taṃ
dadhmuś ca śaṅkhān śaśi|saṃnikāśān
20.10 śrutvā ninādaṃ tv atha Kauravāṇāṃ
harṣād vimuktaṃ saha śaṅkha|śabdaiḥ
senā|patiḥ Pāṇḍava|Sṛñjayānāṃ
Pāñcāla|putro mamṛṣe na kopāt.
tatas tu taṃ vai dvi|radaṃ mah"|ātmā
pratyudyayau tvaramāṇo jayāya
Jambho yathā Śakra|samāgame vai
nāg'|êndram Airāvaṇam Indra|vāhyam.
tam āpatantaṃ sahasā tu dṛṣṭvā
Pāñcāla|putraṃ yudhi rāja|siṃhaḥ
taṃ vai dvi|paṃ preṣayām āsa tūrṇaṃ
vadhāya rājan Drupad'|ātma|jasya.
sa taṃ dvi|p'|êndraṃ sahas" āpatantaṃ
avidhyad agni|pratimaiḥ pṛṣatkaiḥ
karmāra|dhautair niśitair jvaladbhir
nārāca|mukhyais tribhir ugra|vegaiḥ.
tato 'parān pañca|śatān mah"|ātmā
nārāca|mukhyān visasarja kumbhe.
sa tais tu viddhaḥ parama|dvi|po raṇe
tadā parāvṛtya bhṛśaṃ pradudruve.
20.15 taṃ nāga|rājaṃ sahasā praṇunnaṃ
vidrāvyamāṇaṃ vinivartya Śālvaḥ
tottr'|âṅkuśaiḥ preṣayām āsa tūrṇam
Pañcāla|rājasya rathaṃ pradiśya.
dṛṣṭv" āpatantaṃ sahasā tu nāgaṃ
Dhṛṣṭadyumnaḥ sva|rathāc chīghram eva

When they saw the enemy rapidly breaking up, all the eminent warriors in your army cheered King Shalva and
blew their moon-like conches. But, in his anger, the general 20.10
of the Pándavas and Srínjayas—the Panchála prince Dhrishta·dyumna—could not bear to hear the joyful cheers of the Káuravas and the blare of their conches. That hero then swiftly rose up against the elephant in order to defeat it, just as Jambha once attacked Airávana—that king of elephants ridden by Indra—in his battle against Shakra.

When Shalva saw the Panchála prince suddenly attacking him in battle, Your Majesty, that lion among kings quickly drove his elephant forward to kill the son of Drupada. But Dhrishta·dyumna pierced that king of elephants with three fine shafts as it violently charged toward him. Polished by a blacksmith, the sharp arrows flew with fierce velocity and blazed like flames. Great-spirited Dhrishta·dyumna then fired another five hundred excellent shafts into the elephant's forehead. Wounded, the mighty elephant turned around and swiftly fled.

Shalva, however, stopped the king of elephants as it fled 20.15
after being so violently repelled. Using goads and hooks, he drove it swiftly toward the chariot of the Panchála prince. Seeing the elephant attacking him with force, heroic Dhrishta·dyumna took his mace and, with great speed, quickly leaped from his chariot onto the ground, his limbs quivering with fear. With a roar, the mighty elephant fiercely grabbed hold of Dhrishta·dyumna's gold-adorned chariot—as well

gadāṃ pragṛhy' ôgra|javena vīro
bhūmiṃ prapanno bhaya|vihval'|âṅgaḥ.
sa taṃ rathaṃ hema|vibhūṣit'|âṅgaṃ
s'|âśvaṃ sa|sūtaṃ sahasā pragṛhya
utkṣipya hastena nadan mahā|dvi|po
vipothayām āsa vasun|dharā|tale.
Pañcāla|rājasya sutaṃ ca dṛṣṭvā
tad" ârditaṃ nāga|vareṇa tena
tam abhyadhāvat sahasā javena
Bhīmaḥ Śikhaṇḍī ca Śineś ca naptā.
śaraiś ca vegaṃ sahasā nigṛhya*
tasy' âbhito vyāpatato gajasya.
sa saṃgṛhīto rathibhir gajo vai
cacāla tair vāryamāṇaś ca saṃkhye.
20.20 tataḥ pṛṣatkān pravavarṣa rājā
sūryo yathā raśmi|jālaṃ samantāt.
tair āśu|gair vadhyamānā rath'|âughāḥ
pradudruvuḥ sahitās tatra tatra.
tat karma Śālvasya samīkṣya sarve
Pañcāla|putrā nṛ|pa Sṛñjayāś ca
hā|hā|kārair nādayanti* sma yuddhe
dvi|paṃ samantād rurudhur nar'|âgryāḥ.
Pañcāla|putras tvaritas tu śūro
gadāṃ pragṛhy' â|cala|śṛṅga|kalpām
sa|saṃbhramaṃ Bhārata śatru|ghātī
javena vīro 'nusasāra nāgam.
tatas tu nāgaṃ dharaṇī|dhar'|ābhaṃ
madaṃ sravantaṃ jala|da|prakāśam
gadāṃ samāviddhya bhṛśaṃ jaghāna
Pañcāla|rājasya sutas tarasvī.

as its driver and horses—and smashed it onto the ground, hurling it with its trunk.

When they saw that best of elephants tormenting the Panchála prince, Bhima, Shikhándin and the descendant of Shini immediately attacked it with speed.

With their arrows, they fiercely curbed the momentum of the elephant as it charged toward them. Restrained by the charioteers, the elephant staggered as it was held back in battle. King Shalva, however, showered arrows on all sides, 20.20
like the sun emitting a web of rays. Struck by those shafts, the hordes of heroes all fled in every direction.

Seeing Shalva's feat, the Srínjayas and sons of Panchála—fine men that they were—all cried out loud shouts in the battle and blocked off the elephant on every side. The heroic prince of Panchála then quickly seized his mace, which was like a mountain peak. And, with haste, the enemy-slaying hero swiftly pursued the elephant, descendant of Bharata. Brandishing his mace, the fierce Panchála prince then violently struck the frenzied, mountain-like elephant as it secreted juices like a cloud.

sa bhinna|kumbhaḥ sahasā vinadya
mukhāt prabhūtaṃ kṣata|jaṃ vimuñcan
papāta nāgo dharaṇī|dhar'|ābhaḥ
kṣiti|prakampāc calito yath" âdriḥ.

20.25 nipātyamāne tu tadā gaj'|êndre
hā|hā|kṛte tava putrasya sainye
sa Śālva|rājasya Śini|pravīro
jahāra bhallena śiraḥ śitena.
hṛt'|ôttam'|âṅgo yudhi Sātvatena
papāta bhūmau saha nāga|rājñā
yath" âdri|śṛṅgaṃ su|mahat praṇunnaṃ
vajreṇa dev'|âdhipa|coditena.

SAÑJAYA uvāca:

21.1 TASMIṂS TU nihate śūre Śālve samiti|śobhane
tav' âbhajyad balaṃ vegād vāten' êva mahā|drumaḥ.
tat prabhagnaṃ balaṃ dṛṣṭvā Kṛtavarmā mahā|rathaḥ
dadhāra samare śūraḥ śatru|sainyaṃ mahā|balaḥ.
saṃnivṛttās tu te śūrā dṛṣṭvā Sātvatam āhave
śail'|ôpamaṃ sthiraṃ rājan kīryamāṇaṃ śarair yudhi.
tataḥ pravavṛte yuddhaṃ Kurūṇāṃ Pāṇḍavaiḥ saha
nivṛttānāṃ mahā|rāja mṛtyuṃ kṛtvā nivartanam.
21.5 tatr' āścaryam abhūd yuddhaṃ Sātvatasya paraiḥ saha
yad eko vārayām āsa Pāṇḍu|senāṃ dur|āsadām.
teṣām anyonya|su|hṛdāṃ kṛte karmaṇi duṣ|kare
siṃha|nādaḥ prahṛṣṭānāṃ diva|spṛk su|mahān abhūt.
tena śabdena vitrastāḥ Pañcālā Bharata'|rṣabha.
Śiner naptā mahā|bāhur anvapadyata Sātyakiḥ.
sa samāsādya rājānaṃ Kṣemadhūrtiṃ mahā|balam
saptabhir niśitair bāṇair anayad Yama|sādanam.

Its forehead split open, the elephant trumpeted loudly as it poured blood from its face. It then fell to the ground like an earth-bearing mountain toppled by an earthquake.

While that king of elephants was falling down and your 20.25
son's troops were lamenting, the hero of the Shinis* struck off King Shalva's head with a sharp, spear-headed arrow. Shalva fell to the ground beside the mighty elephant, his head chopped off in battle by the Sátvata. He was like a massive mountain peak that had been toppled by a thunderbolt fired by the king of the gods.

SÁNJAYA said:

AFTER THE SLAUGHTER of heroic Shalva, that ornament 21.1
of assemblies, your army rapidly broke up like a great tree broken by the wind. But the great warrior and mighty hero Krita·varman withheld the enemy troops in battle when he saw that the army was dispersing. On seeing the Sátvata warrior standing steady like a rock and being covered with arrows in battle, the Káurava heroes returned, Your Majesty.

A battle then ensued between the Pándavas and the rallied Kuru troops, who had resolved to die rather than flee,
O great king. The Sátvata warrior, Krita·varman, fought an 21.5
incredible battle against the enemy, as he alone restrained Pandu's army, difficult though it was to assail. At this difficult feat, his joyful friends shouted a huge lion-roar that reached the sky.

The Panchálas were terrified by this noise, bull of the Bharatas. But mighty-armed Sátyaki, the grandson of Shini, then advanced. Attacking the powerful king Kshema·dhurti, Sátyaki sent him to Yama's abode with seven sharp

tam āyāntaṃ mahā|bāhuṃ pravapantaṃ śitāñ śarān
javen' âbhyapatad dhīmān Hārdikyaḥ Śini|puṅ|gavam.
21.10 Sātvatau ca mahā|vīryau dhanvinau rathināṃ varau
anyonyam abhidhāvetāṃ śastra|pravara|dhāriṇau.
Pāṇḍavāḥ saha|Pañcālā yodhāś c' ânye nṛp'|ôttamāḥ
prekṣakāḥ samapadyanta tayor ghore samāgame.

nārācair vatsa|dantaiś ca Vṛṣṇy|Andhaka|mahā|rathau
abhijaghnatur anyonyaṃ prahṛṣṭāv iva kuñjarau.
carantau vividhān mārgān Hārdikya|Śini|puṅ|gavau
muhur antardadhāte tau bāṇa|vṛṣṭyā paras|param.
cāpa|vega|bal'|ôddhūtān mārgaṇān Vṛṣṇi|siṃhayoḥ
ākāśe samapaśyāma pataṅgān iva śīghra|gān.
21.15 tam ekaṃ satya|karmāṇam āsādya Hṛdik'|ātma|jaḥ
avidhyan niśitair bāṇaiś caturbhiś caturo hayān
sa dīrgha|bāhuḥ saṃkruddhas tottr'|ârdita iva dvi|paḥ
aṣṭabhiḥ Kṛtavarmāṇam aviddhyat param'|êṣubhiḥ.
tataḥ pūrṇ'|āyat'|ôtsṛṣṭaiḥ Kṛtavarmā śilā|śitaiḥ
Sātyakiṃ tribhir āhatya dhanur ekena cicchide.
nikṛttaṃ tad dhanuḥ śreṣṭham apāsya Śini|puṅ|gavaḥ
anyad ādatta vegena Śaineyaḥ sa|śaraṃ dhanuḥ.

tad ādāya dhanuḥ śreṣṭhaṃ variṣṭhaḥ sarva|dhanvinām
āropya ca dhanuḥ śīghraṃ mahā|vīryo mahā|balaḥ,
21.20 a|mṛṣyamāṇo dhanuṣaś chedanaṃ Kṛtavarmaṇā
kupito 'tirathaḥ śīghraṃ Kṛtavarmāṇam abhyayāt.
tataḥ su|niśitair bāṇair daśabhiḥ Śini|puṅ|gavaḥ

arrows. Wise Krita·varman, the son of Hrídika, then swiftly attacked the mighty-armed bull of the Shinis as he advanced
firing sharp arrows. Wielding their excellent weapons, those 21.10
two powerful Sátvata archers and best of charioteers charged against each other. The Pándavas, Panchálas and other excellent warriors watched these heroes as they fought in that grim battle.

With their calf-toothed arrows, the two mighty warriors of the Vrishnis and Ándhakas struck each other like joyful elephants. Moving around in various directions, the son of Hrídika and bull of the Shinis gradually disappeared from sight because of the shower of arrows that they shot at each other. We watched their shafts flying swiftly through the air like bees, fired with powerful velocity from the bows of the
two Vrishni lions. The son of Hrídika then attacked lone 21.15
Sátyaki, whose deeds are truthful, and wounded his four horses with four sharp arrows. Enraged, like an elephant tormented by a goad, long-armed Sátyaki pierced Krita·varman with eight fine shafts. Krita·varman then struck Sátyaki with three stone-sharpened arrows, which were fired from his bow at full stretch, and sliced through Sátyaki's bow with one more. Discarding that fine, severed bow, the bull of the Shinis quickly took up another bow along with its arrows.

Unable to endure that Krita·varman had cut through his bow, that powerful and mighty champion of all archers
took up an excellent, swift bow and strung it. In his rage, 21.20
that superior warrior then quickly charged against Krita·varman. With ten well-sharpened arrows, the bull of the Shinis

jaghāna sūtam c' âśvāṃś ca dhvajaṃ ca Kṛtavarmaṇaḥ.

tato rājan mah"|êṣv|āsaḥ Kṛtavarmā mahā|rathaḥ
hat'|âśva|sūtaṃ saṃpreksya rathaṃ hema|pariṣkṛtam,
roṣeṇa mahat" āviṣṭaḥ śūlam udyamya māriṣa
cikṣepa bhuja|vegena jighāṃsuḥ Śini|puṅ|gavam.

tac chūlaṃ Sātvato hy ājau nirbhidya niśitaiḥ śaraiḥ
cūrṇitaṃ pātayām āsa mohayann iva Mādhavam.
tato 'pareṇa bhallena hṛdy enaṃ samatāḍayat.

21.25 sa yuddhe Yuyudhānena hat'|âśvo hata|sārathiḥ
Kṛtavarmā kṛt'|âstreṇa dharaṇīm anvapadyata.
tasmin Sātyakinā vīre dvai|rathe virathīkṛte
samapadyata sarveṣāṃ sainyānāṃ su|mahad bhayam.
putrasya tava c' âtyarthaṃ viṣādaḥ samajāyata
hata|sūte hat'|âśve tu virathe Kṛtavarmaṇi.

hat'|âśvaṃ ca samālaksya hata|sūtam arin|dama
abhyadhāvat Kṛpo rājañ jighāṃsuḥ Śini|puṅ|gavam.
tam āropya rath'|ôpasthe miṣatāṃ sarva|dhanvinām
apovāha mahā|bāhum tūrṇam āyodhanād api.

21.30 Śaineye 'dhiṣṭhite rājan virathe Kṛtavarmaṇi
Duryodhana|balaṃ sarvaṃ punar āsīt parāṅ|mukham.
tat pare n' ânvabudhyanta sainyena rajasā vṛtāḥ
tāvakāḥ pradrutā rājan Duryodhanam ṛte nṛ|pam.

killed Krita·varman's charioteer and horses and destroyed his banner.

Krita·varman—that great archer and mighty warrior—became filled with violent fury when he saw that his gold-decked chariot had been stripped of its horses and driver. Raising his lance, he hurled it with a powerful throw, my lord, eager to kill the bull of the Shinis.

But the Sátvata warrior Sátyaki sliced up the lance with his sharp arrows in battle and struck down the pulverized weapon, almost bewildering his Mádhava opponent as he did so. With another spear-headed arrow he struck Krita·varman in the heart.

After his horses and driver were killed in battle by skillful 21.25
Yuyudhána, Krita·varman jumped to the ground. A great fear entered all the Káurava troops when heroic Krita·varman lost his chariot in that duel with Sátyaki. Your son, too, became extremely despondent when Krita·varman was stripped of his chariot and his horses and driver were killed.

However, on seeing that Krita·varman had lost his horses and driver, Kripa charged against the bull of the Shinis, eager to kill him, O enemy-slaying king. Under the eyes of all the archers, Kripa lifted mighty-armed Krita·varman onto his chariot platform and swiftly took him away from the battlefield.

With Shini's grandson in control and Krita·varman bereft 21.30
of his chariot, Dur·yódhana's entire army again took flight. The enemy became invisible, covered by dust from the army, and all your forces fled, Your Majesty, except for king Dur·yódhana.

Duryodhanas tu saṃprekṣya bhagnaṃ sva|balam antikāt
javen' âbhyapatat tūrṇaṃ sarvāṃś c' âiko nyavārayat.
Pāṇḍūṃś ca sarvān saṃkruddho
Dhṛṣṭadyumnaṃ ca Pārṣatam
Śikhaṇḍinaṃ Draupadeyān
Pañcālānāṃ ca ye gaṇāḥ,
Kekayān Somakāṃś c' âiva Sṛñjayāṃś c' âiva māriṣa
a|saṃbhramaṃ dur|ādharṣaḥ śitair bāṇair avākirat.
21.35 atiṣṭhad āhave yattaḥ putras tava mahā|balaḥ.
yathā yajñe mahān agnir mantra|pūtaḥ prakāśavān
tathā Duryodhano rājā saṃgrāme sarvato 'bhavat.
taṃ pare n' âbhyavartanta martyā mṛtyum iv' āhave.
ath' ânyaṃ ratham āsthāya Hārdikyaḥ samapadyata.

SAÑJAYA uvāca:

22.1 PUTRAS TU TE mahā|rāja ratha|stho rathināṃ varaḥ
dur|utsaho babhau yuddhe yathā Rudraḥ pratāpavān.
tasya bāṇa|sahasrais tu pracchannā hy abhavan mahī
parāṃś ca siṣice bāṇair dhārābhir iva parvatān.
na ca so 'sti pumān kaś cit Pāṇḍavānāṃ bal'|ârṇave
hayo gajo ratho v" âpi yo 'sya bāṇair a|vikṣataḥ.
yaṃ yaṃ hi samare yodhaṃ prapaśyāmi viśāṃ pate
sa sa bāṇaiś cito 'bhūd vai putreṇa tava Bhārata.
22.5 yathā sainyena rajasā samudbhūtena vāhinī
pratyadṛśyata saṃchannā tathā bāṇair mah"|ātmanaḥ

When Dur·yódhana saw, from nearby, that his troops were breaking up, he instantly charged against the enemy with speed and repelled all of them on his own. Without wavering, the invincible hero angrily covered all of Pandu's sons with his sharp arrows, as well as Príshata's grandson Dhrishta·dyumna, Shikhándin, the sons of Dráupadi, the Panchála regiments, the Kékayas, the Sómakas and the Sríñjayas, my lord.

Your mighty son stayed on the battlefield, full of exertion. 21.35
Like a huge, bright fire that has been sanctified by mantras in a sacrifice, King Dur·yódhana appeared everywhere in battle. His enemies were unable to assail him in that battle, just as mortals are unable to assail Death.

The son of Hrídika then climbed onto another chariot and joined Dur·yódhana.

SÁNJAYA said:

YOUR SON—that champion of charioteers—looked like 22.1
mighty Rudra as he stood on his chariot, hard to resist in battle, great king. The earth became covered with thousands of Dur·yódhana's arrows. As if pouring torrents of rain over mountains, Dur·yódhana showered the enemy with his shafts. Not one person in that ocean of the Pándava army—nor any horse, chariot or elephant—remained unscathed by Dur·yódhana's arrows. Every warrior that I saw in the battle became shrouded by your son's shafts, descendant of Bharata. Just as troops are enveloped by dust 22.5
that billows from an army's movement, so they were seen covered with the hero's arrows.

bāṇa|bhūtām apaśyāma pṛthivīṃ pṛthivī|pate
Duryodhanena prakṛtāṃ kṣipra|hastena dhanvinā.
teṣu yodha|sahasreṣu tāvakeṣu pareṣu ca
eko Duryodhanaś hy āsīt pumān iti matir mama.
tatr' âdbhutam apaśyāma tava putrasya vikramam
yad ekaṃ sahitāḥ Pārthā n' âbhyavartanta Bhārata.

Yudhiṣṭhiraṃ śaten' ājau vivyādha Bharata'|rṣabha
Bhīmasenaṃ ca saptatyā Sahadevaṃ ca pañcabhiḥ.
22.10 Nakulaṃ ca catuḥ|ṣaṣṭyā Dhṛṣṭadyumnaṃ ca pañcabhiḥ
saptabhir Draupadeyāṃś ca tribhir vivyādha Sātyakim.
dhanuś ciccheda bhallena Sahadevasya māriṣa.

tad apāsya dhanuś chinnaṃ Mādrī|putraḥ pratāpavān
abhyadravata rājānaṃ pragṛhy' ânyan mahad dhanuḥ.
tato Duryodhanaṃ saṃkhye vivyādha daśabhiḥ śaraiḥ.

Nakulas tu tato vīro rājānaṃ navabhiḥ śaraiḥ
ghora|rūpair mah"|êṣv|āso vivyādha ca nanāda ca.
Sātyakiś c' âiva rājānaṃ śareṇ' ānata|parvaṇā
Draupadeyās tri|saptatyā dharma|rājaś ca pañcabhiḥ
aśītyā Bhīmasenaś ca śarai rājānam ārpayan.

samantāt kīryamāṇas tu bāṇa|saṅghair mah"|ātmabhiḥ
na cacāla mahā|rāja sarva|sainyasya paśyataḥ.
22.15 lāghavaṃ sau|ṣṭhavaṃ c' âpi vīryaṃ c' âpi mah"|ātmanaḥ
ati sarvāṇi bhūtāni dadṛśuḥ sarva|mānavāḥ.

We watched bow-wielding Dur·yódhana transform the earth into arrows with his agile hands, O lord of the earth. Indeed, I considered that Dur·yódhana was the only man that existed among the thousands of fighters in both your army and the enemy troops. It was incredible for us to see your son's prowess, descendant of Bharata, as all the Parthas together could not assail him on his own.

Dur·yódhana pierced Yudhi·shthira with a hundred arrows in battle and hit Bhima·sena with seventy and Saha·
deva with five, O bull of the Bharatas. He then wounded 22.10
Nákula with sixty-four shafts, Dhrishta·dyumna with five, the sons of Dráupadi with seven and Sátyaki with three. He then cut through Saha·deva's bow with a spear-headed arrow, my lord.

But Saha·deva, the mighty son of Madri, discarded that severed bow and charged against the king, seizing hold of another, huge bow. He then pierced Dur·yódhana in battle with ten arrows.

Nákula, that heroic and mighty archer, also wounded the king with nine shafts—which were terrifying to behold—and then roared. Sátyaki, too, shot King Dur·yódhana with a straight shaft, as did the sons of Dráupadi with seventy-three arrows, the King of Righteousness with five and Bhima·sena with eighty more.

However, although covered on all sides by the hordes of arrows fired by these heroes, Dur·yódhana—who was under the eyes of the entire army—did not waver, Your Majesty.
All the men watched the agility, skill and energy shown by 22.15
heroic Dur·yódhana, which surpassed every living creature.

Dhārtarāṣṭrā hi rāj'|êndra yodhās tu sv|alpam antaram
a|paśyamānā rājānaṃ paryavartanta daṃśitāḥ.
teṣām āpatatāṃ ghoras tumulaḥ samapadyata
kṣubdhasya hi samudrasya prāvṛṭ|kāle yathā svanaḥ.
samāsādya raṇe te tu rājānam a|parājitam
pratyudyayur mah"|êṣv|āsāḥ Pāṇḍavān ātatāyinaḥ.

Bhīmasenaṃ raṇe kruddho Droṇa|putro nyavārayat.
nānā|bāṇair mahā|rāja pramuktaiḥ sarvato|diśam
n' ājñāyanta raṇe vīrā na diśaḥ pradiśaḥ kutaḥ.
22.20 tāv ubhau krūra|karmāṇāv ubhau Bhārata duḥ|sahau
ghora|rūpam ayudhyetāṃ kṛta|pratikṛt'|âiṣiṇau
trāsayantau diśaḥ sarvā jyā|kṣepa|kaṭhina|tvacau.

Śakunis tu raṇe vīro Yudhiṣṭhiram apīḍayat.
tasy' âśvāṃś caturo hatvā Subalasya suto vibho
nādaṃ cakāra balavat sarva|sainyāni kopayan.
etasminn antare vīraṃ rājānam a|parājitam
apovāha rathen' ājau Sahadevaḥ pratāpavān.
ath' ânyaṃ ratham āsthāya Dharma|putro Yudhiṣṭhiraḥ
Śakuniṃ navabhir viddhvā punar vivyādha pañcabhiḥ
nanāda ca mahā|nādaṃ pravaraḥ sarva|dhanvinām.

tad yuddham abhavac citraṃ ghora|rūpaṃ ca māriṣa
prekṣatāṃ prīti|jananaṃ siddha|cāraṇa|sevitam.

Then, king of kings, Dhrita·rashtra's troops, who had been absent for only a short while, returned to King Dur·yódhana wearing their armor. There was a horrific tumult as they advanced forward, like the sound of the ocean surging in the rainy season. Joining their undefeated king in battle, the mighty archers rose up against the bow-drawing Pándavas.

The furious son of Drona held back Bhima·sena in battle. The heroes on the battlefield became invisible because of the array of arrows that were fired on every side; nor could the major directions be seen, let alone the minor ones.

Both Ashva·tthaman and Bhima were cruel in their ac- 22.20
tions and difficult to repel. Both also had rough skin from drawing their bowstrings. Constantly seeking to counter each other, they fought a contest that was horrifying to see and that filled every direction with terror.

Heroic Shákuni besieged Yudhi·shthira in battle. Slaughtering Yudhi·shthira's four horses, the powerful son of Súbala then roared, provoking all the troops to anger, my lord. Mighty Saha·deva drove away the heroic and undefeated king in his chariot in the battle. Standing on this new chariot, Yudhi·shthira, the son of Righteousness, pierced Shákuni with nine arrows and then again with five more. That champion of all archers then made a huge roar.

The battle was both wonderful and awful, my lord. Attended by *siddhas* and *cháranas*, it brought joy to onlookers.

22.25 Ulūkas tu mah"|êṣv|āsaṃ Nakulaṃ yuddha|dur|madam
abhyadravad a|mey'|ātmā śara|varṣaiḥ samantataḥ.
tath" âiva Nakulaḥ śūraḥ Saubalasya sutaṃ raṇe
śara|varṣeṇa mahatā samantāt paryavārayat.
tau tatra samare vīrau kula|putrau mahā|rathau
yodhayantāv apaśyetāṃ kṛta|pratikṛt'|âiṣiṇau.

tath" âiva Kṛtavarmāṇaṃ Śaineyaḥ śatru|tāpanaḥ
yodhayañ śuśubhe rājan Baliṃ Śakra iv' āhave.

Duryodhano dhanuś chittvā Dhṛṣṭadyumnasya saṃyuge
ath' âinaṃ chinna|dhanvānaṃ vivyādha niśitaiḥ śaraiḥ.
22.30 Dhṛṣṭadyumno 'pi samare pragṛhya param'|āyudham
rājānaṃ yodhayām āsa paśyatāṃ sarva|dhanvinām.
tayor yuddhaṃ mahac c' āsīt saṃgrāme Bharata'|rṣabha
prabhinnayor yathā saktaṃ mattayor vara|hastinoḥ

Gautamas tu raṇe kruddho Draupadeyān mahā|balān
vivyādha bahubhiḥ śūraḥ śaraiḥ saṃnata|parvabhiḥ.
tasya tair abhavad yuddham indriyair iva dehinaḥ
ghora|rūpam a|saṃvāryaṃ nirmaryādam avartata.
te ca saṃpīḍayām āsur indriyāṇ' îva bāliśam.
sa ca tān prati saṃrabdhaḥ pratyayodhayad āhave.
22.35 evaṃ citram abhūd yuddhaṃ tasya taiḥ saha Bhārata
utthāy'|ôtthāya hi yathā dehinām indriyair vibho.

With showers of arrows fired on every side, infinite-spirited Ulúka then attacked the great archer Nákula, who is difficult to conquer in battle. In just the same way, heroic Nákula repelled Súbala's grandson* in battle by firing a vast shower of arrows in every direction. The two heroes were seen fighting one another in battle, both of them great warriors from noble families and both eager to counter the other. 22.25

In a similar manner, enemy-incinerating Sátyaki, the grandson of Shini, looked glorious as he fought against Krita·varman, just as Shakra did in his battle against Bali.

Dur·yódhana, meanwhile, cut through Dhrishta·dyumna's bow in battle and then pierced the bowless hero with his
sharp shafts. But Dhrishta·dyumna picked up an excellent 22.30
weapon and fought the king in battle, while all the archers looked on. The two warriors then engaged in a huge combat on the battlefield, bull of the Bharatas; it was like a contest between two fine, rutting and frenzied elephants.

Filled with battle-fury, Kripa, the heroic grandson of Gótama, then pierced the mighty sons of Dráupadi with numerous straight arrows. His battle against them was terrible, unrestrained and limitless, and resembled the struggle between the embodied soul and the five senses. The five sons of Dráupadi besieged him, just as the senses besiege a fool. Enraged, the grandson of Gótama fought back against
them in battle. In this way, there was a wondrous battle be- 22.35
tween the grandson of Gótama and the sons of Dráupadi, O Bhárata. It was like the never-ending conflict between embodied souls and the senses, my lord.

narāś c' âiva naraiḥ sārdhaṃ dantino dantibhis tathā
hayā hayaiḥ samāsaktā rathino rathibhiḥ saha.
saṃkulaṃ c' âbhavad bhūyo ghora|rūpaṃ viśāṃ pate.
idaṃ citram idaṃ ghoram idaṃ raudram iti prabho.
yuddhāny āsan mahā|rāja ghorāṇi ca bahūni ca.
te samāsādya samare paras|param arin|damāḥ
vyanadaṃś c' âiva jaghnuś ca samāsādya mah"|āhave.

teṣāṃ śastra|samudbhūtaṃ rajas tīvram adṛśyata
vātena c' ôddhataṃ rājan dhāvadbhiś c' âśva|sādibhiḥ.
22.40 ratha|nemi|samudbhūtaṃ niḥśvāsaiś c' âpi dantinām
rajaḥ sandhy'|âbhra|kalilaṃ divā|kara|pathaṃ yayau.
rajasā tena saṃpṛkto bhās|karo niṣprabhaḥ kṛtaḥ.
saṃchādit" âbhavad bhūmis te ca śūrā mahā|rathāḥ.

muhūrtād iva saṃvṛttaṃ nīrajaskaṃ samantataḥ
vīra|śoṇita|siktāyāṃ bhūmau Bharata|sattama
upāśāmyat tatas tīvraṃ tad rajo ghora|darśanam.

tato 'paśyam ahaṃ bhūyo dvandva|yuddhāni Bhārata
yathā|prāṇaṃ yathā|śreṣṭhaṃ madhy'|âhne vai su|dāruṇam.
varmaṇāṃ tatra rāj'|êndra vyadṛśyant' ôjjvalāḥ prabhāḥ
śabdaś ca tumulaḥ saṃkhye śarāṇāṃ patatām abhūt
mahā|veṇu|vanasy' êva dahyamānasya parvate.

Men engaged in battle with men, elephants with elephants, horses with horses, and charioteers with charioteers. Once more the war became chaotic and terrible to see, lord of the people. Here the battle was full of wonder, over there it was awful, and over there it was horrific, my lord. The conflicts were dreadful and numerous, great king. As they attacked and clashed against each other, the enemy-taming warriors roared out loud and killed one another in that great battle.

A fierce cloud of dust came into view, Your Majesty, stirred up by the troops' weapons and billowing because
of the wind and fleeing cavalrymen. Stirred up further by 22.40
the chariot wheels and the snorts of elephants, the dust climbed to the sky, thick as evening clouds. Tainted by the dust, the sun lost its radiance, and the earth and heroic warriors became obscured.

But in a short while, when the earth had been sprinkled with the blood of heroes, everywhere became clear of dust and the fierce and terrifying cloud settled.

Once again, descendant of Bharata, I watched men fight horrific duels at midday, each according to their strength and superiority. Their armor shone with blazing splendor, king of kings, and the noise of their arrows flying in the battle became tumultuous, like the sound of a large bamboo forest burning on a mountain.

SAÑJAYA uvāca:

23.1 VARTAMĀNE TADĀ yuddhe ghora|rūpe bhayānake
abhajyata balaṃ tatra tava putrasya Pāṇḍavaiḥ.
tāṃs tu yatnena mahatā saṃnivārya mahā|rathān
putras te yodhayām āsa Pāṇḍavānām anīkinīm.
nivṛttāḥ sahasā yodhās tava putra|jay'|âiṣiṇaḥ.
saṃnivṛtteṣu teṣv evaṃ yuddham āsīt su|dāruṇam
tāvakānāṃ pareṣāṃ ca dev'|âsura|raṇ'|ôpamam.

pareṣāṃ tava sainye vā n' āsīt kaś cit parāṅ|mukhaḥ.
anumānena yudhyante saṃjñābhiś ca paras|param.
teṣāṃ kṣayo mahān āsīd yudhyatām itar'|êtaram.
23.5 tato Yudhiṣṭhiro rājā krodhena mahatā yutaḥ
jigīṣamāṇaḥ saṃgrāme Dhārtarāṣṭrān sa|rājakān.
tribhiḥ Śāradvataṃ viddhvā rukma|puṅkhaiḥ śilā|śitaiḥ
caturbhir nijaghān' âśvān nārācaiḥ Kṛtavarmaṇaḥ.
Aśvatthāmā tu Hārdikyam apovāha yaśasvinam;
atha Śāradvato 'ṣṭābhiḥ pratyaviddhyad Yudhiṣṭhiram.

tato Duryodhano rājā rathān sapta|śatān raṇe
preṣayad yatra rāj" âsau Dharma|putro Yudhiṣṭhiraḥ
te rathā rathibhir yuktā mano|māruta|raṃhasaḥ
abhyadravanta saṃgrāme Kaunteyasya rathaṃ prati.
23.10 te samantān mahā|rāja parivārya Yudhiṣṭhiram
a|dṛśyaṃ sāyakaiś cakrur meghā iva divā|karam.

SÁNJAYA said:

DURING THIS horrific and terrifying battle, the Pándavas split open your son's army on the battlefield. With a mighty effort, however, your son restrained his great warriors and fought back against the Pándavas' troops. The Pándava warriors, although eager to conquer your son, were repelled with force. At their withdrawal, there was a grim battle between your men and the enemy troops, resembling a war between the gods and demons. 23.1

None of the enemy or your troops turned their backs. They fought one another through signs and inference, and there was a vast massacre as they battled against one another.

King Yudhi·shthira then became filled with huge rage and yearned to attack Dhrita·rashtra's troops in battle, as well as their king. Piercing Kripa, the son of Sharádvat, with three gold-feathered, stone-sharpened arrows, Yudhi·shthira killed Krita·varman's horses with four more. Ashva·tthaman, however, took away Krita·varman, the glorious son of Hrídika, whereupon the son of Sharádvat pierced Yudhi·shthira back with eight shafts. 23.5

King Dur·yódhana then dispatched seven hundred chariots against King Yudhi·shthira, the son of Righteousness, on the battlefield. Swift as the mind or wind, the chariots charged with their charioteers against the vehicle of the son of Kunti in battle. They surrounded Yudhi·shthira on all 23.10
sides, great king, and made him invisible with their arrows, just as clouds conceal the sun.

te dṛṣṭvā dharma|rājānaṃ Kauraveyais tathā kṛtam
n' âmṛṣyanta su|saṃrabdhāḥ Śikhaṇḍi|pramukhā rathāḥ.
rathair aśva|varair yuktaiḥ kiṅkiṇī|jāla|saṃvṛtaiḥ
ājagmur atha rakṣantaḥ Kuntī|putraṃ Yudhiṣṭhiram.

tataḥ pravavṛte raudraḥ saṃgrāmaḥ śoṇit'|ôdakaḥ
Pāṇḍavānāṃ Kurūṇāṃ ca Yama|rāṣṭra|vivardhanaḥ.
rathān sapta|śatān hatvā Kurūṇām ātatāyinām
Pāṇḍavāḥ saha Pañcālaiḥ punar ev' âbhyavārayan.
23.15 tatra yuddhaṃ mahac c' āsīt tava putrasya Pāṇḍavaiḥ
na ca nas tādṛśaṃ dṛṣṭaṃ n' âiva c' âpi pariśrutam.

vartamāne tadā yuddhe nirmaryāde samantataḥ
vadhyamāneṣu yodheṣu tāvakeṣv itareṣu ca,
vinadatsu ca yodheṣu śaṅkha|varyaiś ca pūritaiḥ,
utkruṣṭaiḥ siṃha|nādaiś ca garjitaiś c' âiva dhanvinām,
atipravṛtte yuddhe ca chidyamāneṣu marmasu
dhāvamāneṣu yodheṣu jaya|gṛddhiṣu māriṣa,
saṃhāre sarvato jāte pṛthivyāṃ śoka|saṃbhave
bahvīnām uttama|strīṇāṃ sīmant'|ôddharaṇe tathā,
23.20 nirmaryāde mahā|yuddhe vartamāne su|dāruṇe
prādur āsan vināśāya tad" ôtpātāḥ su|dāruṇāḥ.
cacāla śabdaṃ kurvāṇā sa|parvata|vanā mahī.
sa|daṇḍāḥ s'|ôlmukā rājan kīryamāṇāḥ samantataḥ
ulkāḥ petur divo bhūmāv āhatya ravi|maṇḍalam.
viṣvag|vātāḥ prādur āsan nīcaiḥ śarkara|varṣiṇaḥ.
aśrūṇi mumucur nāgā vepathuṃ c' âspṛśan bhṛśam.

Filled with great fury, the heroes that were led by Shikhándin were unable to endure seeing the Káuravas act in this way against the King of Righteousness. Advancing toward Yudhi·shthira, the son of Kunti, they protected him with their chariots, which were yoked to the finest horses and covered with nets of bells.

There was then a hideous battle between the Pándavas and the Kurus, in which blood flowed like water and which increased the kingdom of Yama. Destroying the seven hundred chariots of the Kuru archers, the Pándavas and the
Panchálas once more repelled them. It was a vast battle be- 23.15
tween your son and the Pándavas, the like of which we had never seen or heard of.

War was then waged without limits in all directions. Troops from both your army and the enemy were slaughtered. Warriors shouted and fine conches blared. Archers bellowed and cried out lion-roars. The battle became extreme, my lord, as vital organs were pierced and soldiers charged about, eager for victory. Destruction occurred everywhere; the earth became full of grief; and multitudes
of noble women tore out their hair. While this dreadful, 23.20
vast battle continued without limits, terrifying omens appeared, spelling destruction. The earth, with its mountains and forests, shook and groaned. Meteors struck the sphere of the sun and fell to the ground from the sky, scattered on every side, along with sticks and blazing coals. Winds arose, swirling in every direction and pouring down gravel. Elephants shed tears and trembled violently.

etān ghorān anādṛtya samutpātān su|dāruṇān
punar yuddhāya saṃyattāḥ kṣatriyās tasthur a|vyathāḥ
ramaṇīye Kuru|kṣetre puṇye svargaṃ yiyāsavaḥ.
tato Gāndhāra|rājasya putraḥ Śakunir abravīt:
«yudhyadhvam agrato yāvat pṛṣṭhato hanmi Pāṇḍavān!»

23.25 tato naḥ saṃprayātānāṃ Madra|yodhās tarasvinaḥ
hṛṣṭāḥ kilakilā|śabdam akurvanta, pare tathā.
asmāṃs tu punar āsādya labdha|lakṣā dur|āsadāḥ
śar'|âsanāni dhunvantaḥ śara|varṣair avākiran.
tato hataṃ parais tatra Madra|rāja|balaṃ tadā
Duryodhana|balaṃ dṛṣṭvā punar āsīt parāṅ|mukham.

Gāndhāra|rājas tu punar
vākyam āha tato balī:
«nivartadhvam! a|dharma|jñā
yudhyadhvaṃ! kiṃ sṛtena vaḥ!»

anīkaṃ daśa|sāhasram aśvānāṃ Bharata'|rṣabha
āsīd Gāndhāra|rājasya viśāla|prāsa|yodhinām.
23.30 balena tena vikramya vartamāne jana|kṣaye
pṛṣṭhataḥ Pāṇḍav'|ânīkam abhyaghnan niśitaiḥ śaraiḥ.
tad abhram iva vātena kṣipyamāṇaṃ samantataḥ
abhajyata mahā|rāja Pāṇḍūnāṃ su|mahad balam.

tato Yudhiṣṭhiraḥ prekṣya bhagnaṃ sva|balam antikāt
abhyanodayad a|vyagraḥ Sahadevaṃ mahā|balam:

Taking no notice of these terrifying and awful portents, the warriors once again became intent on battle. Eager to attain heaven, they held their positions unflinchingly on the delightful and auspicious field of the Kurus. Shákuni, the prince of Gandhára, then exclaimed:

"Fight the Pándavas at the front, while I slaughter them in the rear!"

As we advanced, the swift Madra warriors shouted cheers 23.25
of joy. And the enemy also did the same. Precise in their aim and difficult to assail, the enemy attacked us once more and covered us with showers of arrows as they shook their bows. When they saw that the enemy was slaughtering the king of the Madras' army on the battlefield, Dur·yódhana's troops once again fled, Your Majesty.

However, Shákuni, the powerful prince of Gandhára, shouted: "Turn around! You know what is wrong,* so fight! What is the point of fleeing?"

The Gandhára prince had a contingent of ten thousand horses, which fought with mighty lances, O bull of the
Bharatas. While the massacre of men continued, Shákuni 23.30
attacked the Pándava troops with that force and struck them in their rear with sharp arrows. The vast army of the Pandus broke up, Your Majesty, like a cloud dispersed by the wind in every direction.

But when Yudhi·shthira saw, from nearby, that his army had been broken, he calmly urged on mighty Saha·deva, saying:

«asau Subala|putro no jaghanaṃ pīḍya daṃśitaḥ
sainyāni sūdayaty eṣa. paśya Pāṇḍava dur|matim!
gaccha tvaṃ Draupadeyaiś ca Śakuniṃ Saubalaṃ jahi!
rath'|ânīkam ahaṃ dhakṣye Pañcāla|sahito 'n|agha.
23.35 gacchantu kuñjarāḥ sarve vājinaś ca saha tvayā
pādātāś ca tri|sāhasrāḥ. Śakuniṃ tair vṛto jahi!»

tato gajāḥ sapta|śatāś cāpa|pāṇibhir āsthitāḥ
pañca c' âśva|sahasrāṇi Sahadevaś ca vīryavān,
pādātāś ca tri|sāhasrā Draupadeyāś ca sarvaśaḥ
raṇe hy abhyadravaṃs te tu Śakuniṃ yuddha|dur|madam.

tatas tu Saubalo rājann abhyatikramya Pāṇḍavān
jaghāna pṛṣṭhataḥ senāṃ jaya|gṛddhaḥ pratāpavān.

aśv'|ārohās tu saṃrabdhāḥ Pāṇḍavānāṃ tarasvinām
prāviśan Saubal'|ânīkam abhyatikramya tān rathān.
23.40 te tatra sādinaḥ śūrāḥ Saubalasya mahad balam
raṇa|madhye 'vatiṣṭhantaḥ śara|varṣair avākiran.
tad udyata|gadā|prāsam a|kā|puruṣa|sevitam
prāvartata mahad yuddhaṃ rājan dur|mantrite tava.

upāramanta jyā|śabdāḥ prekṣakā rathino 'bhavan.
na hi sveṣāṃ pareṣāṃ vā viśeṣaḥ pratyadṛśyata.
śūra|bāhu|visṛṣṭānāṃ śaktīnāṃ Bharata'|rṣabha
jyotiṣām iva saṃpātam apaśyan Kuru|Pāṇḍavāḥ.
ṛṣṭibhir vimalābhiś ca tatra tatra viśāṃ pate
saṃpatantībhir ākāśam āvṛtaṃ bahv aśobhata.

"The son of Súbala stands over there, clad in armor. Pummeling our rear guard, he is slaughtering our troops. Look at his villainy, Pándava! Go with the sons of Dráupadi and kill Shákuni, the son of Súbala. Together with the Panchálas I will incinerate their chariot division, virtuous prince. Take with you all the elephants and cavalry, and also 23.35
three thousand foot soldiers. Surrounded by these forces, destroy Shákuni!"

Seven hundred elephants ridden by archers, five thousand horses, three thousand infantrymen, the five sons of Dráupadi and powerful Saha·deva all then charged against Shákuni in battle, who is difficult to defeat in war.

But the mighty son of Súbala overpowered the Pándavas, Your Majesty, and slaughtered their army at the rear, greedy as he was for victory.

Enraged, the cavalrymen of the fierce Pándavas overwhelmed the enemy chariots and penetrated the son of Súbala's army. Taking their stand in the middle of the battle- 23.40
field, the heroic horsemen covered the great army of Súbala's son with showers of arrows. Because of your bad policy, Your Majesty, a huge battle then ensued, in which courage abounded and maces and lances were brandished.

The noise of bowstrings ceased and the charioteers became onlookers. It was impossible to distinguish between our troops and the enemy. Both the Kurus and the Pándavas watched spears fly through the air like flames, hurled by the arms of heroes, bull of the Bharatas. The sky glistened brightly, lord of the people, as it became filled in every direction with radiant, flying javelins. The missiles 23.45
that fell on every side looked like locusts in the sky, best

23.45 prāsānāṃ patatāṃ rājan rūpam āsīt samantataḥ
śalabhānām iv' ākāśe tadā Bharata|sattama.
rudhir'|ôkṣita|sarv'|âṅgā vipraviddhair niyantṛbhiḥ
hayāḥ paripatanti sma śataśo 'tha sahasraśaḥ.

anyonyaṃ paripiṣṭāś ca samāsādya paras|param
āvikṣatāḥ sma dṛśyante vamanto rudhiraṃ mukhaiḥ.
tato 'bhavat tamo ghoraṃ sainyena rajasā vṛte.
tān apākramato 'drākṣaṃ tasmād deśād arin|dama
aśvān rājan manuṣyāṃś ca rajasā saṃvṛte sati.
bhūmau nipatitāś c' ânye vamanto rudhiraṃ bahu
keśā|keśi|samālagnā na śekuś ceṣṭituṃ narāḥ.
23.50 anyonyam aśva|pṛṣṭhebhyo vikarṣanto mahā|balāḥ
mallā iva samāsādya nijaghnur itar'|êtaram
aśvaiś ca vyapakṛṣyanta bahavo 'tra gat'|āsavaḥ.
bhūmau nipatitāś c' ânye bahavo vijay'|âiṣiṇaḥ
tatra tatra vyadṛśyanta puruṣāḥ śūra|māninaḥ.

rakt'|ôkṣitaiś chinna|bhujair apakṛṣṭa|śiro|ruhaiḥ
vyadṛśyata mahī kīrṇā śataśo 'tha sahasraśaḥ.
dūraṃ na śakyaṃ tatr' āsīd gantum aśvena kena cit
s'|âśv'|ārohair hatair aśvair āvṛte vasu|dhā|tale,
rudhir'|ôkṣita|sannāhair ātta|śastrair udāyudhaiḥ
nānā|praharaṇair ghoraiḥ paras|para|vadh'|âiṣibhiḥ
su|saṃnikṛṣṭaiḥ saṃgrāme hata|bhūyiṣṭha|sainikaiḥ.

of Bharatas. Horses dropped down in their hundreds and thousands, their entire bodies drenched in blood because of their wounded riders.

Having crushed one another in close combat, wounded soldiers were seen vomiting blood from their mouths. Dust then arose from the army, bringing terrible darkness. I saw horses and men fleeing from the area, as the battlefield became covered with dust, O tamer of enemies. Others fell to the ground, vomiting large amounts of blood and unable to move because their hair was entangled with the locks of others.

Like wrestlers in combat, the mighty warriors dragged 23.50
each other off horses' backs and slaughtered one another. Many who lost their lives in the battle were carried away by their horses. Here and there, numerous others were seen fallen to the ground—men who had been eager for victory and who were proud of their heroism.

The earth was seen covered with hundreds and thousands of blood-soaked troops, their arms lopped off and their hair ripped away. It was impossible for anyone to move far by horse: the earth was strewn with slaughtered steeds and horsemen, and with soldiers who had fought very close together in battle, seeking to kill each other with a diversity of terrifying weapons. Mostly dead, they were still armed and holding their weapons, and their armor was drenched in blood.

23.55 sa muhūrtaṃ tato yuddhvā Saubalo ’tha viśāṃ pate
ṣaṭ|sāhasrair hayaiḥ śiṣṭair apāyāc Chakunis tataḥ.
tath” âiva Pāṇḍav’|ânīkaṃ rudhireṇa samukṣitam
ṣaṭ|sāhasrair hayaiḥ śiṣṭair apāyāc chrānta|vāhanam.

aśv’|ārohāś ca Pāṇḍūnām abruvan rudhir’|ôkṣitāḥ
su|saṃnikṛṣṭe saṃgrāme bhūyiṣṭhe tyakta|jīvitāḥ:

«na hi śakyaṃ rathair yoddhuṃ kuta eva mahā|gajaiḥ.
rathān eva rathā yāntu kuñjarāḥ kuñjarān api.
pratiyāto hi Śakuniḥ svam anīkam avasthitaḥ.
na punaḥ Saubalo rājā yuddham abhyāgamiṣyati!»

23.60 tatas tu Draupadeyāś ca te mattā mahā|dvi|pāḥ
prayayur yatra Pāñcālyo Dhṛṣṭadyumno mahā|rathaḥ.
Sahadevo ’pi Kauravya rajo|meghe samutthite
ekākī prayayau tatra yatra rājā Yudhiṣṭhiraḥ.

tatas teṣu prayāteṣu Śakuniḥ Saubalaḥ punaḥ
pārśvato ’bhyahanat kruddho Dhṛṣṭadyumnasya vāhinīm.
tat punas tumulaṃ yuddhaṃ prāṇāṃs tyaktv” âbhyavartata
tāvakānāṃ pareṣāṃ ca paras|para|vadh’|âiṣiṇām.

te c’ ânyonyam avaikṣanta tasmin vīra|samāgame
yodhāḥ paryapatan rājañ śataśo ’tha sahasraśaḥ.
23.65 asibhiś chidyamānānāṃ śirasāṃ loka|saṃkṣaye
prādur|āsīn mahāñ śabdas tālānāṃ patatām iva,
vimuktānāṃ śarīrāṇāṃ chinnānāṃ patatāṃ bhuvi
s’|āyudhānāṃ ca bāhūnām ūrūṇāṃ ca viśāṃ pate
āsīt kaṭakaṭā|śabdaḥ su|mahāṃl loma|harṣaṇaḥ.

After he had fought for a while, Shákuni, the son of Sú- 23.55
bala, departed with his remaining six thousand horses, O lord of the people.* Likewise, the blood-soaked army of the Pándavas retreated with their remaining six thousand horses, their animals exhausted.

The blood-soaked cavalrymen of the Pandus, who were ready to give up their lives in that extremely close combat, then said:

"It is impossible to fight here with chariots, let alone with mighty elephants. Chariots should advance against chariots and elephants against elephants. Shákuni has retreated and taken up position in his own regiment. The royal son of Súbala will not again return to battle!"

The sons of Dráupadi and the frenzied, mighty elephants 23.60
then moved toward Dhrishta·dyumna, that great warrior of Panchála. When the dust cloud lifted, Saha·deva proceeded on his own toward King Yudhi·shthira, O king of the Kurus.

After those warriors had proceeded, furious Shákuni, the son of Súbala, once again began to strike Dhrishta·dyumna's army in the flanks. There was then once more a turbulent battle between your troops and the enemy, both sides willing to give up their lives and eager to kill the other.

In that conflict between heroes, Your Majesty, the warriors eyed one another and then charged forward in their
hundreds and thousands. During that destruction of the 23.65
world, lord of the people, heads that had been chopped off by swords thumped loudly like falling coconuts. There was also the loud, thudding noise—making one's hair stand on end—of discarded, lacerated bodies falling to the ground, as well as thighs and weapon-bearing arms, Your Majesty.

nighnanto niśitaiḥ śastrair bhrātṝn putrān sakhīn api
yodhāḥ paripatanti sma yath" āmiṣa|kṛte khagāḥ.
anyonyaṃ pratisaṃrabdhāḥ samāsādya paras|param
«ahaṃ pūrvam ahaṃ pūrvam iti» nighnan* sahasraśaḥ.
saṃghāten' āsana|bhraṣṭair aśv'|ārohair gat'|āsubhiḥ
hayāḥ paripatanti sma śataśo 'tha sahasraśaḥ.
23.70 sphuratāṃ pratipiṣṭānām aśvānāṃ śīghra|gāminām
stanatāṃ ca manuṣyāṇāṃ saṃnaddhānāṃ viśāṃ pate
śakty|ṛṣṭi|prāsa|śabdaś ca tumulaḥ samapadyata
bhindatāṃ para|marmāṇi rājan durmantrite tava.

śram'|âbhibhūtāḥ saṃrabdhāḥ śrānta|vāhāḥ pipāsavaḥ
vikṣatāś ca śitaiḥ śastrair abhyavartanta tāvakāḥ.
mattā rudhira|gandhena bahavo 'tra vicetasaḥ
jaghnuḥ parān svakāṃś c' âiva prāptān prāptān an|antarān.
bahavaś ca gata|prāṇāḥ kṣatriyā jaya|gṛddhinaḥ
bhūmāv abhyapatan rājañ śara|vṛṣṭibhir āvṛtāḥ.
23.75 vṛka|gṛdhra|śṛgālānāṃ tumule modane 'hani
āsīd bala|kṣayo ghoras tava putrasya paśyataḥ.
nar'|âśva|kāyaiḥ saṃchannā bhūmir āsīd viśāṃ pate
rudhir'|ôdaka|citrā ca bhīrūṇāṃ bhaya|vardhinī.

asibhiḥ paṭṭiśaiḥ śūlais takṣamāṇāḥ punaḥ punaḥ
tāvakāḥ Pāṇḍaveyāś ca na nyavartanta Bhārata.
praharanto yathā|śakti yāvat prāṇasya dhāraṇam
yodhāḥ paripatanti sma vamanto rudhiraṃ vraṇaiḥ.
śiro gṛhītvā keśeṣu kabandhaḥ sma pradṛśyate

Like birds greedy for carrion, the warriors rushed around,
killing brothers, sons and friends with their sharp arrows.
Incensed at each other, thousands of troops slaughtered one
another in mutual combat, shouting, "Me first! Me first!"
Horses charged about in their hundreds and thousands,
their riders dead and fallen from their saddles through battle. There was a tumultuous noise of swift horses trem- 23.70
bling and rubbing against each other, of armed men roaring,
and of spears, javelins and arrows piercing the innards of
enemies—and all because of your bad policy, Your Majesty.

Your furious troops then began to withdraw when their
animals grew tired and when they themselves had become
thirsty, wounded by sharp weapons and overcome with fa-
tigue. Many on the battlefield became maddened and deranged by the smell of blood and indiscriminately killed
anyone that they came across, whether their own troops
or the enemy. Many warriors lost their lives in their greed
for victory and fell to the ground, enveloped by showers of
arrows, O king.

On that turbulent day, which brought delight to wolves, 23.75
vultures and jackals, the Kuru army suffered a terrible massacre under your son's very eyes. The earth was covered with
the bodies of men and horses, lord of the people, and it glistened with water-like blood, filling the timid with fear.

Although repeatedly mangled by swords, spears and pikes, neither your troops nor the Pándavas retreated, descendant of Bharata. Warriors rushed around, pouring blood from their wounds and striking their opponents as powerfully as they could, while still preserving their lives. A torso came into view; holding its head by the hair, it wielded a sharp

udyamya ca śitaṃ khaḍgaṃ rudhireṇa pariplutam.
23.80 tath" ôtthiteṣu bahuṣu kabandheṣu nar'|âdhipa
tathā rudhira|gandhena yodhāḥ kaśmalam āviśan.

mandī|bhūte tataḥ śabde Pāṇḍavānāṃ mahad balam
alp'|âvaśiṣṭais tura|gair abhyavartata Saubalaḥ.
tato 'bhyadhāvaṃs tvaritāḥ Pāṇḍavā jaya|gṛddhinaḥ
padātayaś ca nāgāś ca sādinaś c' ôdyat'|āyudhāḥ.
koṣṭhakī|kṛtya c' âpy enaṃ parikṣipya ca sarvaśaḥ
śastrair nānā|vidhair jaghnur yuddha|pāraṃ titīrṣavaḥ.

tvadīyās tāṃs tu saṃprekṣya sarvataḥ samabhidrutān
rath'|âśva|patti|dvi|radāḥ Pāṇḍavān abhidudruvuḥ.
23.85 ke cit padātayaḥ padbhir muṣṭibhiś ca paras|param
nijaghnuḥ samare śūrāḥ kṣīṇa|śastrās tato 'patan.
rathebhyo rathinaḥ petur dvi|pebhyo hasti|sādinaḥ
vimānebhyo divo bhraṣṭāḥ siddhāḥ puṇya|kṣayād iva.

evam anyonyam āyastā yodhā jaghnur mahā|have
pitṝn bhrātṝn vayasyāṃś ca putrān api tathā pare.
evam āsīd a|maryādaṃ yuddhaṃ Bharata|sattama
prās'|âsi|bāṇa|kalile vartamāne su|dāruṇe.

SAÑJAYA uvāca:

24.1 TASMIÑ ŚABDE mṛdau jāte Pāṇḍavair nihate bale
aśvaiḥ sapta|śataiḥ śiṣṭair upāvartata Saubalaḥ.
sa yātvā vāhinīṃ tūrṇam abravīt tvarayan yudhi
«yudhyadhvam iti» saṃhṛṣṭāḥ punaḥ punar arin|damāḥ.

sword that was covered with blood. Several other torsos 23.80
also stood up, and the stench of blood filled the troops with bewilderment.

As the noise diminished, the son of Súbala attacked the great army of the Pándavas with his few surviving horses. The Pándavas then swiftly charged forward, eager for victory and accompanied by infantrymen, elephants and cavalrymen brandishing their weapons. Encircling and surrounding Shákuni on all sides, they struck him with various weapons in their desire to cross to the farther shore of the battle.

On seeing the enemy rush toward them on every side, your chariots, horses, infantrymen and elephants charged
against the Pándavas. Some heroic foot soldiers, who had 23.85
lost their weapons, struck each other in battle with their feet and fists and then fell down. Charioteers fell from their chariots and elephant-riders from their elephants, just as *siddhas* fall from their palaces in the sky when their merit is exhausted.

In this way, the warriors toiled against each other in that great battle and killed fathers, brothers, friends, sons and their enemies. In this way, best of Bharatas, the battle was waged without limits among the horrific confusion of spears, swords and arrows.

SÁNJAYA said:

WHEN THE NOISE had lessened and the Pándavas had 24.1
slaughtered the Káurava army, Shákuni, the son of Súbala, returned to the battle with his seven hundred remaining horses. Quickly approaching the troops, Shákuni urged

aprcchat kṣatriyāṃs tatra kva nu rājā mahā|balaḥ.
Śakunes tad vacaḥ śrutvā tam ūcur Bharata'|rṣabha:
«asau tiṣṭhati Kauravyo raṇa|madhye mahā|balaḥ.
yatr' âitat su|mahac chattraṃ pūrṇa|candra|sama|prabham
yatra te sa|tanu|trāṇā rathās tiṣṭhanti daṃśitāḥ,
24.5 yatr' âiṣa tumulaḥ śabdaḥ Parjanya|ninad'|ôpamaḥ
tatra gaccha drutaṃ rājaṃs tato drakṣyasi Kauravam.»
evam uktas tu tair yodhaiḥ Śakuniḥ Saubalas tadā
prayayau tatra yatr' âsau putras tava nar'|âdhipa
sarvataḥ saṃvṛto vīraiḥ samare citra|yodhibhiḥ.
tato Duryodhanaṃ dṛṣṭvā rath'|ânīke vyavasthitam
sa rathāṃs tāvakān sarvān harṣayañ Śakunis tataḥ
Duryodhanam idaṃ vākyaṃ hṛṣṭa|rūpo viśāṃ pate
kṛta|kāryam iv' ātmānaṃ manyamāno 'bravīn nṛ|pam:
«jahi rājan rath'|ânīkam! aśvāḥ sarve jitā mayā.
n' â|tyaktvā jīvitaṃ saṃkhye śakyo jetuṃ Yudhiṣṭhiraḥ.
24.10 hate tasmin rath'|ânīke Pāṇḍaven' âbhipālite
gajān etān haniṣyāmaḥ padātīṃś c' êtarāṃs tathā.»
śrutvā tu vacanaṃ tasya tāvakā jaya|gṛddhinaḥ
javen' âbhyapatan hṛṣṭāḥ Pāṇḍavānām anīkinīm.
sarve vidhṛta|tūṇīrāḥ pragṛhīta|śar'|âsanāḥ
śar'|âsanāni dhunvānāḥ siṃha|nādaṃ praṇedire.
tato jyā|tala|nirghoṣaḥ punar āsīd viśāṃ pate
prādur āsīc charāṇāṃ ca su|muktānāṃ su|dāruṇaḥ.

them on to battle, saying again and again: "Fight with joy, you enemy-tamers!" Shákuni then asked the warriors where mighty King Dur·yódhana was. In response to his question, O bull of the Bharatas, they said:

"The mighty Káurava is stationed over there in the middle of the battlefield. Go over to where that huge parasol shines like the full moon, where those charioteers stand clad
in mail, their bodies protected by armor, and where that tu- 24.5
multuous noise resounds like Parjánya's thunder—go there quickly, Your Majesty, and you will see the Káurava king."

Addressed in this way by those warriors, Shákuni, the son of Súbala, advanced toward your son, Your Majesty, who was surrounded on all sides by heroes who fought with diverse skill in battle. Seeing Dur·yódhana stationed there in his chariot division, Shákuni joyfully said the following words to Dur·yódhana, raising the spirits of all your warriors, lord of the people. As if believing that all his goals had been achieved, Shákuni said to the king:

"Destroy the Pándavas' chariot division, Your Majesty! I have annihilated their horses already. Yudhi·shthira can be conquered only if one is willing to sacrifice one's life in
battle. When we have destroyed the chariot division that is 24.10
protected by the Pándava, we will slaughter their elephants, foot soldiers and other forces, too."

On hearing Shákuni's speech, your troops swiftly rushed with joy against the Pándavas' army, greedy for victory. Carrying their quivers and grasping their bows, they shouted lion-roars as they shook their bows. Once again, lord of the people, bowstrings and palms made a terrible noise as arrows were expertly fired.

tān samīpa|gatān dṛṣṭvā javen' ôdyata|kārmukān
uvāca Devakī|putraṃ Kuntī|putro Dhanañjayaḥ:
24.15 «coday' âśvān a|saṃbhrāntaḥ! praviś' âitad bal'|ârṇavam!
antam adya gamiṣyāmi śatrūṇāṃ niśitaiḥ śaraiḥ.
aṣṭādaśa dināny adya yuddhasy' âsya Janārdana
vartamānasya mahataḥ samāsādya paras|param.
ananta|kalpā dhvajinī bhūtvā hy eṣāṃ mah"|ātmanām
kṣayam adya gatā yuddhe. paśya daivaṃ yathā|vidham!
samudra|kalpaṃ ca balaṃ Dhārtarāṣṭrasya Mādhava
asmān āsādya saṃjātaṃ goṣ|pad'|ôpamam Acyuta.
hate Bhīṣme tu saṃdadhyāc chivaṃ syād iha Mādhava.
na ca tat kṛtavān mūḍho Dhārtarāṣṭraḥ su|bāliśaḥ.
24.20 uktaṃ Bhīṣmeṇa yad vākyaṃ hitaṃ tathyaṃ ca Mādhava
tac c' âpi n' âsau kṛtavān vīta|buddhiḥ Suyodhanaḥ.
tasmiṃs tu tumule Bhīṣme pracyute dharaṇī|tale
na jāne kāraṇaṃ kiṃ tu yena yuddham avartata.
mūḍhāṃs tu sarvathā manye Dhārtarāṣṭrān su|bāliśān
patite Śantanoḥ putre ye 'kārṣuḥ saṃyugaṃ punaḥ!
an|antaraṃ ca nihate Droṇe brahma|vidāṃ vare
Rādheye ca Vikarṇe ca n' âiv' âśāmyata vaiśasam.
alp'|âvaśiṣṭe sainye 'smin sūta|putre ca pātite
sa|putre vai nara|vyāghre n' âiv' âśāmyata vaiśasam.
24.25 Śrutāyuṣi hate vīre Jalasandhe ca Paurave
Śrutāyudhe ca nṛ|patau n' âiv' âśāmyata vaiśasam.
Bhūriśravasi Śalye ca Śālve c' âiva Janārdana

When Dhanan·jaya, the son of Kunti, saw these troops approaching with speed, wielding their bows, he said this to the son of Dévaki:

"Drive on the horses without wavering! Penetrate this 24.15
sea of soldiers! Today I will finish off the enemy with my sharpened arrows. This is the eighteenth day that both sides have clashed together in this vast battle, Janárdana. The almost limitless army that these heroes used to have will today be destroyed in battle. Observe how fate has been ordained!

Dhrita·rashtra's ocean-like army has become a mere cow's hoofprint after battling against us, Áchyuta.* There could have been happiness in this world, Mádhava, if peace had been made after Bhishma's death. But Dhrita·rashtra—that
stupid fool—did not act in that way. Although Bhishma 24.20
offered proper and true advice, Su·yódhana witlessly disobeyed his words. I do not know why the battle continued after Bhishma fell to the ground in that tumult. I believe that Dhrita·rashtra's followers must be utterly foolish and stupid to have returned to battle after Shántanu's son* had fallen!

Afterward the carnage did not even cease when Drona was slaughtered—that best of Brahma-knowing men—nor when Radha's son* or Vikárna was killed. Nor did the carnage even cease when the Káurava army had only a few survivors and Karna, that charioteer's son and tiger-like man,
was killed together with his son. Nor did the carnage even 24.25
cease when heroic Shrutáyush and Jala·sandha, the descendant of Puru, were killed, together with King Shrutáyudha. Nor did the carnage even cease when Bhuri·shravas, Shalya,

Āvantyeṣu ca vīreṣu n' âiv' âśāmyata vaiśasam.
Jayadrathe ca nihate rākṣase c' âpy Alāyudhe
Bāhlike Somadatte ca n' âiv' âśāmyata vaiśasam
Bhagadatte hate śūre Kāmboje ca su|dāruṇe
Duḥśāsane ca nihate n' âiv' âśāmyata vaiśasam.

dṛṣṭvā vinihatāñ śūrān pṛthaṅ māṇḍalikān nṛ|pān
balinaś ca raṇe Kṛṣṇa n' âiv' âśāmyata vaiśasam.
24.30 akṣauhiṇī|patīn dṛṣṭvā Bhīmasena|nipātitān
mohād vā yadi vā lobhān n' âiv' âśāmyata vaiśasam.
ko nu rāja|kule jātaḥ Kauraveyo viśeṣataḥ
nirarthakaṃ mahad vairaṃ kuryād anyaḥ Suyodhanāt.
guṇato 'bhyadhikāñ jñātvā balataḥ śauryato 'pi vā
a|mūḍhaḥ ko nu yudhyeta jānan prājño hit'|â|hitam?

yan na tasya mano hy āsīt tvay" ôktasya hitaṃ vacaḥ
praśame Pāṇḍavaiḥ sārdhaṃ so 'nyasya śṛṇuyāt katham?
yena Śāntanavo vīro Droṇo Vidura eva ca
pratyākhyātāḥ śamasy' ârthe kiṃ nu tasy' âdya bheṣajam?
24.35 maurkhyād yena pitā vṛddhaḥ pratyākhyāto Janārdana
tathā mātā hitaṃ vākyaṃ bhāṣamāṇā hit'|âiṣiṇī
pratyākhyātā hy a|sat|kṛtya sa kasmād rocayed vacaḥ?
kul'|ânta|karaṇo vyaktaṃ jāta eṣa Janārdana.
tath" âsya dṛśyate ceṣṭā nītiś c' âiva viśāṃ pate.
n' âiṣa dāsyati no rājyam iti me matir Acyuta.

Shalva or the Avánti heroes were slaughtered, Janárdana. Nor did the carnage even cease when Jayad·ratha, the demon Aláyudha, Báhlika or Soma·datta was killed. Nor did the carnage even cease when heroic Bhaga·datta, or the cruel king of Kambója, or Duhshásana was slain.

The carnage did not even cease, Krishna, when they saw that their heroes were slaughtered, kings who ruled over wide territories and who were mighty in war. Nor—whether 24.30
out of folly or perhaps greed—did it even cease when they saw that their army leaders had been slain by Bhima·sena. Except for Su·yódhana, what person born into a family of kings, especially a Káurava, would wage such a huge and pointless feud? What person who is possessed of his senses and aware of profit and disadvantage would knowingly fight against an enemy that is superior in virtue, strength and heroism?

Why would Dur·yódhana listen to another person if he was disinclined to make peace with the Pándavas when you spoke to him with beneficial words? What medicine can there today be for the man who rejected the heroic son of Shántanu, Drona and also Vídura when they sued for peace? Why, Janárdana, would he listen to advice when, out of stu- 24.35
pidity, he ignored his elderly father and also disrespectfully ignored his mother, even though she spoke beneficial words to him and wished him well? It is clear that he was born to destroy his family, Janárdana. His actions and conduct show that this is the case, lord of the people. I do not believe that this man will give us our kingdom, Áchyuta.

ukto 'haṃ bahuśas tāta Vidureṇa mah"|ātmanā
na jīvan dāsyate bhāgaṃ Dhārtarāṣṭras tu māna|da.
yāvat prāṇā dhariṣyanti Dhārtarāṣṭrasya dur|mateḥ
tāvad yuṣmāsv a|pāpeṣu pracariṣyati pāpakaṃ.
na ca śakyo 'nyathā jetum ṛte yuddhena Mādhava
ity abravīt sadā māṃ hi Viduraḥ satya|darśanaḥ.
24.40 tat sarvam adya jānāmi vyavasāyaṃ dur|ātmanaḥ
yad uktaṃ vacanaṃ tena Vidureṇa mah"|ātmanā.

yo hi śrutvā vacaḥ pathyaṃ Jāmadagnyād yathā|tatham
avāmanyata dur|buddhir dhruvaṃ nāśa|mukhe sthitaḥ.
uktaṃ hi bahuśaḥ siddhair jāta|mātre Suyodhane
enaṃ prāpya dur|ātmānaṃ kṣayaṃ kṣatraṃ gamiṣyati.
tad idaṃ vacanaṃ teṣāṃ niruktaṃ vai Janārdana;
kṣayaṃ yātā hi rājāno Duryodhana|kṛte bhṛśam.

so 'dya sarvān raṇe yodhān nihaniṣyāmi Mādhava.
kṣatriyeṣu hateṣv āśu śūnye ca śibire kṛte,
24.45 vadhāya c' ātmano 'smābhiḥ saṃyugaṃ rocayiṣyati.
tad antaṃ hi bhaved vairam. anumānena Mādhava
evaṃ paśyāmi Vārṣṇeya cintayan prajñayā svayā
Vidurasya ca vākyena ceṣṭayā ca dur|ātmanaḥ.
tasmād yāhi camūṃ vīra yāvadd hanmi śitaiḥ śaraiḥ
Duryodhanaṃ mahā|bāho vāhinīṃ c' âsya saṃyuge.
kṣemam adya kariṣyāmi dharma|rājasya Mādhava
hatv" âitad dur|balaṃ sainyaṃ Dhārtarāṣṭrasya paśyataḥ!»

Dear friend and giver of honors, great-spirited Vídura has told me many times that Dhrita·rashtra's son will not give us our share of the kingdom while he is alive. As long as he retains his life-breath, the foolish son of Dhrita·rashtra will act wrongfully toward you, even though you are without sin. Vídura, that exponent of truth, has always told me that Dur·yódhana can be conquered only through battle, Mádhava. Today I realize that heroic Vídura foretold all of evil 24.40
Dur·yódhana's conduct.

It is a foolish man who hears but rejects the proper and true words of Jamad·agni's son;* that person certainly stands in the mouth of destruction. As soon as Su·yódhana was born, the *siddhas* said several times that the warrior race would be destroyed because of that evil man. Their words have come true, Janárdana; for numerous kings have been massacred on behalf of Dur·yódhana.

Today, Mádhava, I will annihilate all their troops in battle. And when I have swiftly killed their warriors and emptied their camp, Dur·yódhana will himself seek battle with
us—to his own destruction. Then the hostilities will come 24.45
to an end. Descendant of Madhu and Vrishni, I have reached this viewpoint through inference, through thinking with my own intellect, and as a result of Vídura's words and evil Dur·yódhana's actions. Therefore advance toward their army, O mighty-armed hero, so that I can slay Dur·yódhana and his troops with my sharp arrows in battle! Under the very eyes of Dhrita·rashtra's son, Mádhava, I will bring security to the King of Righteousness by slaying this weak army!"

SAÑJAYA uvāca:

abhīṣu|hasto Dāśārhas tath" ôktaḥ Savyasācinā
tad bal'|âugham a|mitrāṇām a|bhītaḥ prāviśad balāt.
24.50 śar'|âsana|vanaṃ ghoraṃ śakti|kaṇṭaka|saṃkulam
gadā|parigha|panthānaṃ ratha|nāga|mahā|drumam,
haya|patti|latā|kīrṇaṃ gāhamāno mahā|yaśāḥ
vyacarat tatra Govindo rathen' âtipatākinā.
te hayāḥ pāṇḍurā rājan vahanto 'rjunam āhave
dikṣu sarvāsv adṛśyanta Dāśārheṇa pracoditāḥ.

tataḥ prāyād rathen' ājau Savyasācī paran|tapaḥ
kirañ śara|śatāṃs tīkṣṇān vāri|dhārā ghano yathā.
prādur|āsīn mahāñ śabdaḥ śarāṇāṃ nata|parvaṇām
iṣubhiś chādyamānānāṃ samare Savyasācinā.
24.55 a|sajjantas tanu|treṣu śar'|âughāḥ prāpatan bhuvi.
Indr'|âśani|sama|sparśā Gāṇḍīva|preṣitāḥ śarāḥ.
narān nāgān samāhatya hayāṃś c' âpi viśāṃ pate
apatanta raṇe bāṇāḥ pataṅgā iva ghoṣiṇaḥ.
āsīt sarvam avacchannaṃ Gāṇḍīva|preṣitaiḥ śaraiḥ
na prājñāyanta samare diśo vā pradiśo 'pi vā.
sarvam āsīj jagat pūrṇaṃ Pārtha|nām'|âṅkitaiḥ śaraiḥ
rukma|puṅkhais taila|dhautaiḥ karmāra|parimārjitaiḥ.

te dahyamānāḥ Pārthena pāvaken' êva kuñjarāḥ
Pārthaṃ na prajahur ghorā vadhyamānāḥ śitaiḥ śaraiḥ.
24.60 śara|cāpa|dharaḥ Pārthaḥ prajvalann iva bhās|karaḥ
dadāha samare yodhān kakṣam agnir iva jvalan.

SÁNJAYA said:

Addressed in this way by Savya·sachin, Krishna the Dashárha took hold of the reins and fearlessly penetrated the
mass of the enemy army with force. The army was like a 24.50
terrifying forest of bows. Maces and clubs were its paths, and it teemed with thorns that were spears. Its tall trees were chariots and elephants, and it abounded with creepers made up of horses and infantrymen. Plunging into that army, glorious Go·vinda rampaged with his many-bannered chariot. Urged on by the Dashárha, the white horses could be seen carrying Árjuna everywhere in battle, Your Majesty.

Enemy-scorching Savya·sachin then advanced into battle on his chariot, spraying out hundreds of arrows, like clouds pouring torrents of rain. His straight arrows made a vast noise, as did the men who were covered with Savya·sa-
chin's shafts in battle. Swarms of arrows fell to the ground, 24.55
unimpeded by any armor. The shafts fired from the Gandíva bow crashed like Indra's thunderbolts. Arrows flew on the battlefield like buzzing bees, hitting men, elephants and horses, lord of the people. Everything became covered by shafts fired from the Gandíva and it was impossible to see either the major or the minor directions in the battle. The entire world became full of arrows that were branded with the Partha's name. Polished by blacksmiths, they were feathered with gold and cleansed with oil.

The Káuravas did not flee from the son of Pritha as he slaughtered them with his sharp arrows and incinerated
them like a fire burning elephants. Wielding his bow and 24.60
arrows, the son of Pritha, who was like the blazing sun, scorched the warriors in battle like a fire burning dry grass.

yathā van'|ânte vana|pair visṛṣṭaḥ
kakṣaṃ dahet kṛṣṇa|gatiḥ su|ghoṣaḥ
bhūri|drumaṃ śuṣka|latā|vitānaṃ
bhṛśaṃ samṛddho jvalanaḥ pratāpī,
evaṃ sa nārāca|gaṇa|pratāpī
śar'|ârcir ucc'|âvaca|tigma|tejāḥ
dadāha sarvāṃ tava putra|senām
a|mṛṣyamāṇas tarasā tarasvī.
tasy' êṣavaḥ prāṇa|harāḥ su|muktā
n' âsajjan vai varmasu rukma|puṅkhāḥ.
na ca dvitīyaṃ pramumoca bāṇaṃ
nare haye vā parama|dvi|pe vā.
aneka|rūp'|ākṛtibhir hi bāṇair
mahā|rath'|ânīkam anupraviśya
sa eva ekas tava putra|senāṃ
jaghāna daityān iva vajra|pāṇiḥ.

SAÑJAYA uvāca:

25.1 ASYATĀṂ YATAMĀNĀNĀṂ śūrāṇām a|nivartinām
saṃkalpam akaron moghaṃ Gāṇḍīvena Dhanañjayaḥ.
Indr'|âśani|sama|sparśān a|viṣahyān mah"|âujasaḥ
visṛjan dṛśyate bāṇān dhārā muñcann iv' âmbu|daḥ.
tat sainyaṃ Bharata|śreṣtha vadhyamānaṃ Kirīṭinā
saṃpradudrāva saṃgrāmāt tava putrasya paśyataḥ.
pitṝn bhrātṝn parityajya vayasyān api c' âpare.
hata|dhuryā rathāḥ ke cidd hata|sūtās tath" âpare.
bhagn'|âkṣa|yuga|cakr'|ēṣāḥ ke cid āsan viśāṃ pate.
25.5 anyeṣāṃ sāyakāḥ kṣīṇās tath" ânye bāṇa|pīḍitāḥ.

Just as when forest-dwellers leave a fire at the edge of a wood and the violent, strong and roaring flame completely burns up the forest, which is thick with trees and has canopies of dry creepers; just so, Árjuna blazed fiercely in every direction and, with his arrows as flames, mercilessly incinerated all your son's army with swift speed, scorching them with hordes of shafts.

Árjuna skillfully fired his gold-feathered, life-taking arrows, which were unimpeded by any armor. Nor did he shoot a second arrow against any man, horse or fine elephant. Penetrating the huge chariot division with his various types of arrows, Árjuna destroyed your son's army all on his own, just as thunderbolt-wielding Indra destroyed the demons.

SÁNJAYA said:

WITH HIS Gandíva bow, Dhanan·jaya foiled the aims of 25.1
the Káurava heroes as they hurled their weapons and struggled against him, refusing to retreat. Like a cloud pouring torrents of rain, Árjuna was seen firing arrows that were powerful and irresistible and that crashed like Indra's thunderbolts. Under your son's very eyes, best of Bharatas, the Káurava army fled from the battle as it was slaughtered by diadem-adorned Árjuna.

Some charioteers abandoned their fathers and brothers, while others abandoned their friends. Some lost their horses, others their drivers. Some charioteers, lord of the people,
had shattered axles, yokes, wheels or shafts.* Some warriors 25.5
ran out of arrows, others were pummeled by darts. Op-

a|kṣatā yugapat ke cit prādravan bhaya|pīḍitāḥ.
ke cit putrān upādāya hata|bhūyiṣṭha|bāndhavāḥ
vicukruśuḥ pitṝṃs tv anye sahāyān apare punaḥ.
bāndhavāṃś ca nara|vyāghra bhrātṝn saṃbandhinas tathā
dudruvuḥ ke cid utsṛjya tatra tatra viśāṃ pate.

bahavo 'tra bhṛśaṃ viddhā muhyamānā mahā|rathāḥ
niśvasantaḥ sma dṛśyante Pārtha|bāṇa|hatā narāḥ.
tān anye ratham āropya hy āśvāsya ca muhūrtakam;
viśrāntāś ca vitṛptāś ca punar yuddhāya jagmire.
25.10 tān apāsya gatāḥ ke cit punar eva yuyutsavaḥ
kurvantas tava putrasya śāsanaṃ yuddha|dur|madāḥ.

pānīyam apare pītvā paryāśvāsya ca vāhanam
varmāṇi ca samāropya ke cid Bharata|sattama.
samāśvāsy' âpare bhrātṝn nikṣipya śibire 'pi ca
putrān anye pitṝn anye punar yuddham arocayan.
sajjayitvā rathān ke cid yathā|mukhyaṃ viśāṃ pate
āplutya Pāṇḍav'|ânīkaṃ punar yuddham arocayan.
te śūrāḥ kiṅkiṇī|jālaiḥ samācchannā babhāsire
trai|lokya|vijaye yuktā yathā daiteya|dānavāḥ.
25.15 āgamya sahasā ke cid rathaiḥ svarṇa|vibhūṣitaiḥ
Pāṇḍavānām anīkeṣu Dhṛṣṭadyumnam ayodhayan.
Dhṛṣṭadyumno 'pi Pāñcālyaḥ Śikhaṇḍī ca mahā|rathaḥ
Nākulis tu Śatānīko rath'|ânīkam ayodhayan.
Pāñcālyas tu tataḥ kruddhaḥ sainyena mahatā vṛtaḥ

pressed by fear, some fled all at once, even though they were
uninjured. Some, who had lost most of their relatives, took
hold of their sons and repeatedly called out for their fathers,
while others did the same for their friends. Here and there,
tiger among men and lord of the people, other warriors fled,
abandoning their relatives, brothers and kinsmen.

We saw many great warriors on the battlefield that had
been hit by the arrows of Pritha's son; severely wounded,
they were bewildered and breathing heavily. Some warriors
pulled these men onto their chariots and helped them re-
cuperate for a while; when they had rested and composed
themselves, they once again returned to battle. Others— 25.10
difficult to defeat in war—abandoned such men and obeyed
your son's command by advancing forward, eager to fight
once more.

Some drank water and rested their animals, while others
put on their armor, best of Bharatas. Some helped their
brothers and then left them at camp; others did the same
for their fathers or sons and then once more illuminated the
battle. Some prepared their chariots in order of importance
and then once more illuminated the battle, plunging into
the Pándava army. Draped with nets of bells, the heroes
looked radiant, just like the *daitéya*s or *dánava*s when they
were intent on conquering the three worlds.*

Some of the warriors then suddenly advanced forward in 25.15
gold-adorned chariots and battled against Dhrishta·dyum-
na among the Pándava forces. The Panchála prince Dhri-
shta·dyumna, the great warrior Shikhándin, and Shataníka,
the son of Nákula, all fought against this chariot division.
Filled with violent rage and surrounded by a huge force,

abhyadravat su|saṃkruddhas tāvakān hantum udyataḥ.
tatas tv āpatatas tasya tava putro jan'|âdhipa
bāṇa|saṃghān anekān vai preṣayām āsa Bhārata.
Dhṛṣṭadyumnas tato rājaṃs tava putreṇa dhanvinā
nārācair ardha|nārācair bahubhiḥ kṣipra|kāribhiḥ,
25.20 vatsa|dantaiś ca bāṇaiś ca karmāra|parimārjitaiḥ
aśvāṃś ca caturo hatvā bāhvor urasi c' ârpitaḥ.

so 'tividdho mah"|êṣv|āsas tottr'|ârdita iva dvi|paḥ
tasy' âśvāṃś caturo bāṇaiḥ preṣayām āsa mṛtyave.
sāratheś c' âsya bhallena śiraḥ kāyād apāharat.
tato Duryodhano rājā pṛṣṭham āruhya vājinaḥ
apākrāmadd hata|ratho n' âtidūram arin|damaḥ.
dṛṣṭvā ca hata|vikrāntaṃ svam anīkaṃ mahā|balaḥ
tava putro mahā|rāja prayayau yatra Saubalaḥ.

tato ratheṣu bhagneṣu tri|sāhasrā mahā|dvi|pāḥ
Pāṇḍavān rathinaḥ sarvān samantāt paryavārayan.
25.25 te vṛtāḥ samare pañca gaj'|ânīkena Bhārata
aśobhanta mahā|rāja grahā vyāptā ghanair iva.

tato 'rjuno mahā|rāja labdha|lakṣo mahā|bhujaḥ
viniryayau rathen' âiva śvet'|âśvaḥ Kṛṣṇa|sārathiḥ.
taiḥ samantāt parivṛtaḥ kuñjaraiḥ parvat'|ôpamaiḥ
nārācair vimalais tīkṣṇair gaj'|ânīkam ayodhayat.
tatr' âika|bāṇa|nihatān apaśyāma mahā|gajān
patitān pātyamānāṃś ca nirbhinnān Savyasācinā.

the Panchála prince angrily charged forward, determined to kill your troops. Your son, however, fired several volleys of arrows at Dhrishta·dyumna as he attacked, O lord of the people. Your bow-wielding son then killed Dhrishta·dyumna's four horses, Your Majesty, and shot Dhrishta·dyumna in the chest and arms with numerous swift arrows, as well
as with half-arrows, arrows that had tips like calves' teeth, 25.20
and shafts that were polished by blacksmiths.

But although that great archer was badly wounded, like an elephant pained by goads, Dhrishta·dyumna sent Dur·yódhana's four horses to their death with his arrows. He then struck off the head of Dur·yódhana's charioteer with a spear-headed shaft. On losing his chariot, enemy-taming Dur·yódhana climbed onto the back of a horse and fled to an area that was not too far away. Seeing that his army had lost its courage, Dur·yódhana then proceeded toward the son of Súbala, Your Majesty.

After the Káurava chariots had been crushed in this way, three thousand huge elephants encircled all the Pándava
charioteers on every side. The five warriors looked glorious 25.25
when they were surrounded by this force of elephants in battle, just like planets encompassed by clouds, great king.

With his white horses and dark charioteer, mighty-armed Árjuna, who always hits his mark, then advanced on his chariot, Your Majesty.* Although surrounded on every side by those mountain-like elephants, he battled against the force of elephants with his sharp and gleaming arrows. We watched Savya·sachin pierce the enormous elephants and strike them with one arrow each; some of them had already fallen, others were still falling down. Seeing those elephants,

Bhīmasenas tu tān dṛṣṭvā nāgān matta|gaj'|ôpamaḥ
kareṇ' ādāya mahatīṃ gadām abhyapatad balī
ath' āplutya rathāt tūrṇaṃ daṇḍa|pāṇir iv' Ântakaḥ.
25.30 tam udyata|gadaṃ dṛṣṭvā Pāṇḍavānāṃ mahā|ratham
vitresus tāvakāḥ sainyāḥ śakṛn|mūtre ca susruvuḥ.
āvignaṃ ca balaṃ sarvaṃ gadā|haste Vṛkodare.

gadayā Bhīmasenena bhinna|kumbhān rajasvalān
dhāvamānān apaśyāma kuñjarān parvat'|ôpamān.
prādravan kuñjarās te tu Bhīmasena|gadā|hatāḥ
petur ārta|svaraṃ kṛtvā chinna|pakṣā iv' âdrayaḥ.
prabhinna|kumbhāṃs tu bahūn dravamāṇān itas tataḥ
patamānāṃś ca saṃprekṣya vitresus tava sainikāḥ.

Yudhiṣṭhiro 'pi saṃkruddho Mādrī|putrau ca Pāṇḍavau
gārdhra|patraiḥ śitair bāṇair ninyur vai Yama|sādhanam.
25.35 Dhṛṣṭadyumnas tu samare parājitya nar'|âdhipam
apakrānte tava sute haya|pṛṣṭhaṃ samāśrite,
dṛṣṭvā ca Pāṇḍavān sarvān kuñjaraiḥ parivāritān
Dhṛṣṭadyumno mahā|rāja sahasā samupādravat
putraḥ Pañcāla|rājasya jighāṃsuḥ kuñjarān yayau.

a|dṛṣṭvā tu rath'|ânīke Duryodhanam arin|damam
Aśvatthāmā Kṛpaś c' âiva Kṛtavarmā ca Sātvataḥ
apṛcchan kṣatriyāṃs tatra kva nu Duryodhano gataḥ.
a|paśyamānā rājānaṃ vartamāne jana|kṣaye
manvānā nihataṃ tatra tava putraṃ mahā|rathāḥ
vivarṇa|vadanā bhūtvā paryapṛcchanta te sutam.

mighty Bhima·sena—who himself resembled a maddened elephant—took his huge mace in his hand and rushed forward, swiftly jumping out of his chariot, like Death bearing
his staff. Your troops became terrified when they saw that 25.30
great warrior of the Pándavas wielding his mace, and they soiled themselves with feces and urine. The entire army became alarmed when Vrikódara took his mace in his hand.

We watched as the mountain-like elephants fled, covered with dust, their foreheads cracked open by Bhima·sena with his mace. Struck by Bhima·sena's mace, the elephants ran away and fell down with cries of pain, just like the mountains did when they had their wings cut off. Your troops became terrified when they saw the elephants falling and fleeing here and there in great numbers, their foreheads split open.

Furious Yudhi·shthira and the Pándava sons of Madri also sent the elephants to Yama's abode with their sharp,
vulture-feathered arrows. On seeing that all the Pándavas 25.35
were surrounded by elephants, the Panchála prince Dhrishta·dyumna—after he had beaten the Káurava king in battle and your son had fled on the back of a horse—also charged forward violently and advanced against the elephants, eager to kill them, great king.

Meanwhile, Ashva·tthaman, Kripa and Krita·varman, the Sátvata, asked the warriors on the battlefield where Dur·yódhana had gone, since they could not see him in the chariot division. Unable to see their king during that slaughter of human beings, the great warriors worried that your son had died in the carnage and asked after him with pale faces. Some men replied that Dur·yódhana had fled from the invincible

āhuḥ ke cidd hate sūte prayāto yatra Saubalaḥ
hitvā Pañcāla|rājasya tad anīkaṃ dur|utsahaṃ.
25.40 apare tv abruvaṃs tatra kṣatriyā bhṛśa|vikṣatāḥ:
«Duryodhanena kiṃ kāryaṃ. drakṣyadhvaṃ yadi jīvati!
yudhyadhvaṃ sahitāḥ sarve! kiṃ vo rājā kariṣyati?»

te kṣatriyāḥ kṣatair gātrair hata|bhūyiṣṭha|vāhanāḥ
śaraiḥ saṃpīḍyamānās tu n' âtivyaktam ath' âbruvan:
«idaṃ sarvaṃ balaṃ hanmo yena sma parivāritāḥ.
ete sarve gajān hatvā upayānti sma Pāṇḍavāḥ.»

śrutvā tu vacanaṃ teṣām Aśvatthāmā mahā|balaḥ
bhittvā Pañcāla|rājasya tad anīkaṃ dur|utsahaṃ.
Kṛpaś ca Kṛtavarmā ca prayayur yatra Saubalaḥ
rath'|ânīkaṃ parityajya śūrāḥ su|dṛḍha|dhanvinaḥ.
25.45 tatas teṣu prayāteṣu Dhṛṣṭadyumna|puraskṛtāḥ
āyayuḥ Pāṇḍavā rājan vinighnantaḥ sma tāvakān.
dṛṣṭvā tu tān āpatataḥ saṃprahṛṣṭān mahā|rathān
parākrāntāṃs tathā vīrān nirāśaṃ jīvite tadā
vivarṇa|mukha|bhūyiṣṭham abhavat tāvakaṃ balam.
parikṣīṇa|yudhān dṛṣṭvā tān ahaṃ parivāritān
rājan balena dvy|aṅgena tyaktvā jīvitam ātmanaḥ,
ātmanā pañcamo 'yuddhyaṃ Pāñcālasya balena ha
tasmin deśe vyavasthāya yatra Śāradvataḥ sthitaḥ.
saṃpradrutā vayaṃ pañca Kirīṭi|śara|pīḍitāḥ.
Dhṛṣṭadyumnaṃ mahā|raudraṃ

army of the Panchála prince when his chariot-driver had been killed and that he had proceeded toward Súbala's son.
Other warriors, who had been badly wounded in the battle, 25.40
said:

"What need is there for Dur·yódhana? See if he lives! You should all unite and fight! What will the king do for you?"

As they were pounded by arrows, these warriors, who had injured limbs and had lost most of their animals, then said in unclear tones:

"Let us destroy this entire army that has surrounded us! The Pándavas have all killed the elephants and have advanced upon us!"

Hearing their words, mighty Ashva·tthaman burst through the army of the Panchála prince, even though it was difficult to assail. Heroic Kripa and Krita·varman then left behind the chariot division and advanced toward Súbala's son, armed with strong bows.

As the Káurava warriors advanced, the Pándavas moved 25.45
forward with Dhrishta·dyumna in front of them, slaughtering your men. At the sight of those heroic and mighty warriors charging bravely forward with joy, your troops lost hope for their lives and many of their faces became drained of color. When I saw that our troops were diminishing and surrounded, I, too, offered up my own life, Your Majesty. As a fifth leader, I fought against the army of the Panchála prince with a twofold force, taking up position where the son of Sharádvat stood. The five of us, however, fled, overwhelmed by the arrows of diadem-adorned Árjuna. We

tatra no 'bhūd raṇo mahān;
jitās tena vayaṃ sarve
vyapayāma raṇāt tataḥ.
25.50 ath' âpaśyaṃ Sātyakiṃ tam upāyāntaṃ mahā|ratham
rathaiś catuḥ|śatair. vīro māṃ abhyadravad āhave.
Dhṛṣṭadyumnād ahaṃ muktaḥ kathañ cic chrānta|vāhanāt
patito Mādhav'|ânīkaṃ duṣ|kṛtī narakaṃ yathā.
tatra yuddham abhūd ghoraṃ muhūrtam ati|dāruṇam.
Sātyakis tu mahā|bāhur mama hatvā paricchadam
jīva|grāham agṛhṇān māṃ mūrchitaṃ patitaṃ bhuvi.
tato muhūrtād iva tad gaj'|ânīkam avadhyata
gadayā Bhīmasenena nārācair Arjunena ca.
abhipiṣṭair mahā|nāgaiḥ samantāt parvat'|ôpamaiḥ
n' âtiprasiddh" âiva gatiḥ Pāṇḍavānām ajāyata.
25.55 ratha|mārgaṃ tataś cakre Bhīmaseno mahā|balaḥ
Pāṇḍavānāṃ mahā|rāja vyapākarṣan mahā|gajān.
Aśvatthāmā Kṛpaś c' âiva Kṛtavarmā ca Sātvataḥ
a|paśyanto rath'|ânīke Duryodhanam arin|damam
rājānaṃ mṛgayām āsus tava putraṃ mahā|ratham.
parityajya ca Pāñcālyaṃ prayātā yatra Saubalaḥ
rājño darśana|saṃvignā vartamāne jana|kṣaye.

SAÑJAYA UVĀCA:

26.1 GAJ'|ÂNĪKE HATE tasmin Pāṇḍu|putreṇa Bhārata
vadhyamāne bale c' âiva Bhīmasenena saṃyuge,
carantaṃ ca tathā dṛṣṭvā Bhīmasenam arin|damam
daṇḍa|hastaṃ yathā kruddham antakaṃ prāṇa|hāriṇam.

then fought a huge battle against terrifying Dhrishta·dyumna, but he defeated all of us and we retreated from the battlefield.

I then saw the great warrior Sátyaki attacking with four 25.50
hundred chariots. The hero charged against me in battle. I had somehow escaped from Dhrishta·dyumna because his horses were tired, but I fell among the Mádhava's regiment like a sinner falling into hell. For a while, the battle became fierce and extremely horrific. Mighty-armed Sátyaki struck off my armor and captured me alive as I lay on the ground unconscious.

In a mere moment, our elephant division was slaughtered by Bhima·sena with his mace and by Árjuna with his arrows. The Pándavas' pathway became completely blocked by the huge, mountain-like elephants that lay pressed together on all sides. But powerful Bhima·sena made a chariot- 25.55
path for the Pándavas by dragging away the huge elephants, great king.

Unable to see enemy-taming Dur·yódhana in the chariot division, Ashva·tthaman, Kripa and the Sátvata Krita·varman searched for your son, that king and mighty warrior. As the human massacre continued, they left behind the Panchála prince and advanced toward Súbala's son, desperate to see their king.

SÁNJAYA said:

DESCENDANT OF BHARATA, when the son of Pandu had 26.1
destroyed the elephant division and the Káurava army was being slaughtered by Bhima·sena in war, your surviving sons gathered together in battle after they saw that enemy-taming

sametya samare rājan hata|śeṣāḥ sutās tava
a|dṛśyamāne Kauravye putre Duryodhane tava
sodaryāḥ sahitā bhūtvā Bhīmasenam upādravan.

Durmarṣaṇaḥ Śrutāntaś ca Jaitro Bhūribalo Raviḥ
Jayatsenaḥ Sujātaś ca tathā Durviṣaho 'ri|hā
26.5 Durvimocana|nāmā ca Duṣpradharṣas tath" âiva ca
Śrutarvā ca mahā|bāhuḥ sarve yuddha|viśāradāḥ
ity ete sahitā bhūtvā tava putrāḥ samantataḥ
Bhīmasenam abhidrutya rurudhuḥ sarvato|diśam.

tato Bhīmo mahā|rāja sva|ratham punar āsthitaḥ
mumoca niśitān bāṇān putrāṇāṃ tava marmasu.
te kīryamāṇā Bhīmena putrās tava mahā|raṇe
Bhīmasenam apāsedhan pravaṇād iva kuñjaram.
tataḥ kruddho raṇe Bhīmaḥ śiro Durmarṣaṇasya ha
kṣura|preṇa pramathy' āśu pātayām āsa bhū|tale.
26.10 tato 'pareṇa bhallena sarv'|āvaraṇa|bhedinā
Śrutāntam avadhīd Bhīmas tava putraṃ mahā|rathaḥ.
Jayatsenaṃ tato viddhvā nārācena hasann iva
pātayām āsa Kauravyaṃ rath'|ôpasthād arin|damaḥ.
sa papāta rathād rājan bhūmau tūrṇam mamāra ca.

Śrutarvā tu tato Bhīmaṃ kruddho vivyādha māriṣa
śatena gṛdhra|vājānāṃ śarāṇāṃ nata|parvaṇām.
tataḥ kruddho raṇe Bhīmo Jaitraṃ Bhūribalaṃ Ravim
trīn etāṃs tribhir ānarchad viṣ'|âgni|pratimaiḥ śaraiḥ.
te hatā nyapatan bhūmau syandanebhyo mahā|rathāḥ
vasante puṣpa|śabalā nikṛttā iva kiṃśukāḥ.

Bhima·sena was careering around like staff-bearing Death, who snatches away lives in a rage. Although your son, the Káurava Dur·yódhana, was still absent, the brothers charged against Bhima·sena in unison, Your Majesty.

Durmárshana, Shrutánta, Jaitra, Bhuri·bala, Ravi, Jayat·
sena, Sujáta, enemy-slaying Dúrvishaha, Durvimóchana, 26.5
Dushpradhársha and huge-armed Shrutárvan—all these battle-skilled sons of yours gathered from every side. Attacking Bhima·sena, they blocked him off in every direction.

Bhima then climbed once more onto his chariot and fired sharp arrows at your sons' vital organs, great king. But although they were pelted by Bhima in that great battle, your sons drove Bhima·sena away, like an elephant driven out of a forest. Filled with battle-rage, Bhima swiftly struck Durmárshana's head with a razor-edged arrow and sent it hurtling
to the ground. With another spear-headed arrow that could 26.10
cut through any obstacle, Bhima—that great warrior—then slaughtered your son Shrutánta. With almost a laugh, the enemy-tamer then pierced Jayat·sena with an iron shaft and toppled the Káurava from his chariot platform. Jayat·sena fell from his chariot and quickly died on the ground, Your Majesty.

Wrathful Shrutárvan pierced Bhima with a hundred straight, vulture-feathered arrows, my lord. Furious in battle, Bhima then struck all three of Jaitra, Bhuri·bala and Ravi with three arrows that were like poison or fire. Slaughtered, the great warriors fell from their chariots onto the ground, just as *kim·shuka* trees are cut down in the spring, bearing various colored blossoms.

26.15 tato 'pareṇa bhallena tīkṣṇena paran|tapaḥ
Durvimocanam āhatya preṣayām āsa mṛtyave.
sa hataḥ prāpatad bhūmau sva|rathād rathināṃ varaḥ
gires tu kūṭa|jo bhagno māruten' êva pāda|paḥ.

Duṣpradharṣaṃ tataś c' âiva
Sujātaṃ ca sutaṃ tava
ek'|âikaṃ nyahanat saṃkhye
dvābhyāṃ dvābhyāṃ camū|mukhe.
tau śilī|mukha|viddh'|âṅgau petatū ratha|sattamau.
tataḥ patantam samare abhivīkṣya sutaṃ tava
bhallena pātayām āsa Bhīmo Durviṣahaṃ raṇe.
sa papāta hato vāhāt paśyatāṃ sarva|dhanvinām.

dṛṣṭvā tu nihatān bhrātṝn bahūn ekena saṃyuge
a|marṣa|vaśam āpannaḥ Śrutarvā Bhīmam abhyayāt.
26.20 vikṣipan su|mahac cāpaṃ kārtasvara|vibhūṣitam
visṛjan sāyakāṃś c' âiva viṣ'|âgni|pratimān bahūn
sa tu rājan dhanuś chittvā Pāṇḍavasya mahā|mṛdhe
ath' âinaṃ chinna|dhanvānaṃ viṃśatyā samavākirat.
tato 'nyad dhanur ādāya Bhīmaseno mahā|balaḥ
avākirat tava sutaṃ «tiṣṭha tiṣṭh' êti» c' âbravīt.

mahad āsīt tayor yuddhaṃ citra|rūpaṃ bhayānakam
yādṛśaṃ samare pūrvaṃ Jambha|Vāsavayor babhau.
tayos tatra śitair muktair Yama|daṇḍa|nibhaiḥ śaraiḥ
samācchannā dharā sarvā khaṃ diśo vidiśas tathā.

Bhima, the scorcher of his enemies, then struck Durvi- 26.15
móchana with another sharp, spear-headed arrow and sent him to his death. That best of charioteers fell dead from his chariot onto the ground, just as a tree growing on the crest of a mountain is broken by the wind.

At the front of the army, Bhima·sena then killed—one after the other—Dushpradhársha and your son Sujáta with two arrows each. The two excellent warriors fell down, their limbs pierced by stone-tipped arrows. After watching your son fall in war, Bhima toppled Dúrvishaha with a spear-headed shaft on the battlefield. Under the eyes of all the archers, Dúrvishaha fell dead from his vehicle.

When Shrutárvan saw that his brothers had been killed in battle by a single man, he became overwhelmed by fury and attacked Bhima. Drawing his mighty, gold-adorned bow 26.20
and firing a horde of arrows that resembled poison or fire, he sliced through the Pándava's bow in that great battle, Your Majesty, and then covered the bowless warrior with twenty more shafts. Mighty Bhima·sena, however, took up another bow, covered your son with arrows, and shouted: "Stand still! Stand still!"

A great battle occurred between the two heroes, wonderful to see and terrifying. It was just as when Jambha and Vásava fought in a battle in the past. The entire earth, sky, and major and minor directions became covered with sharp arrows that the two warriors fired in that contest and that resembled Death's staff.

26.25 tataḥ Śrutarvā saṃkruddho dhanur ādāya sāyakaiḥ
Bhīmasenaṃ raṇe rājan bāhvor urasi c' ârpayat.
so 'tividdho mahā|rāja tava putreṇa dhanvinā
Bhīmaḥ saṃcukṣubhe kruddhaḥ parvaṇ' îva mah"|ôda|dhiḥ.
tato Bhīmo ruṣ'|āviṣṭaḥ putrasya tava māriṣa
sārathiṃ caturaś c' âśvāñ śarair ninye Yama|kṣayam.
virathaṃ taṃ samālakṣya viśikhair loma|vāhibhiḥ
avākirad a|mey'|ātmā darśayan pāṇi|lāghavam.
Śrutarvā viratho rājann ādade khaḍga|carmaṇī.
ath' âsy' ādadataḥ khaḍgaṃ śata|candraṃ ca bhānumat
kṣura|preṇa śiraḥ kāyāt pātayām āsa Pāṇḍavaḥ.
26.30 chinn'|ôttam'|âṅgasya tataḥ kṣura|preṇa mah"|ātmanā
papāta kāyaḥ sa rathād vasu|dhām anunādayan.
tasmin nipatite vīre tāvakā bhaya|mohitāḥ
abhyadravanta saṃgrāme Bhīmasenaṃ yuyutsavaḥ.
tān āpatata ev' āśu hata|śeṣād bal'|ârṇavāt
daṃśitān pratijagrāha Bhīmasenaḥ pratāpavān.
te tu taṃ vai samāsādya parivavruḥ samantataḥ.
tatas tu saṃvṛto Bhīmas tāvakān niśitaiḥ śaraiḥ
pīḍayām āsa tān sarvān sahasr'|âkṣa iv' âsurān.
tataḥ pañca|śatān hatvā sa|varūthān mahā|rathān
jaghāna kuñjar'|ânīkaṃ punaḥ sapta|śataṃ yudhi.
26.35 hatvā śata|sahasrāṇi pattīnāṃ param'|êṣubhiḥ
vājināṃ ca śatāny aṣṭau Pāṇḍavaḥ sma virājate.
Bhīmasenas tu Kaunteyo hatvā yuddhe sutāṃs tava

Full of fury, Shrutárvan took up a bow and shot Bhi- 26.25
ma·sena in the chest and arms with his arrows in battle, Your Majesty. But, although badly wounded by your bow-wielding son, Bhima shook with rage, great king, like the ocean when the moon changes. Possessed by fury, Bhima dispatched your son's charioteer and four horses to Yama's abode with his shafts. On seeing Shrutárvan stripped of his chariot, that hero of limitless spirit then displayed his dexterity by shrouding him with feathered arrows.

Chariotless Shrutárvan picked up his sword and shield, Your Majesty. But, as he lifted up the gleaming sword, which was adorned with a hundred moons, the Pándava struck off
his head from his body with a razor-edged arrow. When 26.30
heroic Bhima sliced off his head with a razor-edged arrow, Shrutárvan's body fell from the chariot, making the earth groan.

At the death of this hero, your troops rushed against Bhima·sena in battle, bewildered by fear but eager to fight. As these armored warriors charged swiftly forward from the remaining mass of troops, powerful Bhima·sena stood up against them. Approaching him, they surrounded him on all sides. But, although surrounded, Bhima pounded all your troops with sharp arrows, as if he were thousand-eyed Indra subduing demons.

After destroying five hundred great shielded chariots, Bhima again slaughtered a division of seven hundred elephants in battle. The Pándava looked glorious after he had 26.35
massacred hundreds and thousands of foot soldiers and eight hundred horses with his excellent arrows. Indeed, when Bhima·sena, the son of Kunti, had killed your sons in

mene kṛt'|ârtham ātmānaṃ sa|phalaṃ janma ca prabho.

tam tathā yudhyamānaṃ ca vinighnantaṃ ca tāvakān
īkṣituṃ n' ôtsahante sma tava sainyā nar'|âdhipa.
vidrāvya ca Kurūn sarvāṃs tāṃś ca hatvā pad'|ânugān
dorbhyāṃ śabdaṃ tataś cakre trāsayāno mahā|dvi|pān.

hata|bhūyiṣṭha|yodhā ca tava senā viśāṃ pate
kiñcic|cheṣā mahā|rāja kṛpaṇā samapadyata.

SAÑJAYA uvāca:

27.1 DURYODHANO mahā|rāja Sudarśaś c' âpi te sutaḥ
hata|śeṣau tadā saṃkhye vāji|madhye vyavasthitau.
tato Duryodhanaṃ dṛṣṭvā vāji|madhye vyavasthitam
uvāca Devakī|putraḥ Kuntī|putraṃ Dhanañjayam:

«śatravo hata|bhūyiṣṭhā jñātayaḥ paripālitāḥ.
gṛhītvā Sañjayaṃ c' âsau nivṛttaḥ Śini|puṅgavaḥ.
pariśrāntaś ca Nakulaḥ Sahadevaś ca Bhārata
yodhayitvā raṇe pāpān Dhārtarāṣṭrān sah'|ânugān.
27.5 Duryodhanam abhityajya traya ete vyavasthitāḥ
Kṛpaś ca Kṛtavarmā ca Drauṇiś c' âiva mahā|rathaḥ.
asau tiṣṭhati Pāñcālyaḥ śriyā paramayā yutaḥ
Duryodhana|balaṃ hatvā saha sarvaiḥ Prabhadrakaiḥ.

asau Duryodhanaḥ Pārtha vāji|madhye vyavasthitaḥ
chattreṇa dhriyamāṇena prekṣamāṇo muhur muhuḥ.
prativyūhya balaṃ sarvaṃ raṇa|madhye vyavasthitaḥ.
enaṃ hatvā śitair bāṇaiḥ kṛta|kṛtyo bhaviṣyasi!

battle, he considered that he had achieved his goal and that his birth had borne fruit, my lord.

Your troops could not bear to look at Bhima·sena as he fought and annihilated your men in this fashion, Your Majesty. After he had routed all the Kurus and killed their followers, he terrified the mighty elephants by slapping his forearms.

On losing most of its troops, what little remained of your army became wretched, O lord of the people.

SÁNJAYA said:

THEN, GREAT KING, Dur·yódhana and your son Sudársha, 27.1
who had both survived slaughter, took up position in battle in the middle of the cavalry. When he saw Dur·yódhana standing among the cavalry, Krishna, the son of Dévaki, said to Dhanan·jaya, the son of Kunti:

"The enemy are mostly destroyed, and your kinsmen are protected. Sátyaki, the bull of the Shinis, has returned after capturing Sánjaya. Nákula and Saha·deva are both exhausted, descendant of Bharata, after fighting in battle against the evil troops of Dhrita·rashtra and their followers. Those three men—Kripa, Krita·varman and that great 27.5
warrior the son of Drona—are still standing firm after leaving behind Dur·yódhana. The Panchála prince is stationed over there, graced with the highest glory, after he and all the Prabhádrakas have killed Dur·yódhana's army.

Dur·yódhana has taken up position over there in the middle of the cavalry, O son of Pritha. He looks around continuously under the parasol that is held over him. After rallying his entire army, he has positioned himself in the

gaj'|ânīkaṃ hataṃ dṛṣṭvā tvāṃ ca prāptam arin|dama
yāvan na vidravanty ete tāvaj jahi Suyodhanam!
27.10 yātu kaś cit tu Pāñcālyaṃ «kṣipram āgamyatām iti».
pariśrānta|balas tāvan n' âiṣa mucyeta kilbiṣī.

hatvā tava balaṃ sarvaṃ saṃgrāme Dhṛtarāṣṭra|jaḥ
jitān Pāṇḍu|sutān matvā rūpaṃ dhārayate mahat.
nihataṃ sva|balaṃ dṛṣṭvā pīḍitaṃ c' âpi Pāṇḍavaiḥ
dhruvam eṣyati saṃgrāme vadhāy' âiv' ātmano nṛ|paḥ.»

evam uktaḥ Phālgunas tu Kṛṣṇaṃ vacanam abravīt:
«Dhṛtarāṣṭra|sutāḥ sarve hatā Bhīmena Mādhava.
yāv etāv āsthitau Kṛṣṇa tāv adya na bhaviṣyataḥ.
hato Bhīṣmo hato Droṇaḥ Karṇo Vaikartano hataḥ.
Madra|rājo hataḥ Śalyo hataḥ Kṛṣṇa Jayadrathaḥ.
27.15 hayāḥ pañca|śatāḥ śiṣṭāḥ Śakuneḥ Saubalasya ca.
rathānāṃ tu śate śiṣṭe dve eva tu Janārdana
dantināṃ ca śataṃ s'|âgraṃ tri|sāhasrāḥ padātayaḥ.
Aśvatthāmā Kṛpaś c' âiva Trigart'|âdhipatis tathā
Ulūkaḥ Śakuniś c' âiva Kṛtavarmā ca Sātvataḥ.

etad balam abhūc cheṣaṃ Dhārtarāṣṭrasya Mādhava.
mokṣo na nūnaṃ kālāt tu vidyate bhuvi kasya cit!
tathā vinihate sainye paśya Duryodhanaṃ sthitam.
ady' âhani mahā|rājo hat'|â|mitro bhaviṣyati.
na hi me mokṣyate kaś cit pareṣām iti cintaye.

middle of the battlefield. But you will achieve your goal by killing Dur·yódhana with your sharp arrows! Slaughter Su·yódhana, O enemy-tamer, before all his troops run away when they see that the elephant division has been massacred and that you are attacking them! Send someone to the Pa- 27.10
nchála prince to tell him to come quickly. Then that sinner will not escape, especially when his army is tired.

The son of Dhrita·rashtra has a formidable look about him because he has destroyed all your troops in battle and believes that the sons of Pandu are defeated. When he sees that his own army has been slaughtered and pummeled by the Pándavas, that king will surely enter battle, only to result in his own destruction!"

Addressed in this way, Phálguna* made this reply to Krishna: "Descendant of Madhu, all the sons of Dhrita·rashtra have been killed by Bhima. And the two sons that stand over there, O Krishna, will today exist no longer. Bhishma is dead, Drona is dead, and so is Karna, the son of the sun. Shalya, the king of the Madras, is dead, as is Jayad·ratha, O
Krishna. Shákuni, the son of Súbala, has five hundred horses 27.15
remaining. They have one hundred chariots remaining, two hundred elephants in total, and three thousand foot soldiers. Ashva·tthaman, Kripa, the lord of the Tri·gartas, Ulúka, Shákuni and the Sátvata Krita·varman are also left.

This, Mádhava, is what remains of the son of Dhrita·rashtra's army. How true it is that no one on earth can escape Time! Look at Dur·yódhana standing there, even though his army has been destroyed! On this very day, the great king Yudhi·shthira will have his foes slaughtered. For I do not think that any of the enemy will escape me! Today they

ye tv adya samaraṃ Kṛṣṇa na hāsyanti mad'|ôtkaṭāḥ
tān vai sarvān haniṣyāmi yady api syur na mānuṣāḥ.
27.20 adya yuddhe su|saṃkruddho dīrghaṃ rājñaḥ prajāgaram
apaneṣyāmi Gāndhāraṃ ghātayitvā śitaiḥ śaraiḥ.
nikṛtyā vai dur|ācāro yāni ratnāni Saubalaḥ
sabhāyām aharad dyūte punas tāny āharāmy aham.
adya tā api rotsyanti sarvā Nāga|pure striyaḥ
śrutvā patīṃś ca putrāṃś ca Pāṇḍavair nihatān yudhi.
samāptam adya vai karma sarvaṃ Kṛṣṇa bhaviṣyati.
adya Duryodhano dīptāṃ śriyaṃ prāṇāṃś ca mokṣyati.
n' âpayāti bhayāt Kṛṣṇa saṃgrāmād adya cen mama
nihataṃ viddhi Vārṣṇeya Dhārtarāṣṭraṃ su|bāliśam.
27.25 mama hy etad a|śaktaṃ vai vāji|vṛndam arin|dama
soḍhuṃ jyā|tala|nirghoṣam. yāhi yāvan nihanmy aham!»
Evam uktas tu Dāśārhaḥ Pāṇḍavena yaśasvinā
acodayad dhayān rājan Duryodhana|balaṃ prati.
tad anīkam abhiprekṣya trayaḥ sajjā mahā|rathāḥ
Bhīmaseno 'rjunaś c' âiva Sahadevaś ca māriṣa
prayayuḥ siṃha|nādena Duryodhana|jighāṃsayā.
tān prekṣya sahitān sarvāñ javen' ôdyata|kārmukān
Saubalo 'bhyadravad yuddhe Pāṇḍavān ātatāyinaḥ.
Sudarśanas tava suto Bhīmasenaṃ samabhyayāt
27.30 Suśarmā Śakuniś c' âiva yuyudhāte Kirīṭinā.
Sahadevaṃ tava suto haya|pṛṣṭha|gato 'bhyayāt.

will not escape war. However intoxicated they are by battle-fury, I will kill them all—even if they were not human. Filled with rage in battle, I will today kill the Gandhára 27.20
prince with my sharp arrows and rid King Yudhi·shthira of his long insomnia. I will bring back the treasures that the wicked son of Súbala fraudulently stole at the gambling match in the assembly hall.

All the women in Naga·pura will today weep when they hear that the Pándavas have killed their sons and husbands in battle. On this very day, Krishna, every deed will be fulfilled. Today Dur·yódhana will give up his life and his radiant majesty. If the foolish son of Dhrita·rashtra does not flee from me today in battle, Krishna, then you will know that he is dead, O descendant of Vrishni. This horde of 27.25
steeds will be unable to withstand the sound of my bow-string and palms, O enemy-tamer. Drive on the chariot so that I can slaughter them!"

Addressed in this way by the glorious Pándava, the Dashárha urged on his horses against Dur·yódhana's troops, Your Majesty. Seeing the enemy division, the three armed and mighty warriors—Bhima·sena, Árjuna and Saha·deva—attacked with a lion-roar in their desire to kill Dur·yódhana.

At the sight of those bow-wielding warriors all rushing swiftly forward in a group, Súbala's son charged against the Pándava archers in battle. Your son Sudárshana attacked Bhima·sena, while Sushárman and Shákuni fought against 27.30
diadem-wearing Árjuna. Your son Dur·yódhana advanced on horseback against Saha·deva.

tato hi yatnataḥ kṣipraṃ tava putro jan'|âdhipa
prāsena Sahadevasya śirasi prāharad bhṛśam.
s' ôpāviśad* rath'|ôpasthe tava putreṇa tāḍitaḥ
rudhir'|āpluta|sarv'|âṅga āśī|viṣa iva śvasan.
pratilabhya tataḥ saṃjñāṃ Sahadevo viśāṃ pate
Duryodhanaṃ śarais tīkṣṇaiḥ saṃkruddhaḥ samavākirat.

Pārtho 'pi yudhi vikramya Kuntī|putro Dhanañjayaḥ
śūrāṇām aśva|pṛṣṭhebhyaḥ śirāṃsi nicakarta ha.
27.35 tad anīkaṃ tadā Pārtho vyadhamad bahubhiḥ śaraiḥ.
pātayitvā hayān sarvāṃs Trigartānāṃ rathān yayau.
tatas te sahitā bhūtvā Trigartānāṃ mahā|rathāḥ
Arjunaṃ Vāsudevaṃ ca śara|varṣair avākiran.
Satyakarmāṇam ākṣipya kṣura|preṇa mahā|yaśāḥ
tato 'sya syandanasy' ēṣāṃ cicchide Pāṇḍu|nandanaḥ.
śilā|śitena ca vibho kṣura|preṇa mahā|yaśāḥ
śiraś ciccheda sahasā tapta|kuṇḍala|bhūṣaṇam.

Satyeṣum atha c' ādatta yodhānāṃ miṣatāṃ tava
yathā siṃho vane rājan mṛgaṃ paribubhukṣitaḥ.
27.40 taṃ nihatya tataḥ Pārthaḥ Suśarmāṇaṃ tribhiḥ śaraiḥ
viddhvā tān ahanat sarvān rathān rukma|vibhūṣitān.
tataḥ prāyāt tvaran Pārtho dīrgha|kālaṃ su|saṃvṛtam
muñcan krodha|viṣaṃ tīkṣṇaṃ Prasthal'|âdhipatiṃ prati.

With speed and care, your son then violently hit Saha·deva on the head with a spear, lord of the people. Struck by your son, Saha·deva collapsed on his chariot platform, breathing like a poisonous snake and his limbs all drenched in blood. Saha·deva, however, regained consciousness and furiously covered Dur·yódhana with sharp arrows, lord of the people.

The Partha Dhanan·jaya, that son of Kunti, also advanced in battle and sliced off the heads of heroes who were on
horseback. Pritha's son dispersed that division of troops with 27.35
numerous arrows. Killing all the horses, he then proceeded against the chariots of the Tri·gartas. The mighty warriors of the Tri·gartas, who were gathered together, covered Árjuna and Vásu·deva with showers of shafts. But the glorious son of Pandu hurled a razor-tipped arrow at Satya·karman and cut through the shaft of his chariot. With a stone-sharpened, razor-tipped arrow, famed Árjuna then brutally cut off his head, which was adorned with earrings of refined gold.

While your troops were watching, Árjuna then grabbed hold of Satyéshu, just as a lion in a forest grabs a deer
when it wants to eat, Your Majesty. After killing Satyéshu, 27.40
the son of Pritha pierced Sushárman with three arrows and destroyed all the gold-decorated chariots. The son of Pritha then swiftly advanced against the ruler of Prásthala, releasing the fierce poison of his anger, which he had long kept restrained.

tam Arjunaḥ pṛṣatkānāṃ śatena Bharata'|rṣabha
pūrayitvā tato vāhān prāharat tasya dhanvinaḥ.
tataḥ śaraṃ samādhāya Yama|daṇḍ'|ôpamaṃ tadā
Suśarmāṇaṃ samuddiśya cikṣep' āśu hasann iva.
sa śaraḥ preṣitas tena krodha|dīptena dhanvinā
Suśarmāṇaṃ samāsādya bibheda hṛdayaṃ raṇe.
27.45 sa gat'|âsur mahā|rāja papāta dharaṇī|tale
nandayan Pāṇḍavān sarvān vyathayaṃś c' âpi tāvakān.

Suśarmāṇaṃ raṇe hatvā putrān asya mahā|rathān
sapta c' âṣṭau ca triṃśac ca sāyakair anayat kṣayam.
tato 'sya niśitair bāṇaiḥ sarvān hatvā pad'|ânugān
abhyagād Bhāratīṃ senāṃ hata|śeṣāṃ mahā|rathaḥ.

Bhīmas tu samare kruddhaḥ putraṃ tava jan'|âdhipa
Sudarśanam a|dṛśyaṃ taṃ śaraiś cakre hasann iva.
tato 'sya prahasan kruddhaḥ śiraḥ kāyād apāharat
kṣura|preṇa su|tīkṣṇena sa hataḥ prāpatad bhuvi.
27.50 tasmiṃs tu nihate vīre tatas tasya pad'|ânugāḥ
parivavrū raṇe Bhīmaṃ kiranto vividhāñ śarān.
tatas tu niśitair bāṇais tav' ânīkaṃ Vṛkodaraḥ
Indr'|āśani|sama|sparśaiḥ samantāt paryavākirat.
tataḥ kṣaṇena tad Bhīmo nyahanad Bharata'|rṣabha.

teṣu t' ûtsādyamāneṣu sen"|âdhyakṣā mahā|rathāḥ
Bhīmasenaṃ samāsādya tato 'yudhyanta Bhārata.
sa tān sarvāñ śarair ghorair avākirata Pāṇḍavaḥ.
tath" âiva tāvakā rājan Pāṇḍaveyān mahā|rathān

Árjuna attacked that bowman's horses, best of Bharatas, covering them with a hundred shafts. He then drew an arrow that resembled Yama's staff, took aim and swiftly fired it at Sushárman, almost laughing as he did so. The arrow that bow-wielding Árjuna released, as he blazed with anger, struck Sushárman in battle and pierced through his heart.
His life-breath departed, Sushárman fell to the ground, 27.45
bringing joy to all the Pándavas and terror to your troops, great king.

After killing Sushárman in battle, Árjuna massacred Sushárman's forty-five sons with his arrows, great warriors though they were. After slaughtering all of Sushárman's followers with sharpened arrows, that mighty warrior then advanced against the survivors of the Bhárata army.

Bhima, who was full of battle-rage, almost laughed as he made your son Sudárshana become invisible with arrows, lord of the people. With a laugh, Bhima furiously struck the head off his body with an extremely sharp, razor-tipped arrow. Sudárshana fell to the ground, slain.

At the death of this hero, Sudárshana's followers sur- 27.50
rounded Bhima in battle, spraying out various shafts. But Vrikódara covered your regiment with sharp arrows on every side; their impact was like that of Indra's thunderbolts. Bhima then annihilated that regiment in an instant, bull of the Bharatas.

When these soldiers were massacred, the army leaders—those mighty warriors—confronted Bhima·sena and fought against him, descendant of Bharata. The Pándava, however, covered all of them with dreadful arrows. In a similar manner, Your Majesty, your troops restrained the great Pándava

śara|varṣeṇa mahatā samantāt paryavārayan.
vyākulaṃ tad abhūt sarvaṃ Pāṇḍavānāṃ paraiḥ saha
tāvakānāṃ ca samare Pāṇḍaveyair yuyutsatām.
27.55 tatra yodhās tadā petuḥ paras|para|samāhatāḥ
ubhayoḥ senayo rājan saṃśocantaḥ sma bāndhavān.

SAÑJAYA uvāca:

28.1 TASMIN PRAVṚTTE saṃgrāme gaja|vāji|nara|kṣaye
Śakuniḥ Saubalo rājan Sahadevaṃ samabhyayāt.
tato 'sy' āpatatas tūrṇaṃ Sahadevaḥ pratāpavān
śar'|âughān preṣayām āsa pataṅgān iva śīghra|gān.
Ulūkaś ca raṇe Bhīmaṃ vivyādha daśabhiḥ śaraiḥ
Śakuniś ca mahā|rāja Bhīmaṃ viddhvā tribhiḥ śaraiḥ
sāyakānāṃ navatyā vai Sahadevam avākirat.
te śūrāḥ samare rājan samāsādya paras|param
vivyadhur niśitair bāṇaiḥ kaṅka|barhiṇa|vājitaiḥ
svarṇa|puṅkhaiḥ śilā|dhautair ā|karṇa|prahitaiḥ śaraiḥ.
28.5 teṣāṃ cāpa|bhuj'|ôtsṛṣṭā śara|vṛṣṭir viśāṃ pate
ācchādayad diśaḥ sarvā dhārā iva payo|mucaḥ.
tataḥ kruddho raṇe Bhīmaḥ Sahadevaś ca vīryavān
ceratuḥ kadanaṃ saṃkhye kurvantau su|mahā|balau.
tābhyāṃ śara|śataiś channaṃ tad balaṃ tava Bhārata
andhakāram iv' ākāśam abhavat tatra tatra ha.
aśvair viparidhāvadbhiḥ śara|cchannair viśāṃ pate
tatra tatra vṛto mārgo vikarṣadbhir hatān bahūn.

warriors on all sides with a massive shower of shafts. Everything became confused, O king—both for the Pándavas, who were eager to fight their enemy in battle, and for your men, who were eager to fight the Pándava troops.
Slaughtered by one another, warriors from both armies 27.55
fell down in that conflict, grieving for their relatives, Your Majesty.

SÁNJAYA said:

AFTER THIS battle, Your Majesty, in which elephants, 28.1
horses and men were massacred, Shákuni, the son of Súbala, advanced against Saha·deva. Mighty Saha·deva, however, quickly fired volleys of arrows at Shákuni as he charged forward, which flew swiftly like bees.

Ulúka pierced Bhima in battle with ten arrows, great king, while Shákuni wounded him with three shafts and then covered Saha·deva with ninety more. Confronting one another in battle, the heroes pierced each other with sharp arrows, which were feathered with heron and peacock plumes. Gold-winged and stone-polished, the shafts
were fired from the ear. The shower of arrows that the war- 28.5
riors' arms fired from their bows covered every direction, like torrents of rain from a cloud, lord of the people.

Battle-enraged Bhima and fervent Saha·deva—both of them extremely powerful—careered around in battle, causing destruction. Your army became shrouded by hundreds of their arrows, descendant of Bharata, and everywhere the sky became like darkness. Here and there, lord of the people, the path was blocked by fleeing horses that were covered with arrows and that dragged behind them numerous dead

nihatānāṃ hayānāṃ ca sah' âiva haya|sādhibhiḥ
varmabhir vinikṛttaiś ca prāsaiś chinnaiś ca māriṣa
28.10 ṛṣṭibhiḥ śaktibhiś c' âiva s'|âsi|prāsa|paraśvadhaiḥ
saṃchannā pṛthivī jajñe kusumaiḥ śabalā iva.

yodhās tatra mahā|rāja samāsādya paras|param
vyacaranta raṇe kruddhā vinighnantaḥ paras|param.
udvṛtta|nayanai roṣāt saṃdaṣṭ'|âuṣṭha|puṭair mukhaiḥ
sa|kuṇḍalair mahī cchannā padma|kiñjalka|sannibhaiḥ,
bhujaiś chinnair mahā|rāja nāga|rāja|kar'|ôpamaiḥ
s'|âṅga|daiḥ sa|tanu|traiś ca s'|âsi|prāsa|paraśvadhaiḥ.
kabandhair utthitaiś chinnair nṛtyadbhiś c' âparair yudhi
kravy'|âda|gaṇa|saṃchannā ghor" âbhūt pṛthivī vibho.
28.15 alp'|âvaśiṣṭe sainye tu Kauraveyān mah"|āhave
prahṛṣṭāḥ Pāṇḍavā bhūtvā ninyire Yama|sādanam.

etasminn antare śūraḥ Saubaleyaḥ pratāpavān
prāsena Sahadevasya śirasi prāharad bhṛśam.
sa vihvalo mahā|rāja rath'|ôpastha upāviśat.
Sahadevaṃ tathā dṛṣṭvā Bhīmasenaḥ pratāpavān
sarva|sainyāni saṃkruddho vārayām āsa Bhārata.
nirbibheda ca nārācaiḥ śataśo 'tha sahasraśaḥ
vinirbhidy' âkaroc c' âiva siṃha|nādam arin|damaḥ.
tena śabdena vitrastāḥ sarve sa|haya|vāraṇāḥ
prādravan sahasā bhītāḥ Śakuneś ca pad'|ânugāḥ.
28.20 prabhagnān atha tān dṛṣṭvā rājā Duryodhano 'bravīt:

men. As if dappled with flowers, the earth became strewn 28.10
with cavalrymen and dead horses, with ripped armor and shattered javelins, and with lances, spears, swords, javelins and axes, my lord.

Confronting one another in that war, the warriors on the battlefield careered around furiously, killing each other, great king. The earth was covered with earring-adorned heads; looking like lotus filaments, their eyes glared with anger and their teeth clenched their lips. Lopped-off arms also lay there, great king. Wearing bracelets and armor, and grasping swords, javelins or axes, they were like the trunks of royal elephants. Swathed with hordes of carrion-eating creatures, the earth was a terrible sight, my lord, as mangled torsos rose from the ground and others danced in battle.

In that great battle, the Pándavas joyfully led the Káura- 28.15
vas to the house of Yama, although little of the Kuru army remained.

In the meantime, the powerful and heroic son of Súbala struck Saha·deva forcefully on the head with a javelin. Saha·deva staggered, great king, and collapsed onto his chariot platform. When fierce Bhima·sena saw that Saha·deva was in this plight, he furiously repelled all the Kuru troops, descendant of Bharata. With his iron arrows, that enemy-tamer wounded men in their hundreds and thousands and then shouted a lion-roar. Terrified by that noise, the followers of Shákuni suddenly fled in fear, along with their
horses and elephants. Seeing that these men were breaking 28.20
up, King Dur·yódhana said:

«nivartadhvam! a|dharma|jñā
yudhyadhvaṃ! kiṃ sṛtena vaḥ!
iha kīrtiṃ samādhāya
pretya lokān samaśnute
prāṇāñ jahāti yo dhīro
yuddhe pṛṣṭham a|darśayan.»

evam uktās tu te rājñā Saubalasya pad'|ânugāḥ
Pāṇḍavān abhyavartanta mṛtyuṃ kṛtvā nivartanam.
dravadbhis tatra rāj'|êndra kṛtaḥ śabdo 'tidāruṇaḥ.
kṣubdha|sāgara|saṃkāśāḥ kṣubhitāḥ sarvato 'bhavan.
tāṃs tathā purato dṛṣṭvā Saubalasya pad'|ânugān
pratyudyayur mahā|rāja Pāṇḍavā vijay'|ôdyatāḥ.
28.25 pratyāśvasya ca dur|dharṣaḥ Sahadevo viśāṃ pate.
Śakuniṃ daśabhir viddhvā hayāṃś c' âsya tribhiḥ śaraiḥ
dhanuś ciccheda ca śaraiḥ Saubalasya hasann iva.
ath' ânyad dhanur ādāya Śakunir yuddha|dur|madaḥ
vivyādha Nakulaṃ ṣaṣṭyā Bhīmasenaṃ ca saptabhiḥ.
Ulūko 'pi mahā|rāja Bhīmaṃ vivyādha saptabhiḥ
Sahadevaṃ ca saptatyā parīpsan pitaraṃ raṇe.
taṃ Bhīmasenaḥ samare vivyādha navabhiḥ śaraiḥ
Śakuniṃ ca catuḥ|ṣaṣṭyā pārśva|sthāṃś ca tribhis tribhiḥ.

te hanyamānā Bhīmena nārācais taila|pāyitaiḥ
Sahadevaṃ raṇe kruddhāś chādayañ śara|vṛṣṭibhiḥ
parvataṃ vāri|dhārābhiḥ sa|vidyuta iv' âmbu|dāḥ.
28.30 tato 'sy' āpatataḥ śūraḥ Sahadevaḥ pratāpavān
Ulūkasya mahā|rāja bhallen' âpāharac chiraḥ.
sa jagāma rathād bhūmiṃ Sahadevena pātitaḥ

"Come back! You know what is wrong, so fight! What is the point of your fleeing? The brave who devote themselves to glory in this world, and who give up their lives without showing their backs in battle, attain divine realms when they die."

Addressed in this way by the king, the followers of Súbala's son returned against the Pándavas, resolving to die rather than retreat. They made a horrific noise as they charged on that battlefield, O king of kings. Like the billowing ocean, they surged on all sides. When the Pándavas saw that the followers of Súbala's son were thus confronting them, they rose up against them, intent on victory, great king.

Saha·deva—who is difficult to assail—then recovered, 28.25
lord of the people. Piercing Shákuni with ten shafts and his horses with three, he cut through the bow of Súbala's son with his arrows, almost laughing as he did so. But Shákuni, who is difficult to defeat in battle, took up another bow and pierced Nákula with sixty arrows and Bhima·sena with seven more. Eager to help his father in battle, Ulúka, too, pierced Bhima with seven arrows and Saha·deva with seventy, great king. Bhima·sena, however, wounded Ulúka with nine arrows in the battle, Shákuni with sixty-four, and Shákuni's attendants with three each.

But although struck by Bhima with his oil-soaked shafts, those men covered Saha·deva with showers of arrows in their battle-fury, just as lightning clouds cover a mountain
with torrents of rain. Then, as Ulúka charged forward, the 28.30
mighty hero Saha·deva struck off his head with a spear-headed arrow, Your Majesty. Felled by Saha·deva and his

rudhir'|āpluta|sarv'|âṅgo nandayan Pāṇḍavān yudhi.

putraṃ tu nihataṃ dṛṣṭvā Śakunis tatra Bhārata
s'|âśru|kaṇṭho viniḥśvasya Kṣattur vākyam anusmaran,
cintayitvā muhūrtaṃ sa bāṣpa|pūrṇ'|êkṣaṇaḥ śvasan
Sahadevaṃ samāsādya tribhir vivyādha sāyakaiḥ.
tān apāsya śarān muktāñ śara|saṃghaiḥ pratāpavān
Sahadevo mahā|rāja dhanuś ciccheda saṃyuge.
28.35 chinne dhanuṣi rāj'|êndra Śakuniḥ Saubalas tadā
pragṛhya vipulaṃ khaḍgaṃ Sahadevāya prāhiṇot.
tam āpatantaṃ sahasā ghora|rūpaṃ viśāṃ pate
dvidhā ciccheda samare Saubalasya hasann iva.

asiṃ dṛṣṭvā tathā chinnaṃ pragṛhya mahatīṃ gadām
prāhiṇot Sahadevāya. sā moghā nyapatad bhuvi.
tataḥ śaktiṃ mahā|ghorāṃ kāla|rātrim iv' ôdyatām
preṣayām āsa saṃkruddhaḥ Pāṇḍavaṃ prati Saubalaḥ.
tām āpatantīṃ sahasā śaraiḥ kanaka|bhūṣaṇaiḥ
tridhā ciccheda samare Sahadevo hasann iva.
28.40 sā papāta tridhā cchinnā bhūmau kanaka|bhūṣaṇā
śīryamāṇā yathā dīptā gaganād vai śata|hradā.

śaktiṃ vinihatāṃ dṛṣṭvā Saubalaṃ ca bhay'|ârditam
dudruvus tāvakāḥ sarve bhaye jāte sa|Saubalāḥ.
ath' ôtkruṣṭaṃ mahac c' āsīt Pāṇḍavair jita|kāśibhiḥ
Dhārtarāṣṭrās tataḥ sarve prāyaśo vimukh" âbhavan*.
tān vai vimanaso dṛṣṭvā Mādrī|putraḥ pratāpavān
śarair aneka|sāhasrair vārayām āsa saṃyuge.

limbs all drenched in blood, Ulúka collapsed to the ground from his chariot, bringing joy to the Pándavas in battle.

Seeing his son killed on that spot, Shákuni sighed deeply, his throat choked with tears, descendant of Bharata. Recalling the words of the Kshattri and with his eyes filled with tears, he brooded for a while, sighing. He then attacked Saha·deva and pierced him with three arrows. But mighty Saha·deva warded off those fired shafts and cut through Shákuni's bow with swarms of arrows in the battle, great
king. His bow severed, Shákuni, the son of Súbala, grabbed 28.35
an enormous sword and hurled it at Saha·deva. But as the terrifying sword of Súbala's son suddenly sped toward him in battle, Saha·deva split it in two, almost laughing as he did so, lord of the people.

Seeing his sword shattered in this way, Shákuni took hold of a huge mace and threw it at Saha·deva. But it fell to the ground, missing its mark. Enraged, Súbala's son then hurled a terrifying spear at the Pándava, which he wielded as if it were the night of Time. But as the spear flew violently toward him in the battle, Saha·deva chopped it into three pieces with his gold-adorned arrows, almost laughing as he
did so. Like a blazing thunderbolt falling from the sky, the 28.40
gold-decorated spear fell to the ground, cut into three pieces.

When they saw that the spear was destroyed and that Súbala's son was stricken with fear, your troops all became terrified and ran away, as did Súbala's son. The conquering Pándavas uttered a loud roar and all of Dhrita·rashtra's followers fled in large numbers. Seeing the bewildered Káuravas, Saha·deva, the powerful son of Madri, held them back in battle with several thousand arrows. He then approached

tato Gāndhārakair guptaṃ puṣṭair aśvair jaye dhṛtam
āsasāda raṇe yāntaṃ Sahadevo 'tha Saubalam.
28.45 svam aṃśaṃ avaśiṣṭaṃ taṃ saṃsmṛtya Śakuniṃ nṛ|pa
rathena kāñcan'|âṅgena Sahadevaḥ samabhyayāt.
adhijyaṃ bala|vat kṛtvā vyākṣipan su|mahad dhanuḥ
sa Saubalam abhidrutya gārdhra|patraiḥ śilā|śitaiḥ
bhṛśam abhyahanat kruddhas tottrair iva mahā|dvi|pam.
uvāca c' âinaṃ medhāvī vigṛhya smārayann iva
«kṣatra|dharme sthiro bhūtvā yudhyasva! puruṣo bhava!
yat tadā hṛṣyase mūḍha glahann akṣaiḥ sabhā|tale
phalam adya prapaśyasva karmaṇas tasya dur|mate.
nihatās te dur|ātmāno ye 'smān avahasan purā.
Duryodhanaḥ kul'|âṅgāraḥ śiṣṭas tvaṃ c' âsya mātulaḥ.
28.50 adya te nirhariṣyāmi kṣureṇ' ônmathitaṃ śiraḥ
vṛkṣāt phalam iv' āviddhaṃ laguḍena pramāthinā.»
evam uktvā mahā|rāja Sahadevo mahā|balaḥ
saṃkruddho raṇa|śārdulo vegen' âbhijagāma tam.
abhigamya su|dur|dharṣaḥ Sahadevo yudhāṃ patiḥ
vikṛṣya balavac cāpaṃ krodhena prajvalann iva,
Śakuniṃ daśabhir viddhvā caturbhiś c' âsya vājinaḥ
chattraṃ dhvajaṃ dhanuś c' âsya cchittvā siṃha iv' ânadat.

in battle the fleeing son of Súbala, who was protected by healthy Gandhára horses and still intent on victory. Calling 28.45
to mind that Shákuni was his remaining share, Saha·deva attacked him with his gold-bodied chariot. Stringing his huge and mighty bow, he drew it and charged with fury against the son of Súbala. He then violently struck him with vulture-feathered and stone-sharpened arrows, as if hitting a great elephant with goads. Berating him, intelligent Saha·deva said these words to Shákuni, as if to remind him:

"Be firm in the warrior code and fight! Be a man! O dim-witted fool, receive today the fruit of the deed you committed when you rejoiced while gambling with dice in the assembly hall! We have killed the degenerates who laughed in the past. Dur·yódhana is still alive—that coal who has burned down his family—and you are his uncle.
Today I will take off your head, ripping it off with a razor- 28.50
tipped arrow, just as a fruit is knocked out of a tree by a stick that strikes it."

Saying this, Your Majesty, Saha·deva—that furious and mighty tiger in battle—swiftly attacked Shákuni. After he had advanced forward, that champion of warriors—so difficult to assault—drew his powerful bow. As if blazing with anger, he wounded Shákuni with ten arrows and pierced his horses with four more. Cutting through Shákuni's parasol, banner and bow, he roared like a lion.

chinna|dhvaja|dhanuś|chatraḥ Sahadevena Saubalaḥ
kṛto 'tividdho bahubhiḥ sarva|marmasu sāyakaiḥ.
28.55 tato bhūyo mahā|rāja Sahadevaḥ pratāpavān
Śakuneḥ preṣayām āsa śara|vṛṣṭiṃ dur|āsadām.
tatas tu kruddhaḥ Subalasya putro
Mādrī|sutaṃ Sahadevaṃ vimarde
prāsena jāmbūnada|bhūṣaṇena
jighāṃsur eko 'bhipapāta śīghram.
Mādrī|sutas tasya samudyataṃ taṃ
prāsaṃ su|vṛttau ca bhujau raṇ'|âgre
bhallais tribhir yugapat saṃcakarta
nanāda c' ôccais taras" āji|madhye.
tasy' āśukārī su|samāhitena
suvarṇa|puṅkhena dṛdh'|âyasena
bhallena sarv'|āvaraṇ'|âtigena
śiraḥ śarīrāt pramamātha bhūyaḥ.
śareṇa kārtasvara|bhūṣitena
divā|kar'|ābhena su|saṃhitena
hṛt'|ôttam'|âṅgo yudhi Pāṇḍavena
papāta bhūmau Subalasya putraḥ.
28.60 sa tac|chiro vegavatā śareṇa
su|varṇa|puṅkhena śilā|śitena
prāverayat kupitaḥ Pāṇḍu|putro
yat tat Kurūṇām a|nayasya mūlam.
bhujau su|vṛttau pracakarta vīraḥ.
paścāt kabandhaṃ rudhir'|âvasiktam
vispandamānaṃ nipapāta ghoraṃ
rath'|ôttamāt pārthiva pārthivasya.
hṛt'|ôttam'|âṅgaṃ Śakuniṃ samīkṣya
bhūmau śayānaṃ rudhir'|ârdra|gātram

After severing Shákuni's banner, bow and parasol, Saha·deva badly wounded the son of Súbala with several arrows in all his vital organs. Fierce Saha·deva then once more 28.55
fired an unstoppable shower of arrows at Shákuni. Enraged and alone, the son of Súbala swiftly charged on his own with a gold-adorned spear against Saha·deva, the son of Madri, eager to kill him in that combat. With three spear-headed arrows, however, the son of Madri simultaneously cut through Shákuni's wielded javelin and his well-rounded arms at the front of the battle. He then immediately roared loudly in the middle of the battlefield.

With a spear-headed arrow—which was well crafted, gold-feathered, made of solid iron and capable of penetrating any obstacle—Saha·deva then struck the head off Shákuni's body. The son of Súbala fell to the ground, his head ripped off in battle by the Pándava with that gold-decorated, well-crafted arrow, which shone like the sun.

With a swift, gold-feathered and stone-sharpened arrow, 28.60
the son of Pandu furiously struck off Shákuni's head, that root of the Kurus' evil. The hero also chopped off Shákuni's well-rounded arms. At this, the king's blood-soaked and horrific torso fell quivering from the top of his chariot, Your Majesty.

When your troops saw Shákuni lying on the ground, his head ripped off and his limbs drenched with blood, their spirits were destroyed by fear and they fled in every direc-

yodhās tvadīyā bhaya|naṣṭa|sattvā
diśaḥ prajagmuḥ pragṛhīta|śastrāḥ.
pravidrutāḥ śuṣka|mukhā visaṃjñā
Gāṇḍīva|ghoṣeṇa samāhatāś ca
bhay'|ârditā bhagna|rath'|âśva|nāgāḥ
padātayaś c' âiva sa|Dhārtarāṣṭrāḥ.
tato rathāc Chakuniṃ pātayitvā
mud"|ânvitā Bhārata Pāṇḍaveyāḥ
śaṅkhān pradadhmuḥ samare 'tihṛṣṭāḥ
sa|Keśavāḥ sainikān harṣayantaḥ.
28.65 taṃ c' âpi sarve pratipūjayanto
dṛṣṭvā bruvāṇāḥ Sahadevam ājau:
«diṣṭyā hato naikṛtiko mah"|ātmā
sah'|ātma|jo vīra raṇe tvay" êti.»

SAÑJAYA uvāca:

29.1 TATAḤ KRUDDHĀ mahā|rāja Saubalasya pad'|ânugāḥ
tyaktvā jīvitam ākrande Pāṇḍavān paryavārayan.
tān Arjunaḥ pratyagṛhṇāt Sahadeva|jaye dhṛtaḥ
Bhīmasenaś ca tejasvī kruddh'|āśī|viṣa|darśanaḥ.
śakty|ṛṣṭi|prāsa|hastānāṃ Sahadevaṃ jighāṃsatām
saṃkalpam akaron moghaṃ Gāṇḍīvena Dhanañjayaḥ.
saṃgṛhīt'|āyudhān bāhūn yodhānām abhidhāvatām
bhallaiś ciccheda Bībhatsuḥ śirāṃsy api hayān api.
29.5 te hayāḥ pratyapadyanta vasudhāṃ vigat'|âsavaḥ
caratā loka|vīreṇa prahatāḥ Savyasācinā.
tato Duryodhano rājā dṛṣṭvā sva|bala|saṃkṣayam
hata|śeṣān samānīya kruddho ratha|gaṇān bahūn,
kuñjarāṃś ca hayāṃś c' âiva pādātāṃś ca samantataḥ
uvāca sahitān sarvān Dhārtarāṣṭra idaṃ vacaḥ:

tion, grasping hold of their weapons. Stricken with terror and assaulted by the noise of the Gandíva, dry-mouthed and bereft of their senses, the foot soldiers fled with the son of Dhrita·rashtra, their chariots, horses and elephants destroyed.

The Pándavas and Késhava were filled with delight at toppling Shákuni from his chariot, descendant of Bharata. Extremely joyful in that battle, they blew their conches,
bringing happiness to their troops. All of them then joyfully 28.65
honored Saha·deva after seeing him fight in battle, saying:

"How fortunate it is, brave Saha·deva, that you have killed this vile hero and his son in battle!"

SÁNJAYA said:

THE ANGRY FOLLOWERS of Súbala's son then gave up 29.1
their lives in battle, great king, and surrounded the Pándavas. Árjuna countered them, intent on pursuing Saha·deva's victory, as did splendid Bhima·sena, whose gaze was like that of an irate, venomous snake. With his Gandíva bow, Dhanan·jaya foiled the intentions of Shákuni's troops, who wielded spears, lances and javelins and were eager to kill Saha·deva. With his spear-headed arrows, Bibhátsu sliced through numerous weapons that were brandished by the
charging fighters, and pierced heads and horses, too. Their 29.5
life-breaths departed, the horses fell to the ground, slaughtered by rampaging Savya·sachin, that hero of the world.

When he saw his army being destroyed, furious King Dur·yódhana summoned from every side his surviving elephants, horses, infantrymen and numerous chariot divi-

«samāsādya raṇe sarvān Pāṇḍavān sa|su|hṛd|gaṇān
Pāñcālyaṃ c' âpi sa|balaṃ hatvā śīghraṃ nyavartata!»
tasya te śirasā gṛhya vacanaṃ yuddha|dur|madāḥ
abhyudyayū raṇe Pārthāṃs tava putrasya śāsanāt.

29.10 tān abhyāpatataḥ śīghraṃ hata|śeṣān mahā|raṇe
śarair āśī|viṣ'|ākāraiḥ Pāṇḍavāḥ samavākiran.
tat sainyaṃ Bharata|śreṣṭha muhūrtena mah"|ātmabhiḥ
avadhyata raṇaṃ prāpya trātāraṃ n' âbhyavindata.
pratiṣṭhamānaṃ tu bhayān n' âvatiṣṭhati daṃśitam.
aśvair viparidhāvadbhiḥ sainyena rajasā vṛte
na prājñāyanta samare diśaś ca pradiśas tathā.
tatas tu Pāṇḍav'|ânīkān niḥsṛtya bahavo janāḥ
abhyaghnaṃs tāvakān yuddhe muhūrtād iva Bhārata.
tato niḥśeṣam abhavat tat sainyaṃ tava Bhārata.
akṣauhiṇyaḥ sametās tu tava putrasya Bhārata
ekādaśa hatā yuddhe tāḥ prabho Pāṇḍu|Sṛñjayaiḥ.

29.15 teṣu rāja|sahasreṣu tāvakeṣu mah"|ātmasu
eko Duryodhano rājann adṛśyata bhṛśaṃ kṣataḥ.
tato vīkṣya diśaḥ sarvā dṛṣṭvā śūnyāṃ ca medinīm
vihīnaḥ sarva|yodhaiś ca Pāṇḍavān vīkṣya saṃyuge
muditān sarva|siddh'|ârthān nardamānān samantataḥ,
bāṇa|śabda|ravāṃś c' âiva śrutvā teṣāṃ mah"|ātmanām

sions. The son of Dhrita·rashtra then said these words to all the assembled troops:

"Attack all the Pándavas and their allied regiments in battle! Kill the prince of Panchála and his army and then return swiftly!"

Humbly obeying Dur·yódhana's orders, the troops—who were difficult to defeat in war—advanced against the sons of Pritha in battle, following the instructions of your
son. But as these surviving men charged swiftly forward in 29.10
that great battle, the Pándavas covered them with arrows that resembled poisonous snakes. On entering the battlefield, the troops were destroyed in an instant by the heroic Pándavas, O best of Bharatas. Nor could they find a protector. Fleeing in fear, the armed warriors were unable to hold their ground.

Dust arose from the army and the fleeing horses, and none of the major or minor directions could be seen in the battle. Many men advanced from the Pándava division and in a mere moment massacred your troops in battle, descendant of Bharata. Nothing was left of that army of yours, descendant of Bharata. The Pandus and Sríñjayas destroyed your son's eleven rallied armies in that battle, descendant of Bharata.

Of the thousands of heroic kings in your army, Dur·yó- 29.15
dhana was the only one still visible, although he was severely wounded, Your Majesty. Looking around in every direction, Dur·yódhana saw that the earth was empty. Bereft of all his troops, he watched the Pándavas as they roared with joy on every side, their goals all achieved. When he heard those heroes' shouts and the noise of their arrows, Dur·yódhana

Duryodhano mahā|rāja kaśmalen' âbhisaṃvṛtaḥ
apayāne manaś cakre vihīna|bala|vāhanaḥ.

DHṚTARĀṢṬRA uvāca:

nihate māmake sainye niḥśeṣe śibire kṛte
Pāṇḍavānāṃ bale sūta kiṃ nu śeṣam abhūt tadā.
etan me pṛcchato brūhi kuśalo hy asi Sañjaya:
yac ca Duryodhano mandaḥ kṛtavāṃs tanayo mama
bala|kṣayaṃ tathā dṛṣṭvā sa ekaḥ pṛthivī|patiḥ.

SAÑJAYA uvāca:

29.20 rathānāṃ dve sahasre tu sapta nāga|śatāni ca
pañca c' âśva|sahasrāṇi pattīnāṃ ca śataṃ śatāḥ,
etac cheṣam abhūd rājan Pāṇḍavānāṃ mahad balam
parigṛhya hi yad yuddhe Dhṛṣṭadyumno vyavasthitaḥ.
ekākī Bharata|śreṣṭha tato Duryodhano nṛ|paḥ
n' âpaśyat samare kaṃ cit sahāyaṃ rathināṃ varaḥ.
nardamānān parān dṛṣṭvā sva|balasya ca saṃkṣayam
tathā dṛṣṭvā mahā|rāja ekaḥ sa pṛthivī|patiḥ
hataṃ sva|hayam utsṛjya prāṅ|mukhaḥ prādravad bhayāt.
ekādaśa|camū|bhartā putro Duryodhanas tava
gadām ādāya tejasvī padātiḥ prasthito hradam.
29.25 n' âtidūraṃ tato gatvā padbhyām eva nar'|âdhipaḥ
sasmāra vacanaṃ Kṣattur dharma|śīlasya dhīmataḥ:
«idaṃ nūnaṃ mahā|prājño Viduro dṛṣṭavān purā
mahad vaiśasam asmākaṃ kṣatriyāṇāṃ ca saṃyuge?»

became overwhelmed by weakness, great king, and set his heart on flight, deprived as he was of his army and his horse.

DHRITA·RASHTRA said:

When my army was destroyed and my camp had been made desolate, who still remained in the Pándava army, charioteer? You are skilled in speaking, Sánjaya, so answer me this question: What did foolish Dur·yódhana do—that son of mine and lord of the earth—when he was alone and saw that his army had been destroyed?

SÁNJAYA said:

Two thousand chariots, seven hundred elephants, five 29.20
thousand horses and ten thousand foot soldiers—this is what remained of the Pándavas' mighty army, O king. Dhrishta·dyumna took control of this force and drew up position in battle.

King Dur·yódhana, that champion of charioteers, was alone and could see no ally in battle, best of Bharatas. When he saw the enemy roaring and observed the destruction of his army, that lord of the earth abandoned his dead horse and fled eastward on his own out of fear. Splendid Dur·yódhana, your son and commander of eleven armies, took
hold of his mace and set out on foot for a lake. That ruler 29.25
of men had not walked very far when he remembered the words of the wise and righteous Kshattri:

"Did wise Vídura not previously foresee that this great calamity would afflict my warriors in battle?"

evaṃ vicintayānas tu praviviksur hradaṃ nṛ|paḥ
duḥkha|saṃtapta|hṛdayo dṛṣṭvā rājan bala|kṣayam.

Pāṇḍavāś ca mahā|rāja Dhṛṣṭadyumna|puro|gamāḥ
abhyadravanta saṃkruddhās tava rājan balaṃ prati.
śakty|ṛṣṭi|prāsa|hastānāṃ balānām abhigarjatām
saṃkalpam akaron moghaṃ Gāṇḍīvena Dhanañjayaḥ.
29.30 tān hatvā niśitair bāṇaiḥ s'|âmātyān saha bandhubhiḥ
rathe śveta|haye tiṣṭhann Arjuno bahv aśobhata.

Subalasya hate putre sa|vāji|ratha|kuñjare
mahā|vanam iva cchinnam abhavat tāvakaṃ balam.
aneka|śata|sāhasre bale Duryodhanasya ha
n' ânyo mahā|ratho rājañ jīvamāno vyadṛśyata,
Droṇa|putrād ṛte vīrāt tath" âiva Kṛtavarmaṇaḥ
Kṛpāc ca Gautamād rājan pārthivāc ca tav' ātma|jāt.

Dhṛṣṭadyumnas tu māṃ dṛṣṭvā hasan Sātyakim abravīt:
«kim anena gṛhītena n' ânen' ârtho 'sti jīvatā?»
29.35 Dhṛṣṭadyumna|vacaḥ śrutvā Śiner naptā mahā|rathaḥ
udyamya niśitaṃ khaḍgaṃ hantuṃ mām udyatas tadā.
tam āgamya mahā|prājñaḥ Kṛṣṇa|Dvaipāyano 'bravīt:
«mucyatāṃ Sañjayo jīvan. na hantavyaḥ kathañ cana.»

Dvaipāyana|vacaḥ śrutvā Śiner naptā kṛt'|âñjaliḥ
tato mām abravīn muktvā «svasti Sañjaya sādhaya!»
anujñātas tv ahaṃ tena nyasta|varmā nir|āyudhaḥ
prātiṣṭhaṃ yena nagaraṃ sāy'|âhne rudhir'|ôkṣitaḥ.

Thinking this and with his heart tormented by suffering after seeing his army's destruction, the king became eager to enter the lake, Your Majesty.

The Pándavas, who were led by Dhrishta·dyumna, furiously charged against your army, great king. With his Gandíva bow, Dhanan·jaya foiled the intentions of the roaring Káurava troops, who brandished spears, lances, and javelins.
After slaying those warriors with his sharp arrows, along 29.30
with their companions and relatives, Árjuna shone gloriously as he stood on his white-horsed chariot.

Your army was chopped down like a vast forest after Súbala's son was slaughtered along with his horses, chariots and elephants. Of the several hundreds and thousands of men in Dur·yódhana's army, no great warrior was still seen alive, except for the heroic son of Drona, Krita·varman, Kripa the grandson of Gótama, and King Dur·yódhana, your son.

Dhrishta·dyumna looked at me and, with a laugh, he said to Sátyaki:

"Do you want him captive or dead?"

Hearing Dhrishta·dyumna's words, the grandson of Shi- 29.35
ni, that mighty warrior, wielded his sharp sword, intent on killing me. But wise Krishna Dvaipáyana came up to Sátyaki and said:

"Let Sánjaya be released alive. Under no circumstances must he be killed."

Hearing Dvaipáyana's words, the grandson of Shini paid his respects and, releasing me, he said: "Be prosperous, Sánjaya!" With Sátyaki's permission, I set off for the city in the evening, drenched in blood and without armor or weapon.

krośa|mātram apakrāntaṃ gadā|pāṇim avasthitam
ekaṃ Duryodhanaṃ rājann apaśyaṃ bhṛśa|vikṣatam.

29.40 sa tu mām aśru|pūrṇ'|âkṣo n' âśaknod abhivīkṣitum
upapraikṣata māṃ dṛṣṭvā tathā dīnam avasthitam.
taṃ c' âham api śocantaṃ dṛṣṭv" âikākinam āhave
muhūrtaṃ n' âśakaṃ vaktuṃ atiduḥkha|pariplutaḥ.
tato 'smai tad ahaṃ sarvam uktavān grahaṇaṃ tadā
Dvaipāyana|prasādāc ca jīvato mokṣam ātmanaḥ.

sa muhūrtam iva dhyātvā pratilabhya ca cetanām
bhrātṝṃś ca sarva|sainyāni paryapṛcchata māṃ tataḥ.
tasmai tad aham ācakṣe sarvaṃ pratyakṣa|darśivān
bhrātṝṃś ca nihatān sarvān sainyaṃ ca vinipātitam.

29.45 «trayaḥ kila rathāḥ śiṣṭās tāvakānāṃ nar'|âdhipa
iti» prasthāna|kāle māṃ Kṛṣṇa|Dvaipāyano 'bravīt.

sa dīrgham iva niḥśvasya pratyavekṣya punaḥ punaḥ
asau māṃ pāṇinā spṛṣṭvā putras te paryabhāṣata:

«tvad|anyo n' êha saṃgrāme kaś cij jīvati Sañjaya.
dvitīyaṃ n' êha paśyāmi; sa|sahāyāś ca Pāṇḍavāḥ.
brūyāḥ Sañjaya rājānaṃ prajñā|cakṣuṣam īśvaram:

«Duryodhanas tava sutaḥ praviṣṭo hradam ity uta.
su|hṛdbhis tādṛśair hīnaḥ putrair bhrātṛbhir eva ca
Pāṇḍavaiś ca hṛte rājye ko nu jīveta mādṛśaḥ?»

On the way, Your Majesty, I saw Dur·yódhana standing alone, mace in hand and badly wounded; he had walked the distance of a *krosha.** Although he looked toward me as 29.40
I wretchedly stood there, he was unable to see me because his eyes were full of tears and instead he looked past me. Although I saw him grieving and alone on the battlefield, I was unable to say anything for a while, overwhelmed as I was by extreme anguish. But I then told him everything about my capture and how I had been released alive because of Dvaipáyana's grace.

Dur·yódhana brooded for a moment, recovered his senses and then asked me about his brothers and all the troops. I told him everything, having seen it firsthand—how all his brothers had been killed and how his army had been massacred. And also how Krishna Dvaipáyana had said to 29.45
me when I departed: "It is reported that three warriors still remain in your army, lord of men."

Dur·yódhana sighed deeply, contemplating this again and again. Your son then touched me with his hand and replied:

"Apart from you, Sánjaya, no one else is alive in this battle. I do not see anyone else here; only the Pándavas and their allies. Repeat these words, Sánjaya, to my king and lord, who has wisdom for his eyes:

'Your son, Dur·yódhana, has entered a lake. What man like me could live when he has lost such friends, sons and brothers, and when his kingdom has been seized by the Pándavas?'

29.50 ācakṣīthāḥ sarvam idaṃ māṃ ca muktaṃ mah"|āhavāt
asmiṃs toya|hrade guptaṃ jīvantaṃ bhṛśa|vikṣatam.»
evam uktvā mahā|rāja prāviśat taṃ mahā|hradam
astambhayata toyaṃ ca māyayā manu|j'|âdhipaḥ.
tasmin hradaṃ praviṣṭe tu trīn rathāñ śrānta|vāhanān
apaśyaṃ sahitān ekas taṃ deśaṃ samupeyuṣaḥ,
Kṛpaṃ Śāradvataṃ vīraṃ Drauṇiṃ ca rathināṃ varam
Bhojaṃ ca Kṛtavarmāṇaṃ sahitāñ śara|vikṣatān.
te sarve mām abhiprekṣya tūrṇam aśvān anodayan
upayāya ca mām ūcur:
«diṣṭyā jīvasi Sañjaya!»
29.55 apṛcchaṃś c' âiva māṃ sarve putraṃ tava jan'|âdhipam:
«kac cid Duryodhano rājā sa no jīvati Sañjaya?»
ākhyātavān ahaṃ tebhyas tadā kuśalinaṃ nṛ|pam
tac c' âiva sarvam ācakṣaṃ yan māṃ Duryodhano 'bravīt
hradaṃ c' âiv' âham ācakṣaṃ yaṃ praviṣṭo nar'|âdhipaḥ.
Aśvatthāmā tu tad rājan niśamya vacanaṃ mama
taṃ hradaṃ vipulaṃ prekṣya karuṇaṃ paryadevayat:
«aho dhik sa na jānāti jīvato 'smān nar'|âdhipaḥ!
paryāptā hi vayaṃ tena saha yodhayituṃ parān!»
te tu tatra ciraṃ kālaṃ vilapya ca mahā|rathāḥ
prādravan rathināṃ śreṣṭhā dṛṣṭvā Pāṇḍu|sutān raṇe.
29.60 te tu māṃ ratham āropya Kṛpasya su|pariṣkṛtam
senā|niveśam ājagmur hata|śeṣās trayo rathāḥ.
tatra gulmāḥ paritrastāḥ sūrye c' âstam ite sati
sarve vicukruśuḥ śrutvā putrāṇāṃ tava saṃkṣayam.

Tell him all this and also how I have escaped from the great battle and how I am hiding in this lake of water, alive although badly wounded." 29.50

Saying this, great king, that lord of men entered the huge lake and solidified the water through magic.

After Dur·yódhana entered the lake and I was alone, I saw three warriors who had gathered and come to that area. They were Kripa, the heroic son of Sharádvat; the son of Drona, that best of charioteers; and the Bhojan Krita·varman. They were lacerated by arrows and their horses were tired. Seeing me, they all quickly urged on their horses and approached me, saying:

"What fortune it is that you are alive, Sánjaya!"

All of them asked me about your son, that protector of 29.55
the people: "Is our king Dur·yódhana alive, Sánjaya?"

I told them that the king was well and informed them of everything that Dur·yódhana had said to me and also that the lord of men had entered a lake.

Hearing my words, Ashva·tthaman looked at the huge lake and mourned pitifully, saying:

"Oh! What a calamity that the king does not know that we are alive! We would still be able to fight the enemy if he were alongside us!"

The great warriors lamented for a long while in that place. But when they saw the sons of Pandu on the battlefield, those best of charioteers fled. Lifting me onto Kripa's well- 29.60
adorned chariot, the three surviving warriors drove to the army camp. It was sunset, and when the regiments in the camp heard how your sons had been slaughtered, they all lamented in terror.

tato vṛddhā mahā|rāja yoṣitāṃ rakṣiṇo narāḥ
rāja|dārān upādāya prayayur nagaraṃ prati.
tatra vikrośamānānāṃ rudatīnāṃ ca sarvaśaḥ
prādur āsīn mahāñ śabdaḥ śrutvā tad bala|saṃkṣayam.
tatas tā yoṣito rājan rudantyo vai muhur muhuḥ
kurarya iva śabdena nādayantyo mahī|talam,
29.65 ājaghnuḥ kara|jaiś c' âpi pāṇibhiś ca śirāṃsy uta
luluñcuś ca tadā keśān krośantyas tatra tatra ha.
hā|hā|kāra|vinādinyo vinighnantya urāṃsi ca
śocantyas tatra ruruduḥ krandamānā viśāṃ pate.

tato Duryodhan'|âmātyāḥ s'|âśru|kaṇṭhā bhṛś'|āturāḥ
rāja|dārān upādāya prayayur nagaraṃ prati.
vetra|vyāsakta|hastāś ca dvār'|âdhyakṣā viśāṃ pate
śayanīyāni śubhrāṇi spardhy'|āstaraṇavanti ca
samādāya yayus tūrṇaṃ nagaraṃ dāra|rakṣiṇaḥ.
āsthāy' âśvatarī|yuktān syandanān apare punaḥ
svān svān dārān upādāya prayayur nagaraṃ prati.
29.70 a|dṛṣṭa|pūrvā yā nāryo bhās|kareṇ' âpi veśmasu
dadṛśus tā mahā|rāja janā yātāḥ puraṃ prati.
tāḥ striyo Bharata|śreṣṭha saukumārya|samanvitāḥ
prayayur nagaraṃ tūrṇaṃ hata|sva|jana|bāndhavāḥ.

ā go|pāl'|âvi|pālebhyo dravanto nagaraṃ prati
yayur manuṣyāḥ saṃbhrāntā Bhīmasena|bhay'|ârditāḥ.
api c' âiṣāṃ bhayaṃ tīvraṃ Pārthebhyo 'bhūt su|dāruṇam
prekṣamāṇās tad" ânyonyam ādhāvan nagaraṃ prati.

tasmiṃs tathā vartamāne vidrave bhṛśa|dāruṇe
yuyutsuḥ śoka|saṃmūḍhaḥ prāpta|kālam acintayat:

The old men who protected the women set out for the city with the king's wives, Your Majesty. When these women learned of the army's destruction, there was a huge noise as they wailed and wept on every side. Crying repeatedly and making the earth resound with their clamor as if they
were ospreys, the women pounded their heads with their 29.65
nails and fists and ripped out their hair, screaming in every direction, Your Majesty. Shrieking out loud and beating their chests, they wept in grief and lamentation, lord of the people.

Choked with tears and extremely anguished, Dur·yó-dhana's companions also set out for the city, taking with them the wives of the king. The staff-bearing gatekeepers also quickly left for the city, protecting their wives and taking with them fine couches that were draped with valuable carpets. Riding on chariots that were yoked to she-mules, others, too, set out for the city with their respective wives.

Women who had stayed in their houses and whom the 29.70
sun itself had never seen before were now watched by people as they traveled to the city, great king. These delicate women quickly left for the city, best of Bharatas, their kinsmen and relatives slaughtered.

Stricken with fear of Bhima·sena, the bewildered people ran toward the city, including the very cowherds and shepherds. As they fled toward the city, glancing at each other, they felt an intense and horrific fear of the Parthas.

While this extremely terrible flight continued, Yuyútsu, who was stunned by grief, had these proper thoughts:

29.75 «jito Duryodhanaḥ saṃkhye Pāṇḍavair bhīma|vikramaiḥ
ekādaśa|camū|bhartā bhrātaraś c' âsya sūditāḥ.
hatāś ca Kuravaḥ sarve Bhīṣma|Droṇa|puraḥ|sarāḥ.
aham eko vimuktas tu bhāgya|yogād yad|ṛcchayā.
vidrutāni ca sarvāṇi śibirāṇi samantataḥ.
itas tataḥ palāyante hata|nāthā hat'|âujasaḥ.
a|dṛṣṭa|pūrvā duḥkh'|ārtā bhaya|vyākula|locanāḥ
hariṇā iva vitrastā vīkṣamāṇā diśo daśa.

Duryodhanasya sacivā ye ke cid avaśeṣitāḥ
rāja|dārān upādāya prayayur nagaraṃ prati.
29.80 prāpta|kālam ahaṃ manye praveśaṃ taiḥ saha prabho
Yudhiṣṭhiram anujñāpya Bhīmasenaṃ tath" âiva ca.»

etam arthaṃ mahā|bāhur ubhayoḥ sa nyavedayat.
tasya prīto 'bhavad rājā nityaṃ karuṇa|veditā
pariṣvajya mahā|bāhur vaiśyā|putraṃ vyasarjayat.

tataḥ sa ratham āsthāya drutam aśvān acodayat
saṃvāhayitavāṃś c' âpi rāja|dārān puraṃ prati.
taiś c' âiva sahitaḥ kṣipram astaṃ gacchati bhās|kare
praviṣṭo Hāstinapuraṃ bāṣpa|kaṇṭho 'śru|locanaḥ.

apaśyata mahā|prājñaṃ Viduraṃ s'|âśru|locanam
rājñaḥ samīpān niṣkrāntaṃ śok'|ôpahata|cetasam.
29.85 tam abravīt satya|dhṛtiḥ praṇataṃ tv agrataḥ sthitam:

"Although he was the leader of eleven armies, Dur·yódhana has been conquered in battle by the Pándavas, whose power is terrifying. His brothers, too, have been slaughtered. All the Kurus who were led by Bhishma and Drona have been killed. I alone have escaped, whether by fate or by chance. The entire camp has fled on all sides. Running here and there, they have lost their rulers and their strength. I have never seen them like this before: distraught with anguish and their eyes rolling with fear, they seem like terrified deer as they look around in the ten directions. 29.75

Those who remain of Dur·yódhana's companions have
left for the city with the king's wives. I believe that the time 29.80
has come for me to go with them, my lord, after I have gained the permission of Yudhi·shthira and Bhima·sena."

Mighty-armed Yuyútsu then informed the two heroes of this matter. King Yudhi·shthira, who is always compassionate, was pleased with him and, embracing him, the mighty-armed hero let the son of the *vaishya* woman go.

After he had also arranged for the king's wives to be transported to the city, Yuyútsu climbed onto a chariot and quickly urged on his horses. Accompanied by those women, and with damp eyes and a tear-choked throat, he swiftly entered Hástina·pura at sunset.

Yuyútsu then saw wise Vídura, who had tears in his eyes. He had left his king's side because his mind was tormented
by grief. Bowing to Vídura, Yuyútsu stood before him, at 29.85
which point Vídura, who is firm in the truth, said:

«diṣṭyā Kuru|kṣaye vṛtte asmiṃs tvaṃ putra jīvasi.
vinā rājñaḥ praveśād vai kim asi tvam ih' āgataḥ?
etad vai kāraṇaṃ sarvaṃ vistareṇa nivedaya.»

YUYUTSUR uvāca:

«nihate Śakunau tāta sa|jñāti|suta|bāndhave
hata|śeṣa|parīvāro rājā Duryodhanas tataḥ
svakaṃ hayam samutsṛjya prāṅ|mukhaḥ prādravad bhayāt.
apakrānte tu nṛ|patau skandh'|âvāra|niveśanāt
bhaya|vyākulitaṃ sarvaṃ prādravan nagaraṃ prati.
tato rājñaḥ kalatrāṇi bhrātṝṇāṃ c' âsya sarvataḥ
vāhaneṣu samāropya adhyakṣāḥ prādravan bhayāt.
29.90 tato 'haṃ samanujñāpya rājānaṃ saha|Keśavam
praviṣṭo Hāstinapuraṃ rakṣan lokān pradhāvitān.»
etac chrutvā tu vacanaṃ vaiśyā|putreṇa bhāṣitam
prāpta|kālam iti jñātvā Viduraḥ sarva|dharma|vit
apūjayad a|mey'|ātmā Yuyutsuṃ vākyam abravīt:
«prāpta|kālam idaṃ sarvaṃ bhavato Bharata|kṣaye.
rakṣitaḥ kula|dharmaś ca s' ânukrośatayā tvayā.
diṣṭyā tvām iha saṃgrāmād asmād vīra|kṣayāt puram
samāgatam apaśyāma hy aṃśu|mantam iva prajāḥ!
andhasya nṛ|pater yaṣṭir lubdhasy' â|dīrgha|darśinaḥ
bahuśo yācyamānasya daiv'|ôpahata|cetasaḥ
tvam eko vyasan'|ârtasya dhriyase putra sarvathā.

"What fortune it is that you are alive, my child, when the Kurus have suffered this slaughter! But why have you come here without the king coming, too? Tell me in detail the whole reason for this."

YUYÚTSU said:

"After Shákuni was killed, my lord, along with his kinsmen, son and relatives, King Dur·yódhana—whose surviving retinue had been slaughtered—abandoned his horse and fled eastward out of fear. At the king's departure, everyone ran from the royal camp to the city, distraught with fear. The guards also fled in fear, after they had put all the king's wives and brothers in vehicles. I then asked King Yudhi· 29.90
shthira and Késhava for permission to leave and went to Hástina·pura, protecting the people who had fled."

Hearing these words spoken by the son of the *vaishya* woman, infinite-spirited Vídura, who knows everything that is right, saw that Yuyútsu had acted properly and applauded him, saying:

"It is proper for you to have done all this, given the slaughter of the Bharatas. Through your compassion, you have protected your family law. What fortune it is for us to see you here in the city, arriving from this battle which has destroyed heroes. We are like creatures who see the sun!

The blind king is greedy and does not look far ahead; although he was beseeched several times, his mind was afflicted by fate and he now suffers disaster. You, my child, remain in every way his sole staff.

29.95 adya tvam iha viśrāntaḥ śvo 'bhigantā Yudhiṣṭhiram.»
etāvad uktvā vacanaṃ Viduraḥ s'|âśru|locanaḥ
Yuyutsuṃ samanujñāpya praviveśa nṛ|pa|kṣayam
paura|jāna|padair duḥkhādd hā h" êti bhṛśa|nāditam.
nir|ānandaṃ gata|śrīkaṃ hṛt'|ārāmam iv' āśayam
śūnya|rūpam apadhvastaṃ. duḥkhād duḥkhataro 'bhavat
Viduraḥ sarva|dharma|jño viklaven' ântar|ātmanā
viveśa nagare rājan niśvasaṃś ca śanaiḥ śanaiḥ.

Yuyutsur api tāṃ rātriṃ sva|gṛhe nyavasat tadā.
vandyamānaḥ svakaiś c' âpi n' âbhyanandat su|duḥkhitaḥ
cintayānaḥ kṣayaṃ tīvraṃ Bharatānāṃ paras|param.

Rest here today and go to Yudhi·shthira tomorrow." Saying these words with tears in his eyes and taking leave of Yuyútsu, Vídura entered the king's palace, which echoed loudly with the lamentations of anguished citizens and countrymen. The building looked joyless and seemed to have lost its prosperity and happiness. It appeared empty and decaying. Vídura, who knows everything that is right, experienced even greater pain than before and entered the city with a tormented soul, sighing very quietly, Your Majesty. 29.95

Yuyútsu spent the night in his own house. Although welcomed by his friends, in his anguish he could not rejoice. Instead, he brooded over the terrible destruction that the Bharatas had wrought upon one another.

NOTES

Bold *references are to the English text;* ***bold italic*** *references are to the Sanskrit text. An asterisk (*) in the body of the text marks the word or passage being annotated.*

Incipit **The Victory** refers to the story of the Maha·bhárata that describes the battle at Kuru·kshetra and the triumph of the Pándavas. Naráyana (Vishnu) and Nara (Man) are two gods that are often coupled together and are identified with Krishna and Árjuna respectively.

1.1 **Janam·éjaya** is the great-grandson of Árjuna, and it is at his snake sacrifice that the Maha·bhárata is recited by Vaisham·páyana.

1.2 **Su·yódhana:** "good fighter," another name for Dur·yódhana, which means "he who is difficult to fight." Throughout the text, I have chosen to mark the prefixes *su-* and *dur-* for Su·yódhana and Dur·yódhana in order to highlight the meanings of the two different names.

1.6 **The charioteer's son:** Karna.

1.9 **Bharatas:** The first syllable of Bharata is stressed. However, to distinguish the word from Bhārata (with a long *ā*), the stress has not been marked and only the word Bhārata has had its stress marked, Bhárata.

1.10 **King of Righteousness:** Yudhi·shthira, who is also sometimes called the son of Righteousness.

1.17 **Shakra:** A name for Indra.

1.28 Bhima vows that he will break Dur·yódhana's thigh in the *Sabhā/parvan*; see Critical Edition 2.63.14.

1.33 **Vásu·deva:** A name for Krishna. I have accented the first vowel of Vásu·deva (which has a long *ā*: Vāsudeva) to distinguish it from Vasu·deva (which has a short *a*: Vasudeva).

1.41 The term **Kshattri** refers to the fact that Vídura's mother was from a low caste. It also means "steward."

2.19 **The son of Bharad·vaja:** Drona.

2.19 **The grandson of Gótama:** Kripa.

2.22 **Partha:** means "son of Pritha". The sons of Pritha are: Yudhi·shthira, Bhima, and Árjuna. The word **Partha** often also means the followers of Yudhi·shthira, as may be the case here.

2.40 **Ulúka, the mighty son of the gambler:** Ulúka is the son of Shákuni, whose gambling skills are revealed in the *Sabhā/parvan.*

2.63 **The king of the Madras:** Shalya.

2.67 **The two Mádhavas:** Krishna and Sátyaki.

2.67 **The grandson of Bharad·vaja:** Ashva·tthaman.

3.2 We need to understand a word such as *kṣaye* in *pāda* e. Compare *Śalya/parvan* 8.15: *kṣayaṃ manuṣya/dehānāṃ tathā nāg'/âś-va/saṃkṣayam.*

3.7 *Pratyupāyāma:* see Oberlies §6.3.1.2 for this usage of *-ma* instead of *-maḥ.*

3.10 **Bibhátsu:** A name for Árjuna. The original sense of this was presumably literally, "the tormentor," "the one wishing to harm" (*nomina agentis* of the desiderative of *bādh*): a suitable epithet for a warrior. The commonly seen interpretation as "loathing" [of misdeeds] may be a later attempt to make sense of this unfamiliar meaning of the desiderative. (S. Vasudeva.)

3.10 **Vrikódara:** A name for Bhima; literally, "wolf-bellied."

3.17 **Dhanan·jaya:** A name for Árjuna; lit. "wealth-conquering."

3.18 **Go·vinda:** A name for Krishna.

3.30 **The sons of Madri:** Nákula and Saha·deva.

3.45 **Bali:** a demon that was defeated by Vishnu in his incarnation as a dwarf.

4.12 *Vartayiṣyāma:* see note to 3.7.

4.14 **Indra's bow:** the rainbow.

4.15 **Pancha·janya:** Krishna's conch.

4.15 **Gandíva**: Árjuna's bow.

4.16 **Blinding our eyes**: literally, "stealing the light from our eyes."

4.17 **Wielded**: For this meaning of *āviddha*, compare Critical Edition 4.22.24.

4.36 In *Sabhā/parvan* 61–63 (Critical Edition), Bhima swears to tear open Duhshásana's chest and to break Dur·yódhana's thigh.

Vichítra·virya's son: Dhrita·rashtra.

4.46 **Hrishi·kesha**: Krishna.

5.7 The **dice** game, which results in the Pándavas' exile, is narrated in the *Sabhā/parvan*.

5.8 In *Udyoga/parvan* 87–130 (Critical Edition), Dur·yódhana attempts, but fails, to capture Krishna when he sues for peace as a messenger of the Pándavas.

5.9 Dráupadi's humiliation occurs in the *Sabhā/parvan* (especially chapter 58 onward).

5.10 **The two Krishnas**: Krishna and Árjuna.

5.12 **Abhimányu**, Árjuna's son, dies in the *Droṇa/parvan* 48 (Critical Edition).

5.14 There is word-play here: ***yama*** means "twin" and is also the name of the god of the dead, who is himself a twin.

5.28 **The threefold path** in question involves the pursuit of three qualities (in ascending order of importance): *kāma* ("desire" or "pleasure"), *artha* ("benefit" or "profit"), and *dharma* ("righteousness" or "morality").

5.38 **Venerable grandfather**: Bhishma.

5.38 **Teacher**: Drona.

5.40 ***Dhiṣṭhitāḥ:*** see Oberlies p.xxxv for this form.

6.9 **Sthanu**: A name for Shiva.

6.10 **Áruna's brother**: Gáruda.

6.19 The verse plays on a pun: the name used for Skanda is "he who has a great army" (*mahā/sena*), the very phrase used for Shalya.

6.20 On Skanda's consecration as commander of the gods and his victory over an army of demons, see *Āraṇyaka/parvan* 218-221 (Critical Edition).

6.29 **The son of Fire**: On Skanda's birth from Fire, see *Āraṇyaka/parvan* 214 (Critical Edition).

7.10 We need to understand the word *lokān* in *pāda*s ab. Compare *Mahā/bhārata* 7.28.21, 8.51.8, 12.121.55, 12.327.5 (references are to the Critical Edition).

7.16 The **siddhas** are semi-divine beings of great perfection, and the **chárana** are celestial singers.

7.25 **Artáyani**: a name for Shalya.

7.33 **Mághavat**: a name for Indra, meaning "bountiful". **Shámbara**: a demon that was slain by Indra.

7.35 **Vásava**: a name for Indra, meaning "belonging to the Vasus." **Námuchi**: a demon that was killed by Indra.

7.40 **Thorns removed**: This may be a pun alluding to Shalya's imminent death, as the word for "thorn" is *śalya*.

8.9 **The five major sins and the minor sins**: A list of these crimes is given in *Manu* 11.55-67. The five major crimes are: killing a priest, drinking alcohol, stealing, violating a guru's marriage-bed, and associating with those who commit these crimes. The minor crimes include: killing a cow, abandoning one's guru or parents, killing a woman, servant or ruler, adultery, etc. See DONIGER and SMITH 1991: 256–7.

8.20 The **sárvato·bhadra** was a symmetrical form of military array.

8.26 **The grandson of Gótama**: Kripa.

9.8 The thrust of the passage seems to be that the chaos of the battle has caused a breach in the chivalric code, whereby the proper mode of combat is to fight in duels. *s'/ântar'/āyodhinaṃ* literally means: "fighting with an opponent."

9.24 The flower is red.

9.34 **Fourfold armies** are made up of: foot soldiers, cavalry, elephants and chariots.

10.7 *Dhiṣṭhitam:* see Oberlies p. xxxv.

11.22 **The grandson of Shini**: Sátyaki.

11.42 **Not yet excessively angry**: a reference, it seems, to the uncontrolled violence that Ashva·tthaman unleashes in the *Sauptika/parvan*.

11.49 **Vivásvat's son**: here Yama, the god of the dead.

11.53 For this event, in which Bhima goes to Gandha·mádana in order to get special flowers for Dráupadi, see *Āraṇyaka/parvan* 146–152 (Critical Edition). In that passage, however, Bhima does not actually challenge Kubéra to fight, although he does battle with the *rákshasas* that protect Mount Kailása.

12.24 *Hā/hā/kṛt" âbhavan:* for such double sandhi, see Oberlies §1.8.7.

12.35 **The son of Bharad·vaja**: Drona.

12.36 **Víjaya**: a name for Árjuna.

12.59 **Parjánya**: the god of rain, often associated with Indra.

12.63 **Jambha**: name of a demon conquered by Indra. **Vritra**: also a demon that was slain by Indra; the event is narrated, for example, in *Udyoga/parvan* 9–10 (Critical Edition).

13.3 The verse plays on **Shalya**'s name, which means "spear" or "lance."

13.43 The **gandhárva** are a type of deity or celestial musician; the **dánavas** are a class of demon.

14.14 I follow van Buitenen's translation of *triveṇu* in *Āraṇyaka/parvan* 172.4 (Critical Edition).

14.28 **Effortlessly**: literally, "gently" or "softly."

15.10 There is a pun here between ***yama*** meaning "twin" and **Yama** meaning the god of the dead, who is himself a twin.

15.33 **The Sátvata**: Sátyaki

16.31 *Maghavā iva*: for this absence of *sandhi* between *ā* and *i*, see OBERLIES §1.1.2.1.

17.10 **Mádhava**: here Sátyaki.

17.38 **Indra's brother**: Krishna (Vishnu).

17.45 **Tvashtri**: divine craftsman of weapons such as the thunderbolt.

17.45 **Ishána**: a name for Rudra or Shiva.

17.48 **Ándhaka**: name of a demon.

17.51 **Mountain Krauncha when it was struck by Skanda**: For this event, see *Āraṇyaka/parvan* 214 (Critical Edition).

18.13 **Yuyudhána**: Sátyaki.

19.1 *Vimukh" âbhavan*: for such double *sandhi*, see OBERLIES §1.8.7. Verse 19.4 has a similar example: *nirjit" â/jāta/śatrunā*.

20.2 **Airávata**: Indra's elephant.

20.19 *Nigṛhya:* this may be an example of an absolutive acting as a finite verb; see OBERLIES §9.7.3.

20.21 *Nādayanti:* this seems to be an example of a causative with no causal meaning; see OBERLIES §8.8.1.

20.25 **The hero of the Shinis**: Sátyaki.

22.26 **Súbala's grandson**: Ulúka, the son of Shákuni.

23.28 **You know what is wrong**: alternatively, he would be reviling them as being disloyal for fleeing: "You have no sense of duty. You should fight! Why are you fleeing?"

23.56 The KARBELKAR edition starts a new chapter with this verse.

23.68 *Nighnan:* On such augmentless imperfects, see OBERLIES §6.4.1.

24.18 **Áchyuta**: A name for Krishna.

24.22 **Shántanu's son**: Bhishma.

24.23 **Radha's son**: Karna.

24.41 **Jamad·agni's son**: Parashu·rama.

25.4–14 This passage seems to contain examples of absolutives being used as finite verbs; see OBERLIES §9.7.3.

25.14 The **daitéyas** and **dánavas** are demons.

25.26 The juxtaposition of *śvet'|âśvaḥ* and *Kṛṣṇa|sārathiḥ* suggests that the verse is alluding to the literal meaning of Krishna's name ("dark blue") in order to contrast the light and dark colors, hence the above translation.

27.13 **Phálguna**: a name for Árjuna.

27.32 *S' ôpāviśad:* for this type of double *sandhi*, see OBERLIES §1.8.4.

28.42 *Vimukh" âbhavan:* for this type of double *sandhi*, see OBERLIES §1.8.7.

29.39 The word **krosha** ("league") is derived from the verb *kruś* meaning "call out." Its original meaning was that it designated the distance that a voice can call (see MONIER-WILLIAMS, s.v.).

PROPER NAMES AND EPITHETS

ABHIMÁNYU: Son of Árjuna and Subhádra.

ÁCHYUTA: Name for Krishna. Also used of many others in the epic. Literally, "unfallen," "imperishable."

AGNI: The god of fire.

AIRÁVANA/AIRÁVATA: Elephant of Indra.

ALÁMBUSHA: A demon killed by Ghatótkacha. Fights for the Káuravas.

ALÁYUDHA: A demon killed by Ghatótkacha. Fights for the Káuravas.

ÁMBIKA: Mother of Dhrita·rashtra.

ÁNDHAKA: Name of a people. Also the name of a demon killed by Rudra.

ÁRJUNA: The third of the five Pándava brothers. Son of Pandu and Kunti. Also known as: Bibhátsu, Dhanan·jaya, Pándava, Partha, Phálguna, Savya·sachin, Víjaya.

ARTÁYANI: Name for Shalya.

ÁRUNA: Dawn, the charioteer of the sun. Áruna's brother is the bird Gáruda.

ASHVA·TTHAMAN: Son of Drona and Kripi. Fights for the Káuravas.

AYUTÁYUSH: A warrior that fights for the Káuravas.

BÁHLIKA: Father of Soma·datta. Brother of Shántanu. Fights for the Káuravas.

BALA·RAMA: Elder brother of Krishna.

BALI: A demon that was defeated by Vishnu in his incarnation as a dwarf.

BHAGA·DATTA: King of Prag·jyótisha. Fights for the Káuravas.

BHARAD·VAJA: An ancient seer. Father of Drona. Grandfather of Ashva·tthaman.

BHARATA: Prototypical ruler of North India; ancestor of most of the characters in the Maha·bhárata. In the plural, the Bharatas are the descendants of Bharata (see also Bhárata).

BHÁRATA: Descendant of Bharata. Common in the epic.

Bhima: The second of the five Pándava brothers. Son of Pandu and Kunti. Also known as Bhima·sena, Partha, Vrikódara. Literally, "terrifying."

Bhima·sena: Name for Bhima. Literally, "he who has a terrifying army."

Bhishma: Son of Shántanu and Ganga. Fights for the Káuravas.

Bhoja: Name of a people. Connected with the Vrishnis and Ándhakas.

Bhuri·bala: A son of Dhrita·rashtra.

Bibhátsu: A name for Árjuna. Literally, "the tormentor."

Bhuri·shravas: A warrior that fights for the Káuravas.

Brihad·bala: King of Kósala. Fights for the Káuravas.

Chandra·sena: A warrior that fights for the Káuravas.

Chedi: Name of a people.

Chekitána: A Vrishni warrior. Fights for the Pándavas.

Chitra·sena: A son of Karna. Fights for the Káuravas.

Dashárha: Name of a people. Krishna is a chief of the Dashárhas.

Dévaki: Daughter of Dévaka. Wife of Vasu·deva. Mother of Krishna.

Dhrishta·dyumna: Son of the Panchála king Drúpada, brother of Dráupadi. Born from a sacrificial fire. Fights for the Pándavas.

Dhrita·rashtra: King of the Kurus. Son of Krishna Dvaipáyana and Ámbika. Father of Dur·yódhana and 99 other sons.

Dráupadi: Daughter of Drúpada. Wife of the five Pándava brothers. Also known as Krishná. She has five sons: Prativíndhya, Suta·soma, Shruta·kirti, Shatánika, Shruta·sena.

Drona: Son of Bharad·vaja. Husband of Kripi. Father of Ashva·tthaman. Preceptor of the sons of Pandu and the sons of Dhrita·rashtra. Fights for the Káuravas.

Druma·sena: A warrior that fights for the Káuravas.

Duhshásana: A son of Dhrita·rashtra.

Durmárshana: A son of Dhrita·rashtra.

Durvimóchana: A son of Dhrita·rashtra.

DÚRVISHAHA: A son of Dhrita·rashtra.

DUR·YÓDHANA: Eldest son of Dhrita·rashtra and Gandhári. Also known as Su·yódhana. Literally, "he who is difficult to fight."

DUSHPRADÁRSHA: A son of Dhrita·rashtra.

GANDHÁRI: Wife of Dhrita·rashtra. Mother of Dur·yódhana and 99 other sons. Literally, "princess of Gandhára." Daughter of Súbala.

GANDÍVA: The bow of Árjuna.

GAVÁLGANA: The father of Sánjaya.

GHATÓTKACHA: Son of Bhima and Hidímba. A *rákshasa* (demon). Fights for the Pándavas.

GÓTAMA: An ancient seer. Father of Sharádvat. Grandfather of Kripa.

GO·VINDA: A name for Krishna.

GÚHYAKA: A class of beings; followers of Kubéra.

HRÍDIKA: Father of Krita·varman.

HRISHI·KESHA: A name for Krishna.

INDRA: King of the gods (devas). Also known as Mághavat, Shakra, Vásava.

ISHÁNA: A name for Rudra/Shiva.

JAITRA: A son of Dhrita·rashtra.

JALA·SANDHA: A Mágadha king. Fights for the Káuravas.

JAMAD·AGNI: A seer. Father of Párashu-Rama.

JAMBHA: A demon conquered by Indra.

JANAM·ÉJAYA: son of Paríkshit and Mádravati. At his snake sacrifice, Vaisham·páyana recited the Maha·bhárata for the first time. Literally, "people-trembler."

JANÁRDANA: A name for Krishna. Literally, "people-agitator."

JAYAD·RATHA: King of the Sindhus. Fights for the Káuravas.

JAYAT·SENA: A son of Dhrita·rashtra.

KAILÁSA: A mountain; abode of Kubéra.

KAMBÓJA: Name of a people. Sudákshina or Kambója is their king.

KARNA: Son of Surya (the Sun) and Kunti. Adopted by the charioteer Ádhiratha and his wife Radha. Often known as "the charioteer's son." Fights for the Káuravas.

KÁURAVA: Descendant of Kuru. Often refers to Dhrita·rashtra's sons and their followers but the Pándavas are also sometimes called Káurava (since they too are descendants of Kuru).

KÉKAYA: Name of a people. Also refers to five princes of the Kékayas that joined Yudhi·shthira.

KÉSHAVA: A name for Krishna.

KING OF RIGHTEOUSNESS (DHARMA): Yudhi·shthira.

KRAUNCHA: Name of a mountain.

KRIPA: Son of Sharádvat. Grandson of Gótama. Brother of Kripi. Fights for the Káuravas.

KRISHNA: Son of Vasu·deva and Dévaki. Also identified as Vishnu/Naráyana, the supreme God. Also known as Áchyuta, Go·vinda, Hrishi·kesha, Janárdana, Késhava, Vásu·deva. The "two Krishnas" are Krishna and Árjuna.

KRISHNA DVAIPÁYANA. Son of Sátyavati and the seer Paráshara. Father of Dhrita·rashtra, Pandu, and Vídura. Also known as Vyasa. His name derives from the fact that he was abandoned on an island *(dvīpa)*.

KRITA·VARMAN: A Vrishni ruler. Son of Hrídika. Fights for the Káuravas.

KSHATTRI: A name for Vídura. A term referring to the fact that he was born from a low-caste shudra woman; also meaning "steward."

KSHEMA·DHURTI: A warrior that fights for the Káuravas.

KUBÉRA: King of the Guhyakas, *rákshasas* and *yakshas*. Known for his riches.

KUNTI: Wife of Pandu. Mother of Karna by the god Surya, and mother of Yudhi·shthira, Bhima and Árjuna by Pandu (through the gods Dharma, Vayu, and Indra respectively). Also known as Pritha.

KUNTI·BHOJA: Adoptive father of Kunti. Fights for the Pándavas.

KURU: Ancestor of the Bháratas. "The Kurus" are the descendants of

Kuru and include both the Káuravas and Pándavas, although it often refers only to Dhrita·rashtra's sons and their followers.

LÁKSHMANA: Son of Dur·yódhana.

MÁDHAVA: A name of a people. Descendant of Madhu. A name for Krishna, Sátyaki, and Krita·varman.

MADRA/MADRAKA: A name of a people. Shalya is the king of the Madras.

MADRI: Second wife of Pandu. A princess of the Madras. Sister of Shalya. Mother of the twins Nákula and Saha·deva by the two Ashvins.

MÁGHAVAT: A name for Indra. Literally, "bountiful."

MERU: A mountain at the centre of the cosmos.

MLECCHA: Name of a people. Also means: "barbarian," "non-Aryan."

NÁKULA: One of the Pándava brothers (twin of Saha·deva). Son of Pándu and Madri (by one of the Ashvin gods).

NÁMUCHI: A demon killed by Indra.

NARA: Primeval Man. Often considered a god and coupled with Naráyana. Identified with Árjuna.

NARÁYANA: Name of the god Vishnu. Often coupled with Nara. Identified with Krishna. Also the name of a people.

PANCHA·JANYA: The conch of Krishna.

PANCHÁLA: Name of a people who fight on the side of the Pándavas. The king of the Panchálas is Drúpada.

PÁNDAVA: Son of Pándu = Yudhi·shthira, Bhima, Árjuna, Nákula and Saha·deva. Often also refers to the followers of the sons of Pandu.

PANDU: Son of Krishna Dvaipáyana. Half-brother of Dhrita·rashtra and Vídura. Father of the Pándavas. Husband of Kunti and Madri.

PANDYA: Name of a people. In the singular, it means "king of the Pandyas."

PARÍKSHIT: son of Abhimányu and Úttara. Father of Janam·éjaya.

PARJÁNYA: God of rain, often identified with Indra.

PARTHA: Son of Pritha = Yudhi·shthira, Bhima·sena, Árjuna. Often refers to the followers of the sons of Pritha.

PÁURAVA: Descendant of Puru. Name of a people.

PHÁLGUNA: A name for Árjuna.

PRABHÁDRAKA: A division of the Panchálas.

PRÍSHATA: Father of Drúpada, grandfather of Dhrishta·dyumna.

PRITHA: A name for Kunti.

RADHA: Adoptive mother of Karna. Wife of the charioteer Ádhiratha.

RAMA: A name for Bala·rama.

RAVI: A son of Dhrita·rashtra.

RUDRA: A god. Associations with Shiva.

SAHA·DEVA: One of the Pándava brothers. Twin brother of Nákula. Son of Madri and Pandu (by one of the Ashvin gods).

SAMSHÁPTAKA: A group of Káurava warriors.

SÁNJAYA: Son of Gaválgana. Narrates the events of the great battle to Dhrita·rashtra.

SARÁSVATI: Name of a river and goddess. The goddess is often associated with speech and learning.

SÁTVATA: Name of a people belonging to the Yádavas. Used of Krishna, Krita·varman and Sátyaki.

SATYA·KARMAN: A Tri·garta prince.

SÁTYAKI: A Vrishni. Also called Yuyudhána. Means "son of Sátyaka." Grandson of Shini. Fights for the Pándavas.

SATYA·SENA: A son of Karna.

SATYÉSHU: A Tri·garta prince.

SAVYA·SACHIN: A name for Árjuna. Literally, "he who draws (a bow) with his left hand."

SHAKA: Name of a people.

SHÁKUNI: Son of the Gandhára king Súbala. Father of Ulúka.

SHALVA: King of the Shalvas.

SHALYA: King of the Madras. Brother of Madri. Also known as Artáyani.

SHÁMBARA: A demon slain by Indra.

SHÁNTANU: Father of Bhishma by Ganga.

SHARÁDVAT: Father of Kripa.

SHATANÍKA: Son of Nákula and Dráupadi. Fights for the Pándavas.

SHATÁYUSH: A warrior that fights for the Káuravas.

SHIKHÁNDIN: Son (originally daughter) of Drúpada. Fights for the Pándavas and is pivotal in Árjuna's slaughter of Bhishma.

SHINI: Father of Sátyaka. Grandfather of Sátyaki.

SHIVA: A god. Also known as Ishána and Sthanu.

SHRUTÁNTA: A son of Dhrita·rashtra.

SHRUTÁRVAN: A son of Dhrita·rashtra.

SHRUTÁYUSH: A warrior that fights for the Káuravas.

SKANDA: General of the gods. Son of Agni (Fire) and Svaha.

SOMA·DATTA: Father of Bhuri·shravas. Fights for the Káuravas.

SÓMAKA: Name of a people. Often grouped with the Panchálas.

SON OF RIGHTEOUSNESS (DHARMA): Yudhi·shthira.

SRÍNJAYA: Name of a people. Often grouped with the Panchálas.

STHANU: A name for Shiva.

SUBÁHU: A son of Dhrita·rashtra.

SÚBALA: Father of Shákuni.

SUDÁKSHINA: King of the Kambójas. Fights for the Káuravas.

SUDÁRSHA/SUDÁRSHANA: A son of Dhrita·rashtra.

SUJÁTA: A son of Dhrita·rashtra.

SÚRATHA: A Panchála warrior that fights for the Pándavas.

SUSHÁRMAN: King of the Tri·gartas.

SUSHÉNA: A son of Karna. Fights for the Káuravas.

SUTA·SOMA: Son of Nákula and Dráupadi. Fights for the Pándavas.

SU·YÓDHANA: A name for Dur·yódhana. Literally, "good fighter."

TVASHTRI: Divine craftsman of weapons such as the thunderbolt.

UGRÁYUDHA: A warrior that fights for the Káuravas.

ULÚKA: Son of Shákuni. Fights for the Káuravas.

ÚSHANAS: An ancient seer.

UTTAMÁUJAS: A Panchála warrior fighting for the Pándavas. Brother of Yudha·manyu.

VAISHAM·PÁYANA: Disciple of Krishna Dvaipáyana. Recited the Maha·bhárata at Janam·éjaya's snake sacrifice.

VÁSAVA: Name of Indra.

VÁSU·DEVA: Name of Krishna. Means "son of Vasu·deva."

VÍDURA: Son of Krishna Dvaipáyana and a low-caste shudra woman. Uncle of the Pándavas and sons of Dhrita·rashtra.

VÍJAYA: A name for Árjuna. Literally, "victory."

VIKÁRNA: A son of Dhrita·rashtra.

VIVÁSVAT: Father of Yama.

VRIKÓDARA: A name for Bhima. Literally, "wolf-bellied."

VRISHA·SENA: A son of Karna.

VRISHNI: Name of a Yádava people. Connected with the Ándhakas and Bhojas. Krishna, Sátyaki and Krita·varman belong to this clan.

VRITRA: Name of a demon slain by Indra.

YÁDAVA: Name of a people. Descendant of Yadu. Used of Krishna.

YADU: Son of Yayáti, ancestor of the Yadus (= Yádavas). The Yadus are often synonymous with the Vrishnis.

YAMA: The god of the dead. Son of Vivásvat.

YÁVANA: Name of a people. Connected with Greeks.

YUDHA·MANYU: A Panchála warrior fighting for the Pándavas. Brother of Uttamáujas.

YUDHI·SHTHIRA: Eldest of the Pándava brothers. Son of Pandu and Kunti (by the god Dharma). Also known as the Son of Righteousness (Dharma) and the King of Righteousness.

YUYUDHÁNA: Sátyaki's proper name.

YUYÚTSU: Son of Dhrita·rashtra and a *vaishya* woman. Joins the Pándavas.

INDEX

Sanskrit words are given in the English alphabetical order, according to the accented CSL pronuncation aid. They are followed by the conventional diacritics in brackets.

Permitted finals:

k	ṭ	t	p	ṅ	n	m	(*Except* āḥ/aḥ) ḥ/r	āḥ	aḥ	*Initial letters:*
k	ṭ	t	p	ṅ	n	ṃ	ḥ	āḥ	aḥ	k/kh
g	ḍ	d	b	ṅ	n	ṃ	r	ā	o	g/gh
k	ṭ	c	p	ṅ	ṃś	ṃ	ś	āś	aś	c/ch
g	ḍ	j	b	ṅ	ñ	ṃ	r	ā	o	j/jh
k	ṭ	ṭ	p	ṅ	ṃṣ	ṃ	ṣ	āṣ	aṣ	ṭ/ṭh
g	ḍ	ḍ	b	ṅ	ṇ	ṃ	r	ā	o	ḍ/ḍh
k	ṭ	t	p	ṅ	ṃs	ṃ	s	ās	as	t/th
g	ḍ	d	b	ṅ	n	ṃ	r	ā	o	d/dh
k	ṭ	t	p	ṅ	n	ṃ	ḥ	ā	aḥ	p/ph
g	ḍ	d	b	ṅ	n	ṃ	r	ā	o	b/bh
ṅ	ṇ	n	m	ṅ	n	ṃ	r	ā	o	*nasals* (n/m)
g	ḍ	d	b	ṅ	n	ṃ	r	ā	o	y/v
g	ḍ	d	b	ṅ	n	ṃ	*zero*[1]	ā	o	r
g	ḍ	l	b	ṅ	l̃[2]	ṃ	r	ā	o	l
k	ṭ	c ch	p	ṅ	ñ ś/ch	ṃ	ḥ	āḥ	aḥ	ś
k	ṭ	t	p	ṅ	n	ṃ	ḥ	āḥ	aḥ	ṣ/s
gg h	ḍḍ h	dd h	bb h	ṅ	n	ṃ	r	ā	o	h
g	ḍ	d	b	ṅ/ṅṅ[3]	n/nn[3]	m	r	ā	a[4]	*vowels*
k	ṭ	t	p	ṅ	n	m	ḥ	āḥ	āḥ	*zero*

[1]ḥ or r disappears, and if a/i/u precedes, this lengthens to ā/ī/ū. [2]e.g. tān+lokān=tāl̃ lokān.
[3]The doubling occurs if the preceding vowel is short. [4]Except: aḥ+a=o '.

Final vowels:

a	ā	i	ī	u	ū	ṛ	e	ai	o	au	*Initial vowels:*
' â	" â	y a	y a	v a	v a	r a	e '	ā a	o '	āv a	a
' ā	" ā	y ā	y ā	v ā	v ā	r ā	a ā	ā ā	a ā	āv ā	ā
' ê	" ê	' î	" î	v i	v i	r i	a i	ā i	a i	āv i	i
' ē	" ē	' ī	" ī	v ī	v ī	r ī	a ī	ā ī	a ī	āv ī	ī
' ô	" ô	y u	y u	' û	" û	r u	a u	ā u	a u	āv u	u
' ō	" ō	y ū	y ū	' ū	" ū	r ū	a ū	ā ū	a ū	āv ū	ū
a' r	a" r	y ṛ	y ṛ	v ṛ	v ṛ	' ṝ	a ṛ	ā ṛ	a ṛ	āv ṛ	ṛ
' âi	" âi	y e	y e	v e	v e	r e	a e	ā e	a e	āv e	e
' āi	" āi	y ai	y ai	v ai	v ai	r ai	a ai	ā ai	a ai	āv ai	ai
' âu	" âu	y o	y o	v o	v o	r o	a o	ā o	a o	āv o	o
' āu	" āu	y au	y au	v au	v au	r au	a au	ā au	a au	āv au	au